A constant burden

A constant burden

The reconstitution of family life

Margaret Voysey

Routledge & Kegan Paul
London and Boston

First published in 1975
by Routledge & Kegan Paul Ltd
Broadway House, 68-74 Carter Lane,
London EC4V 5EL and
9 Park Street,
Boston, Mass. 02108, USA
Set in Monotype Scotch Roman by
Kelly Selwyn & Co., Melksham, Wiltshire
and printed in Great Britain by
The Camelot Press Ltd., Southampton
ISBN 0 7100 8183 9

5/77

Contents

Acknowledgments

Acknowledgments are due to the Nuffield Provincial Hospitals Trust which financed the research for three years. I am grateful to Professor Raymond Illsley for his help, especially in the initial stages of the project, and to Professor Ross Mitchell and other members of staff at the Royal Aberdeen Hospital for Sick Children and the Aberdeen Maternity Hospital for their co-operation in identifying families suitable for the study. Many thanks are due to all the parents of disabled children who agreed to let me visit and talk to them.

Dr Tony Wootton was one of the first to help me analyse the material gathered. Over a long period of time I received invaluable help and encouragement from Phil Strong and extensive advice and criticism from Gordon Horobin. At various times I benefited from the comments and suggestions made by friends and colleagues in the Centre for Social Studies and Department of Sociology in Aberdeen, and the Social Research Unit, Bedford College, London. In particular, I should like to mention Dr George Brown, Dr Francis Powell, Dr George Psathas and Professor W. M. Williams, Francis and Margaret Castles, Alan Davis and Jacqueline West.

I should also like to thank other friends and my parents for being a constant source of sympathy and optimism, and Hilary May-Miller for all her assistance in preparing the manuscript and meeting every deadline.

And they blessed the seventh day, in sick hope,
And forgot their eternal life.

And form'd laws of prudence and call'd them
The eternal laws of God.

William Blake, *The Book of Urizen*

Introduction

Over the past twenty years there have been many studies of what can generically be termed 'the effects of a disabled child on his family'. Kelman (1964) provides a critical review of a number of such studies, and points out that they constitute evidence of radical changes in conceptions of the nature of disability and the family. The condition of a child, whether he be disabled 'physically' or 'mentally', is now widely seen as 'reversible', and his family as able to play an important part in effecting such improvement. Such a climate of opinion stands in marked contrast to that of 'hopelessness and defeatism in which little more than diagnostic services and custodial care was made available to . . . families . . . [and] scientific interest . . . was largely limited to investigations of parental or familial roles as etiologic agents or correlates' (*ibid.*, p. 78).

The new climate of opinion provides a common rationale for studying disability and the family. This is that it is important to discover what problems having a disabled child presents to parents, in order that appropriate services and facilities may be made available to help them overcome these problems and develop the child's ability to its full potential. I similarly hope that the study reported here will contribute something to changing the situation of parents who have a disabled child. It is, however, essential to distinguish the social from the sociological problem. Failure to do so results in a misrepresentation of the parents' situation, which in practice may make change in that situation unlikely.

Like most studies of disability in the family, mine is based on parents' responses to questions about what it is like to have a disabled child, and my research focus was the effects of a disabled child on family life. Two questions are then raised. Firstly, why do parents say what they say, and secondly, what, if anything, does what they say tell us about the experience of having a disabled child? Any answer to the second question depends on that given to the first. In chapter 1, I look at two typical approaches to these questions, examining their similarities and differences. These are illustrated by a limited number of studies of disability and the family, which are both comparatively recent and intended to be representative of their kind. Both are found inadequate in their treatment of parents' responses, and thus unable to provide a satisfactory account of the consequences of having a disabled child. A major difference, however, lies in their conceptualization of the nature of disability; specifically, of the significance of parents' definitions of their child's condition in relation to the historical fact of its identification as disabled. Hence, before examining these other studies, I present some of the available evidence on disability, whether in a child or an adult, which indicates the importance of examining parents' conceptions of their child's condition. Evidently, my critique of the approaches adopted in the other studies presented is informed by my own. Some anticipation of this is therefore necessary.

I wish to argue that, in a certain sense, parents' responses tell us nothing about what it is like to have a disabled child in the family, but a lot about other people's ideas of what it ought to be like. Indeed, that an adequate explanation of what parents say about their child and his effects on family life can be derived from an examination of the ways in which help is made available to them, since such intervention is aimed at producing an ideal adjustment to the experience of having a disabled child.

This ideal is based on a conception of normal family life in which child-rearing is the central activity. In general, parents are supposed to subjugate their own interests to those of their children, and moreover to enjoy any sacrifices thus incurred. This conception bears a questionable relationship to the experience of *any* parents, and is even less likely to reflect that of those who have a disabled child. However, because it is widely legitimated and, further, actively implemented by agents accredited with official responsibility for the care and control of children, parents of the disabled are constrained to present their experience in such a way that they appear to be fulfilling the demands of normal parenthood.

From what they said when interviewed, the majority of parents appear able to make sense of the presence of disability in their child; his behaviour was more or less understandable to them in its terms (see chapter 5). However, it cannot then be assumed that parents 'accept' or believe that their child is disabled. Rather, this

evidence provides the grounds for others making such an assumption. Since the adequate care and control of any child evidently
depends on the ability to understand or make sense of his
behaviour, parents thereby appear to be performing this essential
activity. Similarly, most parents appear to be maintaining the
family's good reputation in encounters outside the home, to be
fulfilling their responsibilities to their other children by not
discriminating unfairly against them in favour of the disabled
child, and to be maintaining harmonious family relations (see
chapter 6). Again, this does not necessarily mean that parents
have managed a good familial adjustment to the presence of a
disabled child, that the other children are not suffering, or that
others outside the family may not be aware of such matters, but
rather that those to whom such an appearance is presented can
thereby make such an interpretation.

Of course, it is unlikely that anyone would assume that having a
disabled child is just like having a normal child, that it is anything
but undesirable, and that it does not present problems that parents
would not otherwise face. The fact that parents do claim that their
family life is congruent with the normal order may then be taken
as evidence of 'strength of character' or a 'deeper understanding'
of life. I, however, show in chapter 8 that parents sustain their
predominantly calm and cheerful appearance by asserting other
interpretations of their situation which deny its undesirability
and legitimate any suffering on their part. Such interpretations
are grounded in certain theories which are culturally defined as
relevant to, and which are expressed in, the activities of those
agents officially empowered or otherwise in a position to intervene
in the parents' situation. The theories examined are religion and
its commonsense equivalents, medical science, psychiatry and
sociology; the agents: doctors, social workers, voluntary associations for the disabled, and also magazines and newspapers. The
expressions of such agents together constitute the nature of the
good adjustment in terms of which parents are held accountable
for their actions. This then provides an overall or underlying order
to parents' statements about their disabled child and their family
life.

What parents say can be systematically understood as expressions of the objective meanings of their situation available to them
as competent members of society, as persons who can be reasonably
assumed to know what behaviour is expected of parents in general,
and even to have some knowledge relevant to their specifically
disadvantaged situation: as I show, many of the legitimations
which they express are 'commonsense'. To do this, no reference

need be made to parents' conscious processes; the only outstanding problem is how it is that observers manage to see these meanings 'in' parents' statements. Some sociologists would regard this as all that can be said from the evidence available, thus excluding both questions of why parents do say what they say, and what relation their statements bear to the 'real' meaning of having a disabled child. Others might allow a single imputation of motivation: that parents say what they say *in order* to impress the observer in a particular way.

My argument, as has already been implied, is partly in terms of 'external' constraints, constituted in inter-personal contexts. Parents say what they say *because* such responses are legitimated by others, and other responses negatively sanctioned. This does not mean that parents' definitions are determined by others' expectations, or that there is only one way in which they can be honoured. In chapter 6 I relate typical differences in parents' appearances, or inter-personal style, to negotiated definitions of the ways in which the parents' situation differs from that of normal parents. However, in chapter 8 I also attempt to show that there are no other definitions of their situation likely to be available to parents. Moreover, that this itself can be related to the actions of official agents of control, since these constitute an absolute morality for the whole society, to which the 'normal family' and parents' good adjustment are central. For these reasons, I conclude that what parents say to me may 'reflect' a large part of their experience of having a disabled child: there are few situations in which they are likely to be able to say anything else, and in any case little else for them to say. Hence, an examination of what they say in terms of the meanings they make use of in constructing their statements can tell us a lot about the meaning of having a disabled child to his parents.

The grounds of this argument will be developed in chapters 1 and 2. It is developed mainly through an examination of existing work specific to disability and the family, on the family in general and on disability. I begin with some of the available evidence on disability, as it is commonly divided into 'mental subnormality' and 'physical disability'.

1 Underlying pathology and apparent normality

THE 'FACTS' OF DISABILITY

As defined in the Mental Health Act (1959), mental subnormality indicates a state of mind. As Soddy (1972, p. 18) says:

> *Severe subnormality* is a state of arrested or incomplete development of mind so severe that the patient is incapable of leading an independent life, or of guarding himself against serious exploitation (or, in the case of a child, that he will be so incapable when adult); and *subnormality* is a state of arrested or incomplete development of mind, which includes subnormality of intelligence and requires special care or training, but does not amount to severe subnormality.

There is, however, very little evidence of qualitatively different states of mind.

At least half of those identified as mentally subnormal appear to have no neuro-physiological defect. Of a total of 7,800 first admissions of mental defectives to eighty-nine public institutions for mental defectives and epileptics in the USA in 1949, 24·8 per cent were classified as 'undifferentiated' and 30·7 per cent as 'familial'. Since the latter diagnosis indicates only a history of mental subnormality in the family, from which inheritance is merely assumed, 55·5 per cent can be considered to be 'unclassified' (Perry, 1954). Furthermore, most of the remaining categories are differentiated on the basis of apparent physiological concomitants, such as cranial abnormalities and epilepsy, and not from specific qualitative differences in the intellectual dysfunctioning that they are assumed to produce.

More recently, Birch *et al.* (1970) reported that half of all the mentally subnormal children they investigated had clear indication of central nervous system (cns) damage. Such damage was found three times more frequently amongst children with IQs below sixty, but also in more than a quarter of those children with

IQs of sixty or more. However, Birch (1964) found evidence of cns damage without associated subnormal functioning, which, as Birch et al. (op. cit.) point out, indicates that in some of the cases they studied the association between neurological findings and behaviour may not be causal. These writers argue that 'If mental handicap is severe, if clinical evidence of central nervous system damage is present and/or if specific metabolic chromosomal or gene defects can be demonstrated, biological determinance can be presumed' (ibid., p. 160). Phenylketonuria and mongolism are cases in point. Zigler and Harter (1969) cite many other hypothesized causal mechanisms, such as: relative impermeability of the boundaries between regions of the cognitive structure, malfunctioning disinhibitory mechanisms and inadequate neural satiation, which may yet be located.

However, the relationship between any identifiable pathology and observed behavioural differences will still require explanation, and it is unlikely that this will be unilinear. Research in many particular areas of mental subnormality shows that different conditions are associated with the 'same' level of functioning, and the 'same' condition, e.g. mongolism, can be present in cases demonstrating very different levels of functioning (Penrose, 1963). Birch et al. (op. cit.) found that mental subnormality, with and without cns damage, occurred more frequently among children in the lower social classes. Moreover, almost all mildly retarded children with IQs of sixty or more came from families in manual classes, whilst there were almost no cases of children from non-manual classes with IQs of fifty or more and no cns damage. To quote Tizard (1972, p. 278):

> A simple genetical hypothesis cannot account for the absence or comparative absence of neurologically normal, mentally retarded children in families of the upper social groups. Instead the task is to explain why it is that mental retardation without demonstrable clinical signs of brain damage occurs relatively frequently among children of parents in the lower classes.

Despite such evidence Soddy, in the same book (1972, pp. 19–20), says that:

> to the doctor, the so-called subnormal individual differs only in degree, and not in phase or status from the so-called severely subnormal. This is important to note, because nowadays many people are inclined to regard 'high grade' subnormality as not being a medical or clinical problem, however freely they may recognise the medical nature of so-called severe subnormality.

He acknowledges that in the majority of cases 'there is no obvious or declared cause of any mental handicap' (*ibid.*, p. 26), but later gives a list of 'reliable guides to disease patterns' (*ibid.*, p. 30). Some of these, such as cerebral tumours and congenital syphilis, are 'rare'. Those relating to obstetric complications, which he regards as the most common, are associated with social class. Birch *et al.* show that when those mentally subnormal children at high risk from obstetric complications were divided into upper and lower social class categories, fourteen of the seventy-one cases (20 per cent) fell into the lower group, whereas only one of the twenty-one cases (5 per cent) fell into the upper social class category (*op. cit.*, p. 159).

The ascription of mental subnormality, however, does not depend on the demonstration of pathology or etiological processes. Rather, its basis is an individual's performance of tasks designed to assess his intellectual and social competence. Zigler (1966) and Perry (*op. cit.*) suggest that measures of 'social competence' are most appropriate if the aim is to decide whether or not to accord normal status to an individual. Apart from the dangers of thereby misclassifying, for example, psychotics and criminals as subnormal (but then the reverse is as often true), even 'operational' definitions are problematic. Thus, if 'ability to hold down a job' is a criterion, what happens to the person who is sacked? Such an event may be an indicator of economic recession, the employer's attitude to subnormals in general, or the individual in particular, as much as of the competence of the individual concerned. Zigler (*op. cit.*) suggests that the best criterion may be *post hoc*; that is, ability to stay out of an institution. He notes, however, that the criteria for institutionalization need not be the individual's competence, but whether he comes from a 'poor home background'.[1] Again, parents may decide to place a child in an institution because they can no longer cope with him, rather than because of a deterioration in his condition.[2]

In the case of children, IQ tests of some kind are the most common method of assessment. Criticisms of these are familiar. For example, they do not measure intelligence as a general ability, but emphasize certain verbal skills, thus favouring those individuals from middle-class backgrounds in which such skills are more common. It can be argued that even in a population of geniuses, a given proportion would be classified as 'subnormal', and regional differences in standards of application mean that the same individual would be differently classified according to where he lived.[3]

Whatever dimensions are used in evaluating performance, the demarcation of what is to be considered 'normal' functioning must, in the final analysis, be arbitrary. A good assessment will be based on as full an appreciation of the total 'symptom picture' as possible, but, as will be seen shortly, what counts as a symptom is not unproblematic. In any case, it should be apparent that neither upon the grounds of underlying defect, nor level of performance, should the mentally subnormal be regarded as uniquely different from persons of normal ability.

Unlike mental subnormality, physical disability is not identified on the basis of some generalized conception of physical competence, in terms of which the performance of every individual will be evaluated at some stage in his career. Dexter (1964) sees this as a product of a cultural emphasis on intellectual skills, and imagines a society in which physical incompetence would be similarly devalued and tests of 'gawkiness quotient' constructed. Physical disability is ascribed on the basis of specific anatomical or physiological impairments of divers origin, which are regarded as limiting an individual's functioning over a long or indefinite period of time. Nagi (1965) notes that analytically it 'overlaps' with illness, where the impairment is due to some active pathology that has not been arrested or eliminated, and in practice, is treated in rehabilitation programmes which have come to include impairments associated with long-term diseases. However, for certain purposes the adult disabled are now treated as a general category.

The Chronically Sick and Disabled Persons Act (1970) states the duty of local authorities to inform themselves of the numbers of, and to 'make arrangements' (later detailed) for, persons defined in the National Assistance Act (1948). That is, persons 'who are blind, deaf or dumb, and other persons who are substantially and permanently handicapped by illness, injury or congenital deformity, or such other disabilities as may be prescribed by the Minister' (1948, c. 29, s.1). The power to define chronic illness or disability is now similarly invested in the Secretary of State for Health.

Some idea of what the Department of Health and Social Security means by disability, in so far as it is a product of industrial injury, can be gained from a pamphlet giving information to the public on claiming disablement benefit. It refers to a 'loss of physical or mental faculty' which (1970, p. 3):

> means some impairment of the power to enjoy a normal life. It includes disfigurement, even though this causes no bodily handicap. It is expressed as a certain percentage of disablement, and is assessed by a comparison of the claimant's condition as a result of the injury with the condition of a normal, healthy person, of the same age and sex.

Unlike the statutory definition of blindness,[4] assessment 'in no way depends upon the nature of the claimant's employment, or upon loss of earning power' (*ibid.*), for which there are additional allowances and supplements.

The assessments for 'clearly defined injuries' are laid down in a scale. Thus it would be 100 per cent for loss of sight, very severe facial disfigurement, or loss of a hand and foot, and usually 60 per cent for loss of a hand and 14 per cent for loss of an index finger. If the effects of an industrial injury or disease are more disabling to a person who already had something wrong with him, the assessment will take account of this, but not the disability which the pre-existing disability would have caused in any event.

Hence, as officially defined, disability is not regarded as a solely medical phenomenon. Compensation recognizes impairments which are irrelevant to bodily functioning, and that the effects of a given impairment vary according to an individual's occupation – an executive may be less incapacitated by leg injuries than a miner. In the case of industrial injuries, the merits of individual claims are assessed in 'medical tribunals'. The evidence relevant to assessment of an individual's 'power to enjoy a normal life' is that provided by doctors, or, in the case of suspected 'functional overlay', psychiatrists, employed by the DHSS on a full-time or occasional basis. An individual may appeal, usually through a trade-union representative, but the conception of a 'normal healthy person' of a given age and sex which prevails is that held by the doctors or psychiatrists consulted.

Whatever agents are involved in the process, the identification and assessment of the impact or 'severity' of a given impairment is not unproblematic. Different methods of assessment can discover different amounts of disability, as in the case of functional *versus* audiometric tests of hearing, or ophthalmoscopic *versus* photographic investigation of the eyes. Different countries, and even different states within a country, operate different definitions of 'total' and 'near' blindness or partial sight (Lemert, 1951). Nor does an individual's own assessment of his condition provide an objective indicator. Pain thresholds vary between different cultures (Zborowski, 1952), so that, for example, middle-class women are more likely to recognize back pain. A given defect may be so common in a particular culture that it is defined as normal. Thus rickets was an expected deformity in nineteenth-century working-class areas; and smallpox scars so common in the seventeenth century that wanted criminals might be distinguished by their lack of pock marks. Obesity is common in certain sub-cultures, such as the Italian-American or West Indian, and, even if it is seen as impairing activity and reducing life expectancy, given the social importance of eating, it may be preferred to the reduced participation in family life that dieting would entail (Bloom, 1963).

The signs and symptoms of a defect may be 'normalized'; that is, interpreted in such a way that they are contained within a normal framework of explanation. The diagnosis of cases of, for example, coeliac disease and diabetes, may at least be delayed, since the symptoms can be readily explained as 'tiredness', or 'lack of appetite', or simply 'ageing'. The identification of disability may further vary according to the particular situation: clothing may hide scars which evening dress would reveal. Finally, an individual's assessment of his disability is likely to depend not only upon his normal occupational, but his recreational, activities. An impairment of mobility is a greater disability to a man who likes to go dancing, or play football, than to one who prefers sedentary pastimes. Evidently, the relevance of such contingencies may not be apparent in a given assessment encounter, or to the particular assessing agent.

Hence, 'social factors' are, in various ways, important in the identification and assessment of both mental subnormality and physical disability, and in neither case, with the noted exception of a small minority of cases of severe subnormality, can the behaviour of the disabled be directly attributed to some underlying pathology. Most people would perhaps agree with such conclusions. As noted earlier, interest in the effects of a disabled child on his family, and the growth of rehabilitation programmes, indicates a belief that even where an underlying defect is known or assumed to exist, its consequences may be modifiable. Penrose (*op. cit.*) and Sarason (1953) show the 'reversibility' of 'permanent' defects. The work of O'Connor and Tizard (1956) has demonstrated that intensive training programmes and improved institutional conditions enable 'borderline' individuals to function successfully in normal life.

Such evidence has provided the most effective arguments against solely medical explanations of disability. It does not, however, provide an alternative explanation – not, of course, that this is the purpose of rehabilitation. Bialer (1968) argues that since, theoretically, one could only say what was 'really' the case in terms of capacity and curability when an individual dies, it is better to suspend questions of etiology and classification, and to consider an individual's future status in terms of the likelihood of development or reversibility as 'empirical matters'. The processes by which individuals come to be identified and treated as disabled are thereby taken as given. Failure to examine these processes, however, has important consequences for subsequent interpretation of the behaviour of those so identified.

Bialer (*ibid.*) presents a review of experimental work comparing retarded with normal children. This consistently shows a lack of unique differences in their performance on a number of psychological tests. For example, a significant proportion of retarded children responded to learning tasks in the way predicted for normal children; no single set of patterns characterized the retarded and normal children: a retarded child's identification of significant others was no different from that of a normal child.

Bialer's explanations of such phenomena impute psychopathological mechanisms. The retarded children were 'manifesting over-confidence as defensive compensation for feelings of inferiority', or 'denying their inferiority of which they were aware' (*ibid.*, pp. 61–2). He thus ignores the significance for an individual of being identified as mentally subnormal. As Edgerton points out, this implies a total lack of competence, and constitutes a threat to an individual's very status as human. He says that 'passing [as normal] and denial [of subnormality] are as much a matter of life and death as the deceptions of a spy behind enemy lines' (1967, p. 208), but presents such behaviour, not as further evidence of underlying pathology, but as situated inter-personal tactics. These indicate considerable ingenuity. For example, when asked to tell the time the adult retarded might say that his watch had stopped; to read an official form, that he had forgotten his glasses.

Shallenberger and Zigler (1961) further argue that certain differences or 'abnormalities' in the behaviour of retarded children can be interpreted as normal adaptations to situational demands. Thus, 'attention-seeking' and 'perseveration' observed in children in institutions for the subnormal can be explained as the result of deprivation and therefore 'heightened motivation to interact with supportive adults', rather than by, for example, 'cognitive rigidity'. Normal children display similar behaviour after hospitalization of a few days' duration (Perry, *op. cit.*), while experimental work shows that, for any individual, prolonged experience of failure leads to the expectation and 'achievement' of failure, even on tasks which were previously within his competence (Zeaman and House, 1963).

Bialer cites Butterfield and Zigler (1965) as arguing that the facilitative effect of failure on the performance of both retarded and normal children can be ascribed to the child's desire to win the experimenter's approval. However, nowhere does he conclude that such normal explanations might be adequate for understanding the behaviour of retarded children, but persists in treating this as a special research topic: 'a good deal of work is necessary before we can answer the jackpot question: how does the retarded respond to the various . . . factors outlined above?' (*op. cit.*, p. 72).

He proposes an explanation based on Lewinian Field Theory, which is aimed at understanding 'the dynamic interaction of the individual with his specific environment' (*ibid.*, pp. 73–4). Investigation is then a matter of defining 'which parts of the physical and social environment . . . are transformed into goals, barriers, or boundaries, and the other psychological factors that constitute the individual's life-space' (*ibid.*, p. 77). Assessment, using video-recordings of the behaviour of retarded children, would require dividing his behaviour into units or episodes on the basis of observable changes in the child's environment, behaviour, or both, and 'analysing the units one by one into categories and factors which allow for systematic study of the individual's interaction with his milieu' (*ibid.*, pp. 79–80). Such an approach, however, includes no rationale for deciding what would count as an 'observable change', nor what that change would signify. The observer's processes of interpretation and categorization are implicitly treated as unproblematic.[5] In this case, it appears unlikely that any of a child's responses would induce questioning of his status as retarded.

The behaviour of the physically disabled may be similarly subject to competing explanations. From an extensive survey of the literature Barker (1948) drew the following generalizations: (1) the physically disabled are more frequently 'maladjusted' than the normal; (2) the long-term physically disabled are more likely to be maladjusted than the short-term; and (3) the severely disabled have more frequent and severe adjustment problems. Richardson *et al.* (1961) found that physically disabled children show more self-depreciation, greater lack of confidence, more concern with the past, and compare themselves less with others. Further, Barker (*op. cit.*) also found that the type of maladjustment is not peculiar to the disabled, and no relationship between the type of disability and behaviour. Moreover, as Barker *et al.* (1951) document at length, whether or not atypical, physique normally influences behaviour. It is an important basis for social distinction and related to this an important part of self-concept.

Hence, as Meyerson (1948) suggests, the social-psychological problems of the disabled might better be seen as an inability to attain simple universally achieved goals. The inability to recognize a friend unless spoken to may be more of a disability to the blind than that to appreciate art; the deaf suffer more from the lack of normal conversation than of music. Such skills are taken for granted by normal people: they are the necessary basis for ordinary everyday interaction. Those lacking in such respects are thus automatically disadvantaged, and must constantly be made aware of their 'inferiority'. Further, they may frequently be forced to make others aware of it as they ask for help and tolerance, which necessitates an invasion of privacy that most normals suffer only by chance or in certain situations. Not, of course, that such intrusion is always necessary: the disabled may neither need nor want help or tolerance in a particular situation. Blind people may need to know what bus has arrived, but require no help in getting on it: lower status is more often ascribed by others than it is deserved because of 'actual' inferiority (Ladieu *et al.*, 1948). But repeated experience of such devaluation by others may foster self-devaluation, and help may then become expected by, and even essential to, the disabled.

Similarities in the behaviour of the disabled may then be understood as resulting from similar social experiences, as adaptations to similar situations. The severely disabled demonstrate more 'abnormal' behaviour because they are disadvantaged in a wider range of situations. The longer an individual has been disabled the more devaluation he is likely to have experienced, and the greater the likelihood of adaptive behaviour. Hence, maladjustment of the physically disabled is not so much an indicator of pathological processes resulting from the inherent nature of the specific defect, as a particular pattern of adjustment, given a reduced repertoire of normal interactive skills and the devaluating responses of normals.

In conclusion, observed similarities and differences in the behaviour of the disabled do not reflect objective characteristics of that behaviour which have an independent observable existence in a separately identifiable environment, but are differences in the ways in which that behaviour is identified. The 'same' behaviour, whether in a mentally subnormal or physically disabled individual, child or adult, may be differently defined according to the considerations invoked by the defining agent. Where these considerations include the definitions of others concerned with the disabled, his behaviour is explicable within the context of everyday interaction. 'Social factors' constitute both necessary and sufficient conditions for its understanding, and any identified defect is significant in so far as it differentiates others' responses to the disabled individual. Where others' definitions are excluded from consideration, observed similarities and differences in the behaviour of the disabled are attributable solely to imputed characteristics of the underlying defect, of which the individual is simply the means of expression.

Administrative classifications, as Richardson (1969) points out, foster the assumption of 'neat single effects' of disability, or of what Meyerson (*op. cit.*) notes to be Aristotelian explanations: the deaf are suspicious 'because' they are deaf; the blind apathetic because they are blind. Such explanations rest on a fundamental separation of the individual from his environment. At most, social factors become conditions which allow more or less of the effects of disability to become apparent. Thus Soddy acknowledges that 'when it comes to the questions of prognosis, equal if not greater weight must be given to the question of the child's environment', but in the preceding sentence treats 'social conditions' as something which may simply 'complicate the diagnosis', and for which therefore 'some allowance' must be made (*op. cit.*, p. 46). He notes the higher prevalence of identified subnormality amongst school children, but argues that this is because 'school life exposes subnormal children to the situation which they are least able to sustain' (*ibid.*, p. 25). Similarly, the greater numbers of persons identified as subnormal with increasing industrialization indicates 'the creation of special problems for its subnormal members by an industrial society' (*ibid.*, p. 26).

The question of how social factors ought to be considered will be taken up again later in this and the next chapter. Differences already indicated in conceptualization of the phenomena of disability are an important source of differences in and explanations of the effects of a disabled child on his family. These I now consider.

THE 'EFFECTS' OF DISABILITY

Two main approaches in the literature on disability and the family can be distinguished. I shall examine, first, their typical characteristics and, second, their underlying assumptions. Initially they conceive differently the effects of a disabled child on family life, and this is based on a fundamentally different perspective on social life in general, but in terms of my own perspective both are ultimately found inadequate.

The first approach is typified in the following quotation (McMichael, 1971, p. 15):

We are beginning to realise that a physical handicap, of itself, constitutes an emotional hazard and sooner or later will become an emotional challenge, both for the child and his family. The handicap will involve the family from time to time in crises which they can either surmount, thus strengthening their own personalities and relationships, or evade, so weakening and distorting them.

No examination of the processes by which a child was identified as disabled is thereby made. If it is, this is treated as a matter of solely historical interest: parents may be asked how they 'found out' that their child was disabled, to name their 'sources of information'. In either case, the presence of disability is taken as an established fact. This is of course partly because studies necessarily occur after the identification of disability, but the implication is that there is an objective meaning of the child's condition which parents may or may not have discovered. Where parents disagree with others' interpretations of the child's condition, it is their assessments which require explanation. Finding differences between mothers' and doctors' evaluations of the severity of handicap in the child on a basis of a number of pre-defined categories, McMichael says that 'the mothers appeared unable to accept the grave outlook' (*ibid.*, p. 35). Similarly, where mothers disagreed with teachers' ratings of their child's adjustment 'in general the observations of the teachers are likely to be more objective' (*ibid.*, p. 83). Given that the facts of disability are regarded as independent of the effects, or parents' responses to them, the research problem is one of categorizing parents' responses in relation to them.

In 1964 Kelman pointed to the consensus in the literature that the effects of a disabled child are necessarily 'noxious'. The continuing assumption of pathology in family life is evident in the earlier quotation or in the following: 'The family is slowed up in its affectional and emotion-satisfying performances' (Meyerowitz and Kaplan, 1967, p. 253). This assumption variously informs methodology. McMichael (*op. cit.*) presents her results in seven chapters, each dealing with one of the 'kinds of problems' that parents face, and devotes considerable space to scoring the amount of 'rejection' of their child shown in parents' responses. Fowle (1968) presents the two central hypotheses of her investigation as: (1) the marital integration of parents who have kept their severely retarded children at home tends to be lower than that of parents who have institutionalized them; and (2) the role tension of siblings between the ages of six and seventeen in families who have kept the retarded child at home tends to be higher than in those who have institutionalized the child. Accordingly, it is 'marital integration' and 'sibling role tension' that are measured. Kelman (*op. cit.*) provides some illustrations from his own research of the consequences of such selective definition of the 'relevant' areas for investigation. For example, that parents of mongoloid children visit outside the home less than those of non-mongoloid children might be adduced as evidence of their 'special isolation' were it not that they are *visited* more.

The basis for choosing indicators of such variables is obscure. Rejection could be shown by parents in their reported feelings of shame and embarrassment, their refusal to accept child-guidance, or by the father's physical desertion of the family. Marital integration and sibling role tension are regarded as having two aspects: the integration of ends and the integration of means, which in turn are defined in terms of husbands' and wives' ranking of 'domestic values' and the 'mutual co-ordination of domestic roles' respectively. Both of these indices are based on the assumption that conflict and frustration in family integration can be indexed by a parent's identification of his spouse or child in terms of uncomplimentary personal attributes.

It appears that anything parents say or do can show the effects of having a disabled child. The fact that a cystic fibrotic child requires a lot of attention results in parents having a 'felt need for eternal vigilance'; buying him a pet reflects parents' guilt regarding their role in the etiology of the condition, or paternal hostility to the child because of occupational disabilities. Parents who seek counselling services manifest their 'severe dependency needs', and the fact that those who have lost a child through death are more likely to have another is a 'guilt-denial-of-guilt reaction' (Meyerowitz and Kaplan, *op. cit.*, pp. 252–8).

If parents' responses counter the assumption of pathology, they may be variously reinterpreted in accordance with the observer's categories. The role tension of oldest boys in families which kept their retarded child at home was not significantly greater than in those who had institutionalized the child, but 'the trends are however in the predicted direction for the significance level of ·09 is not far removed from the acceptable level of ·05' (Fowle, *op. cit.*, p. 471). Again 'the mothers' responses could be seen as an attempt perhaps to put a good face on it, or as an unwillingness to admit to difficulties in handling the child at home' (McMichael, *op. cit.*, p. 84); 'the mothers' inability to recognise the seriousness of their child's condition appears to arise . . . from a general attitude of guilt and rejection, and . . . from an unwillingness to acknowledge [the child's] severe limitations in both physical and mental development' (*ibid.*, p. 35). Hewett observes: 'if families of handicapped children do not break down there is a strong possibility that they will become too cohesive, and . . . that the handicapped children will be "over-dependent" because their mothers are "over-protective"' (1970, p. 77).

The third main characteristic of this approach is apparent. This is that the effects of having a disabled child are primarily conceptualized in terms of intra-psychic, or intra-familial processes and relationships. McMichael (*op. cit.*) devotes four chapters to 'emotional' problems, treating 'social' problems separately, despite the social basis of 'shame' and 'embarrassment' evident in examples cited of people staring at and making remarks about the disabled child. Moreover, inadequate housing and financial difficulties are things that parents 'must face'. Meyerowitz and Kaplan (*op. cit.*) similarly translate social considerations into psychic terms and examine three 'levels of response': the intra-psychic, intra-familial and family-community.

Where they are not so transformed, social factors may provide a further source of what Garfinkel (1967) characterizes as '*ad hoc*' considerations for explaining otherwise discrepant results.[6] Thus Meyerowitz and Kaplan (*op. cit.*) adduce such factors as the age of parents, distribution of children between well and ill, or the prior death of a child, with no apparent grounding in their findings. Fowle (*op. cit.*) suggests that the reason why the marital integration of parents who kept their severely retarded children at home was not significantly different from that of parents who had institutionalized them was that the former used community day centres. If the reader can 'see' the relevance of such factors, and thereby understand 'what might be going on' in the families investigated, it is because he shares the knowledge, or the 'background expectancies' which inform such interpretations. In this case, the source of such meanings is a certain conception of normal family life in which the presence of a disabled member 'must' create certain problems according to the structure of the particular family concerned. These points will be taken up in this and the next chapter.

In the second kind of approach to the question of the effects of a disabled child on his family, an examination of the processes by which parents identified their child as disabled is central. Hewett (*op. cit.*) gives many case examples of these, and concludes that the majority of parents (70 per cent) thought that doctors should tell parents as soon as they suspect that something is wrong with the child, even though they may not be sure what it is. However, she found in practice that 'doctors (and other professional people) are opponents rather than allies to be approached with a mixture of caution and militance, rather than confidence' (*op. cit.*, p. 46) from whom it is difficult to obtain satisfaction.

Meadow (1968) relates the problems of doctor–parent interaction, partly to the medical ambiguities of a particular condition, that of congenital deafness. Considering both participants' perspectives, she analyses the events of diagnosis and prescription in three stages: (1) the 'diagnostic funnel', defined as that period of time after parents suspect that something is wrong with their child, but before a diagnosis has been confirmed; (2) when a positive diagnosis is made, and (3) when, following diagnosis, some prescription is made by the doctor. Focusing on the events following diagnosis of poliomyelitis, Davis (1963) conceptualizes two major strategies by which parents seek to sustain their definition of the child as normal. These are 'normalization', where parents seek validation from others, and 'disassociation', where parents avoid audiences which might invalidate their definition.

Consideration of such issues has two important features. Firstly, the independent significance of parents' definitions of their child's behaviour is asserted. '[The mother] needs above all else to be taken seriously' (Hewett, *op. cit.*, p. 30): 'One really needs to see cerebral palsied children to understand how their disordered movements affect their general appearance' (*ibid.*, p. 38). This author bases her classifications of severity of disability solely on mothers' judgments. Davis (*op. cit.*) found that medical evaluations of the severity of impairment were not directly related to the level of the child's later performance. Thus a 'severely' disabled girl learnt to participate in many activities with normal children, whilst a 'moderately' disabled boy became increasingly housebound. Differences in their performance are attributed to differences in their parents' behaviour, but this is identified not in terms of general attitudes of acceptance or rejection, but to specific everyday management practices.

Secondly, far from being suddenly disrupted, family life is found, with this approach, to be continuous with its existing style and structure. Observing that a disabled child is as likely to be born into a family with pre-existing strains and stresses as not, and thus without a prior assumption of pathology, Hewett finds that mothers attempt to use their experience with normal children in bringing up a disabled child, only trying to adapt when difficulties arise. Moreover, she emphasizes the normality of many such difficulties. How much a child is taken out always depends on the area in which the family lives, the number of children, whether they have a car, and 'above all, the preferences, tastes and finances of the particular family' (*op. cit.*, p. 27). The weather, carrying shopping, and getting on to buses constitute the everyday context in which mothers find difficulties in using a wheelchair. From this perspective, the inadequacy of concepts like 'guilt', 'acceptance' and 'adjustment' is made apparent: 'What are parents guilty *about*? Acceptance and adjustment . . . describe complex patterns of feelings, attitudes and circumstance in terms so grossly over-simplified as to distort, almost out of recognition, the original response . . . of the individual parent' (*ibid.*, p. 204).

Farber (1964) similarly argues that one should not treat parents' adjustments as more or less unique reactions, but regard the onset of disability as the initiation of a *new process*. 'The ways by which families meet critical events are not generally as well conceptualized as are the stimuli' (*ibid.*, p. 392). He emphasizes 'what action is to be taken to counteract a series of events over which the family are concerned' (*ibid.*, p. 394). Davis (*op. cit.*) proposes the 'summary concept' of 'emergence' to indicate that reactions displayed by families are not in any strict sense 'determined' by the objective events, nor that they stem from personality characteristics, attitudes or inter-personal configurations. Rather, this regards reactions in terms of an ongoing developmental process, an improvisatory 'building up'. The actual undergoing of the process sets its own conditions for future action, the conditions being 'an existential amalgam of previously emergent responses and events' (*ibid.*, p. 10). Davis says that this defies causal reduction, and if, *post hoc*, certain regularities can be found in the process, this is not to say that the end states are wholly contained in the beginnings.

Accordingly, in using the concept of crisis, he refers to underlying perceptual-interpretative processes, whereby the family is 'carried from' a state of relative security concerning its members to one that is perceived as very threatening, and he observes that this still suggests more order than there actually is. He regards the family as a 'simmering vessel of primary social life' (*ibid.*, p. 110), to which nearly all individual experience is brought home for synthesis and transformation, and thus finds that families do not get alienated, disorganized, or detached from a historic sense of who and what they were. Continuity of identity is preserved as a result of the emergent character of the ongoing adjustment process, with its redefinitions, re-evaluations and retrospective reconstructions. The changes that do occur, which are usually denied by families, are mediated by a 'variety of psychological masking devices that disguise their experiential contour and give them the stamp of a familiar and known past' (*ibid.*, p. 11).

Having a disabled child appears, then, with this approach to be, like the interpretations of the behaviour of the disabled examined earlier, understandable in terms consistent with normal behaviour. This presentation is primarily achieved on the basis of (a) attempting to give parents' versions of their experience and (b) providing background information on the family situation as the context to which their responses refer. One can then understand parents' lack of expressions of dissatisfaction at having no inside toilet: they never had one and the disabled child is incontinent (Hewett, *op. cit.*, p. 48); or that for low-income families the hardships arising from the disability were additive on a base of daily struggle, in which priorities were assigned to more urgent family health and social problems (Farber, *op. cit.*). However, other considerations are invoked and these, as in the other approach, are essentially psychological.

Davis regards parents' statements about 'greater solidarity and amity [as having] relevance primarily at the testimonial level' since he says 'strains and tensions soon became evident in the functioning of most of the families' (*op. cit.*, p. 116). As his major example, he gives parents' acknowledgment that their normal children became spoiled whilst the polio child was in hospital. His explanation of families' failure to experience a loss of identity is based on Gestalt psychology: the normal aggregate of family pursuits, interests and relations retained enough of its contour and detail, so that alterations in the figure fail to induce perceptual reorganization of the total field. When discussing how mothers do eventually manage to take their cerebral palsied child out, Hewett only says 'equanimity in the face of friends and of curious strangers has been hardly won over a period of time' (*op. cit.*, p. 120).

Farber's central aim is to differentiate types of crisis: 'tragic' and 'role-organizational' as different ways in which family members perceive disruption and to associate this with socio-economic status. Parents of high socio-economic status perceive the disruption as tragic because it is a frustration of their hopes and aspirations for the child and the family as a whole. Parents of low status see the problem rather as one of coping with a seemingly interminable care problem. His conceptualization of the intervening processes appeals to differences in parents' attitudes to socialization: emphasis on the development of self-control where socialization is primarily the child's activity *versus* emphasis on parental control to achieve obedience and responsiveness to parental authority. He again provides examples which indicate the referents of such variables. Thus, in the tragic case, the parents regard themselves as implicated and cannot blame the child for his condition, and so they cannot rationalize their hostility towards him. However, he still does not show how parents resolve such problems: 'the resolution of this conflict lies in the priorities assigned by the parent to his conformity with conventional norms and obligations as compared with personal gratification' (op. cit., p. 416).

Further, although he indicates how, for example, the 'revision of extra-familial commitments' might differentially support new modes of family organization in that parents discontinue relations with those who do not support such modes, he does not consider the circumstances in which families may take such non-supportive reaction seriously, nor in either case the relationship between outsiders' actions and the organization of family life. Like the studies examined earlier, he ultimately adduces other factors such as religion and moral principles which might also influence the 'distortion of family coalitions'.

Nor does Davis leave us submerged in the irreducible complexity of social life, but attempts to show how parents' experiences may have some common structure. Thus, the optimism of parents whose child has only recently contracted polio is 'buttressed' by their 'great faith in medicine'; their concern about their own responsibility for the child's condition reflects a 'key assumption in American values that misfortune does not touch those who take proper precautions and measures' (op. cit., p. 36). Parents are constrained to enact their roles with 'that blend of sorrow, courage, altruism and solidarity that American mores define as appropriate in such situations' (ibid., p. 115) and the sudden paralysis of their child 'appeared to challenge in a number of fundamental respects the parents' conceptions of themselves as responsible and devoted mothers and fathers' (ibid., p. 36). Such conceptualizations are undeniably more sophisticated than those hitherto considered, but they are grounded in a similar theoretical inadequacy.

In both approaches, the analysis depends ultimately upon the kind of conceptual operation pointed out by Blumer (1956), as 'short-comings in contemporary variable analysis'. He says first (op. cit., p. 683):

> there seems to be little limit to what may be chosen or designated as a variable . . . variables may be selected on the basis of a specious impression of what is important, on the basis of conventional usage, on the basis of what can be secured through

a given instrument or technique, on the basis of the demands of some doctrine, or on the basis of imaginative ingenuity in devising a new term.

Second, that variables have no fixed or uniform indicator: 'it seems clear that indicators are tailored and used to meet the peculiar character of the local problem under study' (*ibid.*, p. 685), and, third, that though the data and findings on which analyses are based are here-and-now, yet the here-and-now context is excluded in presentation. There are, however, as has been indicated, important differences between the two approaches in the ways that they treat parents' statements, and these will now be examined in detail.

In the first approach, parents' responses suggest nothing of their conception of themselves and their family life. Such issues have been settled in advance: the entry of a disabled child necessarily disrupts normal family functioning. This assumption is sustained, first by treating the families as having no life prior to, or other than, that which is ordered by the presence of a disabled member; second, by selective definition of the relevant areas for investigation; and, third, by methods of relating parents' responses to such variables, whereby any can count as evidence of the effects of having a disabled child. Since it is assumed that having a disabled child necessarily creates various problems, parents' statements are treated as indicators of their intra-psychic and intra-familial adjustments to such problems. Their overt behaviour is taken as designating certain internal states, which are then seen as causing that behaviour. Parents say and do what they say they do because they have not accepted the child's disability, are guilty and rejecting, or have problems in managing the disabled or other children. The only purpose that parents might have in the immediate situation is that of denying that they have any problems. As Walsh (1972) points out in his criticism of behaviourism, this excludes the possibility that the same overt behaviour may designate different intentions on the parents' part, and that they might act differently in different situations. Differences in parents' observed behaviour that are unaccountable within the existing framework are explained by importing additional considerations, again based on the observer's commonsense notions of the kinds of structures which are typically associated with such behaviour.

Hence, like some of the studies of disability cited earlier, this approach substitutes practical for analytic concerns. If parents' responses are categorized as indicating a more or less undesirable state of affairs, the evident corollary is that something should be done to change it. What is at issue here is not whether having a disabled child does present problems, but that this assumption does not make sense in terms of the evidence of parents' statements.

In the second approach, there is no prior assumption of family pathology. Rather, an attempt is made to treat parents' responses as indicators of their conception of what it is like to have a disabled child, and as such, of complex conscious processes of perception and interpretation. Rather than attempt to explain parents' statements from an independent standpoint, they are interpreted on the basis of what parents themselves say about their family situation, both in the past and present. The relevant variables are then largely those which parents themselves suggest, and the apparent normality of their situation is understandable within the contexts they provide. Thus far, this approach displays some of the features of the phenomenological method, as presented by Bruyn (1968). However, no means for understanding similarities and differences in parents' statements is thereby provided. As some of Davis's work suggested, and as Douglas (1971a) says of phenomenology and Gestalt psychology in general, an emphasis on the contextual determination of meaning becomes, in an extreme form, a kind of 'sociological solipsism', which makes all observations and analyses completely dependent on the situations in which they occur. Further, the question of the relationship between parents' statements and their family life is of course excluded, since no inference to other situations can be made.

However, the writers examined do assume that parents' here-and-now statements should be valid indicators of their behaviour in other situations. As in the first approach, they then are faced with the same discrepancy between what parents say and what they 'ought' to say, given the undesirability of having a disabled child. They similarly import other considerations, such as parents' attitudes to socialization; norms, mores; religious and other principles to make sense of this discrepancy. How such variables might produce parents' responses is more explicit, but similarly identified not in parents' observed responses, but on the basis of unobservable intervening psychological processes. They are 'given independent status *vis-à-vis* the actor, in the sense that he is seen as a passive vehicle of their operation' (Walsh, *op. cit.*, p. 42). Hence, whether parents are seen as rational or denying, coping or rejecting, what they actually say has to be variously reinterpreted in order to sustain the observer's conception of what it 'really' means to have a disabled child.

Both presentations remain within what various writers have termed the 'normative paradigm' of social life. In this, 'interaction is viewed as rule-governed in the sense that an observed pattern of action is rendered intelligible and is explained by referring to rules in the forms of dispositions and expectations to which actors are subject' (Wilson, 1971, p. 60). The major problem with this, however, is that if rules are to account for observed or imputed similarities in action in different situations, or over time, there must be an assumption of 'substantial cognitive consensus'. Actors must agree not only that a situation is one in which a particular rule should be followed, but on what counts as evidence that it is being followed. As any lawyer knows, neither matter is unproblematic.

'Attitudes', 'values', 'mores', 'rules', other 'factors' and the conceptions of normality which embody them, are constructs which typically mystify both the processes to which they refer and the methods by which they are constructed. Various writers have made such points. For example: attitudes are 'abstract expressions of values or preferences given in interview situations, i.e. divorced from concrete, everyday situations' (Douglas, *op. cit.*, p. 172). Values are 'abstractions inferred from acts . . . the act of valuation is a sorting out and ordering process which occurs when events are mediated by the cognitive processes of the cerebral cortex, which results in preferences for various courses of action' (Lemert, 1967, p. 6). The inadequacy of such terms is apparent when one recognizes that everyday action is necessarily context-bound, hence continually 'new' and 'different', and yet actors manage most of the time to sustain a sense of continuity and order, and others recognize similarities or orderly properties in their actions.

If an attempt to account for order or common structures in social action is to be made, then one must examine in what sense such structures 'exist'. Blumer says that this is 'only as they enter into the process of interpretation and definition, out of which joint actions are formed' (1965, p. 543). Rules, norms and values are 'reference points' or, as Cicourel (1970) argues, at the very most formally stated or written rules, which are invoked by actors in formulating their actions to achieve their purposes. Hence, if one is to account for orderly interaction, one must examine the actual ways in which actors invoke such rules, and not impose them on the data.

An adequate account of the apparent normality of the situation of parents with disabled children as presented by them is not then to be sought in the imputation of psychological states, whether 'desirable' or otherwise, nor in the imposition of social factors which might produce them. Rather, an attempt must be made to examine parents' actual statements as ways of making it so appear, to see how parents invoke normality as an adequate account of their situation. Evidently this will not refute the assumption of underlying pathology in family life. Indeed, in itself, it says nothing about family life at all.

2 Normal appearances and official morality

The explanation of any behaviour cannot be based simply on descriptions of external bodily movements or characteristics and the external situations in which such phenomena occur. Man is not an organism which passively responds to influences from either the 'outside' environment or his 'inside' characteristics, or both. Rather, he acts towards the world and constructs his behaviour according to the way he interprets or defines the situation and his own intentions or purposes in that situation. The 'same' outward phenomenon may have many different meanings. Meaning is not given or inherent in 'things'; rather, we have to 'make sense' of what is 'happening to us'.

Its construction, however, is not an individual enterprise; it is produced in interaction with others. An individual's action is formulated on the basis of his perception of the other inter-actants, and since such perception is necessarily a product of inference from appearances rather than directly known 'testing inferences ... is a continuing element in interaction ... inter-action is an essentially interpretative process in which meanings evolve and change over the course of interaction' (Wilson, 1971, p. 67).

This, in essence, is the 'interpretive paradigm' of social life as proposed by Blumer (1956; 1965) and variously interpreted in analyses ascribed to social phenomenology, symbolic interaction-ism and ethnomethodology. I shall not attempt a systematic presentation of the development of such perspectives, nor of their contemporary inter-relationships, but shall continue to appeal to those aspects which are relevant to my aims.[1]

I want to say something about what it is like, or what it means to parents, to have a disabled child. This, I have argued, depends upon an examination of parents' statements in the interview situation. Over all, the majority of parents claim that their disabled child has not had deleterious effects on their family life.

The question is, how they construct such claims in the face of questioning which implicitly asserts the contrary.

Parents do not deny any differences between their situation and that of normal parents. Moreover, they talk about various problems and especially in certain areas such as the nature of the child's condition and interaction with him and others outside the home. Evidently, they talk about other situations, their encounters with other persons, and there are differences amongst them in the ways that they make such talk.

I shall relate differences in what parents told me about their interaction in other situations to differences in their appearances in the interview situation. That is, I shall examine their interview talk to see what meanings they invoke in 'describing' their experiences, but I locate the sources of these meanings in situations other than the interview. To do this, I draw on other studies of phenomena which I consider to be analytically or substantively 'similar'. In the next chapter, I attempt some historical reconstruction of this argument; this chapter is intended as an analytic account.

I shall examine parents' statements as they appear to refer to three substantive topics: (1) the child's disability (chapter 5); (2) their own relationships with others inside and outside the home (chapter 6); and (3) differences between their situation and that of normal parents (chapter 8). The methods of treating parents' statements adopted in these chapters are outlined here and shown as informed principally by symbolic interactionist (or 'labelling') and ethnomethodological accounts of deviant and normal behaviour. The central theme is that of the relationship between objective or other-given meanings of the parents' situation and their own situational constructions. This is discussed first in the context of parents' statements about their child's condition and second in that of sociological and other conceptions of 'the family'. Basically, I argue that parents' statements on each topic constitute the appearance of normal family life because it is as normal parents that others, both informal and formal agencies, treat them.

DEVIANCE AND ACCOUNTABILITY

Historically, analyses based on the interpretive paradigm were most developed in studies of deviant behaviour such as crime, drug-addiction and mental illness (see e.g. Rubington and Weinberg, 1968). From this perspective (Becker, 1966, pp. 9–14):

deviance is *not* a quality of the act the person commits, but rather a consequence of the application by others of rules and sanctions to an 'offender'. The deviant is one to whom that label has successfully been applied; deviant behaviour is behaviour that people so label. . . . Deviance is not a quality that lies in behaviour itself, but in the interaction between the person who commits an act and those who respond to it.

Lemert (1951) argues that it is essential to distinguish between 'primary' deviation which has only marginal implications for the self-concept and identity of the person concerned when the deviance is perceived as a normal variation ('normalized'), or as one which can be dealt with through nominal controls, and 'secondary' deviations. In this case the imputed labels or others' categorizations of the behaviour concerned 'become central facts of existence for those experiencing them, altering psychic structure producing specialized organization of social roles and self-regarding attitudes' (Lemert, 1967, p. 41). Such categories thus make fundamental assertions about a person's underlying 'nature'. They constitute a 'total identity' (Garfinkel, 1956) and act to turn attention away from an individual's other attributes, which might otherwise qualify him for 'normal' status and therefore sustain normal interaction.

Goffman (1968) gives an extensive analysis of these processes as they may affect a wide variety of persons with a 'stigma' or mark of moral inferiority. He says that by definition we believe the person with a stigma is 'not quite human', but shows the contextual dependence of secondary deviation. The 'evidentness' of a stigma symbol is a product of situational considerations, and even 'visible' signs of deviance, e.g. mongoloid features, may not be evident to those with little knowledge of the condition. Others, such as facial scars, may not be perceived in fleeting encounters or darkened rooms. In the absence of outward signs, the discredited condition must be 'known about', e.g. that the individual is subnormal, or diabetic. Stigmatization may depend on the 'obtrusiveness' of a condition, i.e. the extent to which it actually interferes with interaction in a given situation. The subnormality of a child may become evident, though not previously known about, nor outwardly visible, if interaction demonstrates his lack of normally expected skills. Finally, the meaning of a particular condition may be influenced by conceptions of its 'perceived focus'; that is, in what situations it is seen to disqualify the individual from effective action. Facial scars or blindness can be irrelevant in telephone conversations; the inability to walk need be no disadvantage, though quite evident, in a sedentary activity.

Given the situational sources of variation, Goffman goes on to show how the individual with a stigma and other participants may actively manage a situation in such a way that the stigma is not apparent or its implications disattended. He thus argues that secondary deviation should be seen as a relational concept and as one which refers simply to 'the extreme of a graded series of moral adaptations found among "normal" persons, as well as those with . . . stigma' (Lemert, 1967, p. 41). Most people have some attribute which makes them potentially discreditable, though they may not be discredi*ted* in any specific situation.

Freidson (1965) takes up Goffman's argument in his analysis of disability as a form of deviance. He examines classificatory schemes whereby different types of disability can be located in relation to forms of deviance. The first is constructed in terms of two dimensions: those of 'personal responsibility' and 'imputed prognosis' – whether deviance is believed to be 'curable' or 'incurable'. Together these differentiate some of the ways in which any given deviance is managed or controlled by others. Imputed responsibility is critical since it bears on the moral identity of the person concerned and on the obligations others may feel towards him. Where deviance is thought to be curable, its management is likely to be temporary; where incurable it may be permanent, with execution as the extreme. Freidson (*ibid.*, p. 77) gives Table 1 in illustration.

TABLE 1

Imputed prognosis	Responsible	Not responsible
Curable	Limited punishment	Treatment, education and correction
Incurable	Execution; Life imprisonment	Protective custody

Freidson notes, however, that the management of incurability, whether or not responsibility is imputed, is not always markedly different. Institutions for the mentally subnormal are similar in many ways to maximum security prisons in Goffman's (1961a) analysis of 'total institutions'. Moreover, many disabilities are neither curable nor incurable, but 'improvable', which constitutes a distinctly different state. Freidson (*op. cit.*) further argues that a simple moral dichotomy of responsibility does not allow for those 'graded moral adaptations' analysed by Goffman (1968) and incorporates Goffman's conception of stigma as well as the category of 'improvable but incurable'. In a second table (*ibid.*, p. 80) he differentiates between e.g. crippling as stigmatized, and hearing loss as not, though both are 'not responsible' and 'improvable but not curable', and between both and dwarfism, for which an individual again is not held responsible, but which is stigmatized, incurable and unimprovable (see Table 2).

TABLE 2

Imputed prognosis	Responsible		Not responsible	
	No stigma	Stigma	Stigma	No stigma
Curable	Parking violation	Syphilis	Leprosy	Pneumonia
Improvable but not curable		Burglary	Crippling	Hearing loss
Incurable and unimprovable		Sex murder	Dwarfism	Cancer

Other authors variously pursue the situational variability of others' treatment of the disabled. Haber and Smith argue that we should focus rather on 'the elaboration of behavioural alternatives within existing role relationships, rather than the proliferation of specialized role repertoires' (1971, p. 37). The behaviour of the disabled individual may be normalized: it may not, therefore, constitute secondary deviation. Mercer (1965) provides more evidence of how this may arise. Focusing on the question of why the families of some individuals take them back home after a period of institutionalization in a hospital for the retarded, while other families do not, despite similar officially-defined degrees of deviance, she offers an explanation in terms of divergences in definition between the families concerned and official agents of control. Lower-status families are more likely to reject the official definition of the child as retarded, whilst higher-status families share the same definitions.

Such arguments, however, as Lemert points out, ignore several distinctive characteristics of secondary deviation. First, 'beyond the cognitive, dramatic details of face to face interaction' are 'organizational forces of social control through which public and private agencies actively define and classify people . . . set limits to social interaction and induct deviants into special segregated environments' (1967, p. 41). Second, that individuals so defined respond to themselves as moral types, even though they may successfully manage the appearance of normality, because, third, the objective meanings of stigma symbols are grounded in definitions which depict polarized moral opposites.

Thus, whether or not, as Mercer finds, families agree with official definitions of their child's retardation (that he is disabled) it is these which are more 'powerful', in that it is these which will be implemented when the child is assessed for schooling, and as Freidson notes, his later treatment may then resemble that of a criminal. Moreover, however a disabled individual is treated by his family or by official agents, his 'disability' is recognizable in terms of some conception of a normally 'able' person of a comparable age, and this concept does appear to have some status as an absolute category.

Recent philosophical work on the problems of what is necessary to ascribe 'person' suggests that an entity must be recognized as possessing both physical characteristics and a state of consciousness. Puccetti (1968) points out that this can include animals, and excludes incorporeal persons such as God. He examines the practical uses of the concept, and shows that two conditions must be satisfied. First, that the object of ascription has a distinct *intellectual* character, which presupposes access to, and familiarity with, a conceptual scheme, i.e. an ability to use symbols (unlike animals), and, second, that it has a *moral* character, that it is capable of assimilating a conceptual scheme in which moral words and phrases have a place. Hence, he concludes that the concept of a person *is* the concept of a moral agent, an entity to whose behaviour one can properly impute a moral character.

Some experimental findings may be interpreted to illustrate this analysis. Richardson *et al.* (1961) discover great uniformity in children's preferences for pictured children with and without various visible physical handicaps. Moreover, the hierarchy of preferences is related not to degree of functional impairment, as one might commonsensically suppose, but to the distance of the impairment from the face. The authors note the prime importance of the face is initial assessment of another person. In other words, children's preferences are related to their ability to ascribe a (moral) character to the pictured child. Further, a picture of an obese child is consistently rated lowest, and as Richardson (1970) says, referring to Maddox *et al.* (1968), this is a condition for which people are held responsible: it indicates a lack of self-control or a morally reprehensible character.

When moral character is *not* imputed, the entity concerned is not regarded as a person. Since the ascription of intellectual character is a necessary condition of that of moral character, and to the extent that ascription of intellectual character is influenced by physical characteristics, then the disabled individual may not be regarded as a person. It should be noted that on this analysis a human child is a non-person, but he is of course expected to become one after a (negotiable) age. Richardson (*ibid.*) found that younger children did respond more to degree of functional impairment perceiving the pictured children as relatively 'strange' in terms of their more limited experience of a range of physical types. In terms of the above analysis, they had not yet learned to use the 'appropriate' moral categories. When the child is disabled, however, this expectation becomes problematic – in what ways and with what implications for interaction I shall discuss in chapter 6.

Here I examine what such analyses of deviance might tell us about parents' statements about their disabled child's condition. This requires spelling out some of the main ideas involved.

Definitions of the child's condition may vary through time as well as space: different contexts favour the construction of different meanings. This does not mean that all definitives are 'situationally specific', that there are as many meanings of the phenomenon as there are definitional situations. The range of possible definitions is 'primarily constrained by the shared cultural meanings that are culturally defined as relevant to the phenomena' (Douglas, 1967). A child who does not respond to auditory stimulation may be asleep, deaf, distracted or subnormal, but not, in our society, bewitched or fixated by the evil eye. Those who hope that a child whose muscles are severely contracted may become a champion footballer are likely to be regarded as deluded and irrational. Most phenomena, however, 'are' sufficiently ambiguous for several different meanings to be generally seen as appropriate. Thus, the various others concerned with defining the phenomenon may disagree as to which is 'the' (true) meaning. The process by which such conflict is resolved, or what Scheff (1968) calls 'negotiation', is not influenced solely by the 'nature' of the phenomenon itself. As has already been seen, the type of assessment methods used, or the availability of treatment services, may produce a different outcome.

Further, as Scheff (*op. cit.*) argues, the relative 'power' of the interactants may decide whose definition gets accepted as the 'right' one. Those with authority in a particular area, such as psychiatrists or doctors, can not only appeal to their 'expert' knowledge, but often give or withhold their services, disregarding the opinion of the individual in question or his representative (e.g. parent). Meadow (1968) recounts the difficulties parents encountered in persuading doctors that their child was deaf rather than they themselves over-anxious.

The decision of the defining agent may of course be strongly influenced by the behaviour of the individual in an assessment encounter,[2] but the situation may constrain such behaviour so that it is not necessarily typical. Thus it may not constitute adequate evidence for predicting behaviour in other situations, and hence for constructing a valid 'overall' definition.

Zigler (1966) argues that the formal assessment of mental subnormality is likely to produce anxiety which has been shown to depress performance levels. From this perspective an analysis of the face-to-face situations in which definitions are constructed is then essential. Crucial to this is a consideration of how the inter-actants may actively try to influence each other's definition of the situation through attempting to 'manage' the impression that their behaviour makes on the other, thus constraining the other to categorize it according to their respective intentions.

Definitions may also vary through time as different 'others' become involved and thus different patterns of negotiation take place. Again, however, this does not mean that definitions need remain in constant flux. Of course, some may 'shift' more than others. As will be seen in chapter 5, parents may often wonder if their child is 'really' retarded, and more at certain times than others. Generally, the longer a definition has provided adequate explanation of an individual's behaviour, the more resistant to change it will become. But, once certain decisions as to the meaning of a phenomenon have been made, former alternatives may be cut off. That is, particular decisions may act as 'turning points' or 'points of no return' (Lemert, 1967). Once a child has been formally diagnosed as 'a mongol', negotiation then centres around the questions of the severity of the condition and what action, if any, should be taken.

The process of definition through time is often conceptualized as a 'career' since, as in an occupation, the individual is pro-gressively transformed in the eyes of others and himself. For example, the academic is transformed from the ambiguous status of student to fully-fledged professional standing with a permanent university post. The 'mentally subnormal' is produced through a process beginning with doubts as to an individual's intellectual ability to his eventual placement in an institution. Different careers may have very different consequences for the individuals concerned. It is important to discover what agents become involved with his behaviour; what decisions they make with what consequences for later negotiation and decisions. For example, whether or when behaviour defined by certain others as 'odd' is referred to the attention of an expert, the kind of expert may greatly influence how the individual is categorized and with what consequences. If parents can arrange to have their child privately educated, then he may never be officially labelled as educationally subnormal. How an individual is categorized therefore depends on those with whom he comes into contact (Cicourel, 1968).

Further, the processes of definition are dynamic. Labelling can change the nature of what is labelled through modifying patterns of interaction concerning the phenomenon. For instance, once parents 'know' that their child is a mongol, and even though they may want and try to treat him as normally as possible, they may think that there is something that they could do to help him and attempt to find out what behaviour it is appropriate to adopt towards a child of 'this kind'.

Sustained interaction with another person is hazardous if not impossible without developing some idea of what that person is 'really like'. Turner (1968) argues that 'person conceptions' enable us both to interpret the other's behaviour with some degree of confidence and to act appropriately towards him. Not only do person conceptions *direct* interaction, they are *produced* in interaction. Initial tentative conceptions of an other or others are modified until a fairly stable picture emerges which serves to account for most of the other's behaviour. This tends to be defined as the 'real' other which becomes increasingly impervious to counter-conceptions of him and which acts to interpret the inherent ambiguity of many actions.

For most parents interaction with their child is relatively unproblematic. Not only do they 'know' what children in general are like, but close and continuous interaction with a particular child enables them to develop, or at his birth to expect to be able to develop, a reliable conception of what he is or will be like. But the discovery that one's child is 'different' in some way calls into question the normal recipes of child-rearing. To the extent that parents must rely on 'objective' knowledge of their child's condition, so their conceptions of him may be constituted more out of characteristics typical of persons suffering from that condition than of those signifying normality or peculiar to himself. Interaction directed by such a conception is likely to be self-fulfilling in two ways. First, given the above analysis: instances of behaviour which 'fit' the typical picture will reinforce that conception; those which do not may be discounted; and those which are ambiguous may become 'sensible' within its framework. 'Objective knowledge' of the typical characteristics of mongolism may direct parents' perception of and hence interaction with their particular mongol child in this way, so that he is increasingly seen as 'really like' or 'a typical' mongol.

Second, such interaction may be self-fulfilling in so far as person conceptions can become, or at least heavily influence, self-conceptions. That is, others' expectations become self-expectations which constrain behaviour accordingly and, in turn, confirm the expectations of others. This is not a sign of 'weak-will' or 'suggestibility'. Rather, as Mead (1956) argues, this is precisely what 'the self' *is*. An individual can only 'know what he is like' through social interaction, from the categorizations made of his behaviour by others. Judgments or standards of behaviour are not instinctive or given, but must be learnt. The self cannot be understood as a constant entity existing 'inside' the person, but rather as emerging from and through interaction with others. Not only is the self then created by others' definitions, but it requires constant validation from others to be maintained. Certainly, a particular individual's self-conception is unique to him, but it is constructed out of elements that are social in origin.

Others' definitions of behaviour may vary through time and space. So too, therefore, may definitions of self. Changes in others' definitions may produce corresponding changes in definitions of self. Moreover, many such changes are socially patterned in such a way that they are undergone by most members of a society. A major example of this is changes in behaviour with age. Though these may be loosely and variously defined, there are typically different expectations of what behaviour is appropriate in a baby, child, or adolescent. People are expected to 'grow up' and 'be' their age, and this is achieved through interaction so that an individual sees himself as a child and not a baby, an adult no longer an adolescent, and is constrained to behave accordingly.

Evidently there is not always perfect congruence between others' and self-definitions. One may reject others' interpretations as untrue, 'not really me', but great and long-standing discrepancies are generally taken account of with modifications in self-conception, person conceptions, or both. Nor do self-concepts change with every different definition and in every context. The opinions of some audiences are more significant to one than others. If subordinates at work label their new foreman the 'boss's man', then this may be less salient or important to him than his increased standing with his family and friends. Similarly, the handicapped child is likely to be far more influenced, in his early years at least, by the definitions of his family than by those of his peers, strangers and so on.

This analysis suggests that what parents say about their child may reflect less their own constructions than the imputations of others, notably doctors, and especially once a formal diagnosis has been made. It still, however, provides no means of seeing how parents actually do make sense of their child's behaviour when talking about his condition. The interpretive procedures through which they relate available objective meanings to specific items of his observed behaviour, presenting it as instances of those meanings, remain implicit. Cicourel (1970) makes a similar criticism of the analyses of Goffman (1959, 1961b), Mead (1956) and Turner (1968). In each, the model of the actor is one which assumes that he possesses such procedures. My analysis of the concept of the person similarly remains at the level of formal rules which, when used in specific situations, may construct the same individual as a person or non-person successively. Thus, the waiter is symbolically transformed as he enters the dining room; the servant as he goes 'below stairs'. To paraphrase McHugh (1968), parents' methods of interpretation have been put over their heads but not in their mouths.

Garfinkel (1967) takes as his central topic the study of the methods people use in everyday life in constructing social reality. Ethnomethodology is principally concerned with the problem of how members go about seeing what the other is saying. That is, how they 'produce and sustain the *sense* that they act in a shared, orderly world in which actions are concerted in stable, repetitive ways that are recognizable and reportable' (Wilson, 1971, p. 28), or in Garfinkel's own words, 'detectable, countable, recordable, reportable, tell-a-story-aboutable, analysable – in short, *accountable*' (*op. cit.*, p. 33).

The general method used is that of 'documentary interpretation'. This consists of identifying an underlying pattern 'behind' a series of appearances so that each appearance is seen as referring to that pattern. However, the pattern itself is identified through its concrete appearances 'so that the appearances reflecting the pattern and the pattern itself mutually determine one another' (Wilson, *op. cit.*, p. 67). Wilson notes that this is the same as in Gestalt analyses of the mutual determination of the 'part' and the 'whole'. Garfinkel refers to it as 'indexicality'. However, an indexical particular or particular appearance is interpreted partly on the basis of what the pattern projects as the future course of events, and subsequent events may then act to revive earlier interpretations. Members see what others say as indicating 'what someone like that could mean', 'what I could see that he could be talking about' and also as referring to 'what has been talked about so far' or 'what will have been talked about in the end' (Wieder, 1971, p. 133).

The sense of order, then, in any setting, is informed, organized, or constituted by identified particulars of that setting and activities within it, but at the same time it informs, organizes, or constitutes identification of those particulars. Thus, as was seen in chapter 1, a diagnosis of mental subnormality informs interpretations of children's behaviour as 'symptoms' of his condition, whilst at the same time that diagnosis is informed or 'confirmed' by such 'evidence'.

In an earlier article, Garfinkel proposes an analytic distinction between these two aspects of documentation. 'Basic rules' or 'constitutive expectancies' are definitions of the constitutive events of a situation. They 'define the situation and normal events . . . for persons who seek to act in compliance with them' (1963, p. 190). 'Preferential rules' refer to those considerations which are within an actor's discretion (*ibid.*, p. 192):

> to comply with or not in accordance with whatever definitions of 'correct procedure' he might invoke, as for example, considerations of efficiency, efficacy, aesthetic preference, conventional play . . . and the rest. The possibilities that preferential rules can deal with are provided by basic rules . . . the decisions that [the actor] makes must satisfy the basic rules.

Garfinkel makes no later mention of this distinction, but Cicourel retains it in his discussion of 'basic' and 'normative' rules whilst emphasizing that it is an analytic distinction. 'The basic rules provide a sense of social order that is fundamental for a normative order to exist or be negotiated and constructed. The two orders are always in interaction, and it would be absurd to speak of the one without the other' (1970).

A 'medical examination' provides an illustration of this distinction. Here the nominal constitutive expectancies are that a 'doctor' adopts some recognizably 'medical' procedure such as taking a case-history, temperature or blood sample from another, the patient, or where he is a child, his parents. If the doctor only tells jokes or chats about the weather, then an examination is not accomplished, though he may know 'enough' from the case-notes or laboratory reports to make a diagnosis without seeing the patient at all, and the patient himself be quite satisfied with the encounter. Which particular actions the doctor performs, however, are within his discretion according to his decision of, for example, what is necessary to make a diagnosis. It should be evident, especially in such a situation of unequal 'knowledge', that a variety of behaviour items can constitute appearances of a given type of activity. Thus, as Ball (1967) shows, medically 'irrelevant' features of an abortion clinic such as white coats and face-masks constitute it as a properly hygienic medical setting for its medically ignorant patrons. Equally, as will be seen in chapter 7, parents may not 'see' that anything distinctively medical has been accomplished where no diagnosis or 'treatment' is offered.

In chapter 5, I shall examine parents' statements about their child's condition, using Garfinkel's (1963) analysis as modified and extended by McHugh (*op. cit.*). This specifies the various components on which particular appearances are judged and evaluated in constituting an orderly definition. My major focus is an attempt to characterize typical methods adopted by parents in making such judgments in terms of typical differences in the pattern of components on which observed items of the child's behaviour are evaluated. I show that these methods vary according to parents' definitions of the disability on the dimension of 'speed of onset', 'clarity of diagnosis' and 'certainty of prognosis'. Evidently these definitions are constituted in and through parents' perception of items of the child's behaviour, but at the same time the three dimensions differentiate the contexts, or define the situations in which individual perceptions are constructed. They are the basic rules which such perceptions must satisfy. However, ultimately this analysis is insufficient for my purposes.

Douglas (1971a, p. 175) criticizes ethnomethodology as over-emphasizing the situational determination of meaning, thereby denying or refusing to treat its trans-situational or context-independent elements. Ethnomethodologists (or some of them) regard this as a members' problem rather than the sociologist's (Wieder, *op. cit.*, p. 138):

the possibility of producing trans-situational descriptions of e.g. 'definition of the situation', 'actor's orientation to his situation', 'cognitive maps' etc. . . . *is abandoned as the analyst's task* and becomes a further instance of the work that members do in making the *orderly* property of the setting in which they act visible to each other.

Their concern with 'order' is only with how it is made visible both to societal members and sociologists through members' accounting practice. I do not wish to reinstate what several writers (e.g. Douglas, *op. cit.*; Wilson, *op. cit.*) have pointed to as the asymmetrical tendency of many symbolic interactionists' analyses, whereby members are the helpless pawns of a fate embodied in societal definitions of them, but I do want to take up a point raised by my earlier analysis of deviance.

Parents' statements about their child may indicate less their own constructions than the imputations of others, especially doctors. The implications of this are basically expressed in two of Lemert's (1967) criticisms of Goffman (1968). That is, at least some definitions, and, as I showed, this includes disability, are grounded in moral opposites and are thus more 'powerful' both at a point and through time, and that, in the case of deviant behaviour, one should not exclude consideration of the activities of public and private agencies of social control.

The situation of parents of the disabled can be regarded as an example of a 'natural experiment' since the basic expectancies of normal child-rearing are variously called into question. Garfinkel (1967) details several such experiments in which various strategies are adopted to breach members' expectancies which are normally taken for granted, and thus make them observable in the methods that members use in attempting to reconstitute a sense of order. The most important of these basic expectancies is that one member's evaluation of a particular appearance could be seen by another person if their positions were exchanged. That is, that the context of interpretation is not a matter of personal preference, but 'consists of a standardized system of symbols, and . . . "What Anyone Knows" i.e. a pre-established corpus of socially warranted knowledge' (*ibid.*, p. 56). Given this context, an evaluation is required as a matter of 'objective necessity', it is a 'fact of nature'. Examples of 'socially-sanctioned-facts-of-life-in-society-that-any-bona-fide-member-of-the-society-knows [are] such matters as the conduct of family life . . . , distributions of . . . competence . . . , responsibility . . . , motives among members . . . and the presence of good and evil purposes behind the apparent workings of things' (*ibid.*, p. 76).

The distinctive feature of parents' experience of incongruity is that it is not necessarily produced through their own evaluations of the child's appearances as discrepant with those of a normal child. Rather, definitions of his condition in terms of the three dimensions of onset, diagnosis and prognosis may be initially and ultimately those of doctors. It is they who act to provide the basic rules in terms of which parents' evaluation of their child's behaviour must then make sense. Moreover, because such definitions are grounded in polarized moral categories, they constitute an absolute order which cannot be revised whatever present and subsequent discrepancies are apparent to parents.

The implication of this is that parents cannot assume that others will see their child as they do were they to change positions. The 'facts of the matter' are independent of their observations and to the extent that parents do make use of medical definitions of the child's condition they must variously discount the validity of their own experience. I show that from what parents say, their methods of making sense of their child's behaviour do differ according to the meaning imputed to his condition by doctors and others. However, this is not to show that what parents say does indicate their perception of their child's behaviour, or the meanings they attribute to it when in interaction with him. How, then, may their statements be regarded?

Douglas (1970, 1971a, 1971b) suggests a perspective which is based essentially on an integration of Lemert's (1967) two criticisms noted above, and, as a result, reaches a different conclusion on the third distinctive feature of secondary deviation: the relation between the imputation of deviance and an individual's conscious processes. Specifically, Douglas analyses the relationship between the activities of official agencies of control and the existence of absolute moral categories, thus focusing on the question of precisely how and in what sense objective meanings constrain situational actions. Some elaboration of his arguments is necessary.

In a pluralist society where differences and disagreements in the negotiation of the meaning of phenomena are by definition inevitable, individuals enjoy great freedom in constructing situational meanings which will yet be seen as legitimate and plausible. Douglas gives as an example the justification of extramarital sex: 'any reasonably sophisticated young American would come to such a situation well equipped with a barrage of resources from which he would hope to construct a fine legitimization for whatever he intends to do' (1971a, p. 199). According to the audience and his particular purpose, he might appeal to Freudian theory, Kinsey, Eastern glorifications of communication with one's inner being, or birth-control manuals.

Such freedom is maintained in small groups of friends, the family, or in isolated communities which are more or less autonomous from larger social institutions. In such stable groups meanings tend to become routinized, so that there is a high degree of agreement on the appropriate situational uses of rules, but an individual does not see such meanings primarily as constraints, and in any case is not of course simply swayed by others' imputed meanings, but must construct them by his own efforts. However, outside these groups members are faced with conflicting definitions, endemic 'strangeness' and a resulting untrustworthiness, and if they are to work together in such situations they must reach some agreement as to what rules can be invoked and in what way, in order to achieve their particular purposes.

One important device for reaching agreements acceptable to most members of the society derives from a distinction between 'public' and 'private' situations. Douglas observes that this can be called a *'rule of relevance*: it specifies what situations are subject to the invocation and enforcement of rules by those not normally involved. In public situations "outsiders" are legitimate enforcers while in private ones they are not' (*ibid.*, p. 227). Private places may be physical locations such as the home, school, or factory, the legal occupants of which can deny entry to others, including public officials, unless these can claim legal cause.[3] The protection of privacy may also be maintained by symbolic means. Rules of discretion and tact so proscribe the mutual acknowledgment of certain deviations that situational agreement can be maintained as if no conflict existed. There are also various forms of public rules which are recognized as relevant only to the public realm of life.

Public rules are concerned with such matters as tolerance, courtesy, decency, respectability, presentability and so on. Knowledge of such rules enables individuals whose private lives are widely disparate and who are strangers to one another to sustain a common order in public places. Douglas points to several features of what he calls the 'publicity effect'. These are, first, that such public behaviour as being able to 'get along with others', be 'nice' and 'correct' are an important basis for judging a person's character: 'Being seen to take "public appearances" seriously and giving them their "due" is itself important' (*ibid.*, p. 241). Second, in formulating their actions people take into account their conception of what 'the public' response will be: 'the generalized conception of the public and of the nature of the public morality, ideas, feelings, tendencies to action, and so on lead an individual to respond in a different way from the way he would respond if thinking only what he and the people he knows directly would think and do' (*ibid.*, p. 242). The net effect is to produce a *'least-common denominator morality which is the public morality* – a communicative strategy aimed at offending the fewest possible people . . . with . . . a minimum of specific commitments to

anything other than a celebration of the least-common denominator, public morality and beliefs' (*ibid.*, p. 242). This is not, however,
solely the result of publicity effects. To a large extent it is due to
the activities of official agencies of control.

Douglas points to the massive growth in the size and power of
official agencies in the USA over the past century; evidently, the
same can be said of Britain. For every phase and aspect of an
individual's life there is at least one agency empowered to plan
or intervene, so that he will be constrained to act in identified
ways. Some obvious examples are the various central government
departments concerned with matters of taxation, social security
payments and benefits, local authority social service departments,
school medical officers, schools and psychologists. These have
been created for different purposes in different situations with
different powers and constraints on their activities, but 'the central
idea is that of controlling what goes on in our society . . . . The
official agencies of control then are used by the members of our
society, or, at least, by the government officials who construct
them, to try to produce . . . order' (*ibid.*, p. 320).

Official agencies both construct and maintain an absolute
public morality. Individuals may believe that there is an absolute
morality governing their lives and act in accordance with it, even
if privately they do not agree with its rules. They may believe
others do agree, or not know that they disagree, since in most
relationships they lack knowledge of each other's personal beliefs
and background. It is safer, therefore, not publicly to challenge
or violate the public morality. Even if an individual suspects
that most others do agree with him in his opposition to some
aspect of the public morality, public commitment is risky, since
the official agencies have established organized interests and
legal sanctions. Of course, some suffer the consequences, but for
most there is more incentive in acting as if they agree with the
public morality in co-operating with others to maintain a public
fiction of morality and normality. An individual, then, does not
have to 'be' normal in the sense that he judges himself in terms
of absolute moral categories; rather, he has to maintain a
respectable appearance. Whether or not he agrees with the
official morality is irrelevant, since it is to this that he is held
accountable for those of his actions that are public or 'private'
but held to have consequences for the public realm.

I shall, then, treat parents' statements to me about their
disabled child's behaviour as 'public accounts' which are so
formulated that they appear to satisfy the basic rules of the
medical 'facts' of the disability. The different methods by which

this is accomplished may then bear no relation to their practices of making sense of the child's behaviour and interaction with him in other situations. Actually, I conclude in chapter 5 that there are strong grounds for assuming that parents' definitions of their child are as they appear, but to the extent that they are not, the question remains as to why parents do not say what they 'really' think, why it is 'risky' for them to do so. I wish to argue that this is because of others' treatment of parents as *parents* and this is understandable within the same terms as the preceding analysis of deviance and accountability. Current conceptions of disability do not generally legitimate holding parents responsible for the occurrence of the child's condition, and certainly not as having chosen their position. Hence their treatment by others, like that of the disabled themselves, and unlike other types of deviance, cannot be legitimated in terms of any pre-existing personality traits (cf drug-addicts or mental patients) or intended gains to themselves (cf prostitutes, criminals). They are, however, held responsible as parents: they are the child's accountable agents. In the next section I argue that they are held accountable to a conception of normal parenthood which bears a questionable relationship to the experience of any parent. However, since it is actively implemented by agencies officially empowered to control family-related activities, it acts as an official morality which constitutes parents' public appearances. For these reasons, I then regard parents' statements not only about their disabled child, but also about his effects on their family life, as expressions of the official morality which maintain their appearance as normal parents.

THE NORMAL FAMILY

The meaning of the concept of the family, like that of the person, is grounded in members' usage. Harris notes its complexity in commonsense thought. In saying 'the family' people can refer to all their relatives, then distinguish between their 'own' and their 'in-laws'; to offspring, or to parents and their offspring, or to a household. Even if the family is geographically dispersed, it can be 'kept together', individuals 'still do not cease to be members of the family – whatever that means' (1969, p. 63).

Harris argues that in the case of domestic, residential and descent groups, membership cannot be defined in terms of biological relations, since each individual has a unique set of persons to whom he is biologically related. Recruitment is achieved by ignoring some ties of equal genealogical closeness, and this is the product either of individual agreement by the persons concerned, or, where it is done in the same way throughout a society, of a societal *rule*. Hence, societies which use kinship as a basis for the allocation of individuals to exclusive categories have to 'cheat' and ignore ties through men or through women.

The biological or procreative group is a special case, however, because 'the activities which distinguish it prescribe its member-ship' (*ibid.*, p. 66) since these activities *universally* demand a man, a woman and a sexual relationship between them, and the biological necessity of care for immature offspring demands their presence. However, there is no biological necessity that a man and a woman, having procreated offspring, should stay together; nor that either of them should continue to care for their offspring. Even if 'rearing' is recognized as involving 'satisfaction of the conditions required for the development of the personality of a child in such a way that he may be able to co-operate with other individuals for the purposes of survival and procreation' (*ibid.*, p. 87), all that necessarily follows is that there should be a stable group consisting of an adult person and immature persons whom the adult rears. 'To ask "Is the nuclear family universal?" is to ask whether the biological activities which occur in all societies universally result in the creation of groups having the membership defined by those activities' (*ibid.*, p. 87). Hence, in *all* cases it is only by knowledge of the relevant rules which define membership that members can recognize the 'existence' of 'the family' in the activities observed.

Evidently, following Garfinkel (1967), it is only in and through such activities that the rules are constituted and made observable to participants and observers alike. What many sociologists have done is to treat observed activities as biologically or socially necessary or 'given' and requiring explanation in terms of some other constructs, usually norms and values. As competent members of their society and unlike anthropologists,[4] sociologists 'know' what activities can 'count' as evidence of a family and this taken-for-granted knowledge of how a family is constituted is used to identify activities as what a family does and to legitimate the continued existence of the family.

Thus, great variations in its appearances can be recognized. The family may be found in an urban or rural setting, in a 'nuclear' or extended form; it may be of any size. Parents may have a different division of labour in the home, adopt 'authori-tarian' or 'egalitarian' child-rearing practices. Children may move away and adopt different 'life styles'; spouses may die or divorce, in which case we have 'fatherless' or 'motherless' families.[5] As the latter two examples suggest, at any one point in time some differences may be seen as 'social problems'. Ball (1972) argues that family-related problems such as divorce and un-sanctioned unions are only identifiable in terms of particular definitions of the family whether held by professionals or laymen (they are often the same), and they are seen as departures from those definitions which define the desirable rather than necessarily the observable.

A similar kind of theorizing has already been met in relation to disability and its effects. Gouldner typifies such theorizing as 'a symbolic effort to overcome social worlds that have become unpermitted' (1971, p. 486) by intimating 'the goodness of the powerful'. He says that this is essentially what functionalist accounts do by showing that those social objects that survive have an ongoing 'usefulness' since in our world to be useful is to be good.

For example, Farmer (1972) argues that the family cannot just be seen as a biological unit centred on reproduction and perpetuation of the species because it is 'reinforced' by institutions that are 'indubitably social' ones. However, from this it is deduced that this is what distinguishes the human family, not that, for example, other social institutions might well perform the activities concerned. Similarly, it is not an 'end in itself' but 'it exists' to solve the problems involved in meeting certain universal human needs and 'it is an intensely active agency in doing so' (1972, p. 20). I would add that accounts of the family which escape such criticisms do so only by excluding the question of the relationship between the family and wider social institutions. They focus on intra-familial and intra-psychic processes, thus ignoring what is distinctive about family behaviour as compared to that in other small groups.

Of course, conceptions of the family have been influenced by observed differences and changes in members' activities. However, as Gouldner (op. cit.) says, their empirical importance or statistical frequency is typically deprecated. Cross-cultural differences are discounted, notably the revision of early Soviet attempts to destroy the pre-revolutionary form of the family (abolishing marriage ceremonies, divorce virtually on demand, abortion freely permitted and children urged to place party loyalties before that of parents and kin) and the shift of emphasis from the collective towards the family in the Israeli kibbutz. Harris (1969, pp. 90–9) argues that the latter might rather be explained by the fact that the stable community groups which constitute the kibbutzim have become increasingly identifiable in terms of multi-generational kin ties, and thus provide the conditions which encourage the emergence of kin-related activities.

In the Soviet case, he says that the rise in divorce and increase in abortion and delinquency could show the instability of the nuclear family when not socially sanctioned, and anyway it has not been shown that they *were* caused by the changes in family law. He also considers the possibility that the Soviet leaders who reversed the changes might have recognized the indispensability of the family, but concludes that it is much more likely that all the increases in divorce, abortion and delinquency were closely related to contemporary housing conditions. Moore (1969) offers the more satisfactory explanation that there were more pressing objectives in such fields as health and industry, and that, like the Tsarist middle classes, existing family structures expedited their achievement – grandmothers could look after children while their mothers went to work in the factories – and that, from the 1930s on, Soviet leaders deliberately fostered such behaviour, recognizing its appropriateness in a totalitarian state.

Changes produced by industrialization and urbanization, together with the increasing transfer of the education of children to state-controlled institutions, were interpreted thirty years or so ago, as Farmer (*op. cit.*) notes, as heralding the disappearance of the family as a decaying, outworn institution.

Musgrove argues that this prediction was based on a mis-representation of history: 'it is nonsense to talk of the mid twentieth century family as representing a decline from an earlier Golden Age . . . in fact, the family was commonly grudging and inept in the social training it afforded the young' (1966, pp. 22–3). He presents evidence that in the 1860s, of Manchester children between the ages of three and twelve years, only 6 per cent were at work, 40 per cent were at school and 54 per cent were at neither: 'compulsory schooling did not "usurp" the parent, he had long been usurped by the street gang' (*ibid.*, p. 30). Harris suggests that the 'loss of functions' thesis was partly a product of the 'unwillingness of bureaucratic institutions to accept in practice that they do share "functions" and that untrained and non-specialized individuals . . . can be of assistance to them in the successful performance of their activities' (*op. cit.*, p. 108).

Today, as will be seen shortly, agencies concerned with the family express different sentiments. Why this might be, or the question of the relationship or 'fit' between an industrializing society and the family, has been the subject of much discussion.[6] I shall merely note a few points. In the intervening years Farber (1964) notes that studies of family-related problems have followed current conceptions of insufficiencies in therapeutic or alleviatory institutions. Thus, in the latter part of the Depression the issue was the effects of unemployment on family relationships; in wartime, those of the husband's absence on military service, and increasing concern over mental health has been accompanied by studies of mental illness in the family. Quarantelli (1960) and Young (1954) similarly argue that studies of disasters have commonly demonstrated the role of the extended family as the major source of aid to the afflicted nuclear family, which they note is just as well since the formal agencies could never cope in the absence of such mutual aid patterns.

Current conceptions of the family stress two important spheres of activity or functions. The fact that most people spend most of their lives in a biological group is now seen as showing that the family has 'proved extremely resilient' (Farmer, *op. cit.*, p. 1). In the 'process' of 'nuclearization' it has 'adapted' so that it 'is now concerned with a more detailed and refined satisfaction of needs than hitherto' (Fletcher, 1966, p. 16). Quoting Edmund Leach as saying in his 1967 Reith lectures that 'far from being the basis of a good society the family with its narrow privacy and tawdry secrets is the source of all our discontents', Farmer interprets this as a 'full-scale attack' on the family (*ibid.*, p. 2).

In his critique of contemporary American sociology of the family, Moore (*op. cit.*) similarly locates the major theme of the 'almost axiomatic' nature of the assertions of the universality of the family, as that it is making up for lost economic functions by providing better emotional service. Thus (Wynn, 1972, pp. 34–5):

> the family is . . . the centre of social life for most people in the present . . . . Home and family compensate for deficiencies of many people's working lives . . . [and] are at the centre of ambition and self-respect for ordinary men and women. The family provides the supreme comfort and support for persons of all ages . . . . Family joys and family griefs are the most keenly felt joys and griefs for most men and women. However successful a man may be in his job . . . family life is still important.

The statistics on marriage and divorce are commonly interpreted as evidence of this. Compared with 1890, a much bigger proportion of the adult population of the USA is married, but a *much* bigger proportion has been divorced. Moore (*ibid.*) says that it is often argued that divorce strengthens emotional functions by allowing more freedom to choose congenial partners, but points out that this goes a long way towards the opposing view that marriage may be superfluous. Berger and Kellner (1964) argue that people divorce not because they regard marriage as unimportant but because it is so important that they have no tolerance for the less than completely successful arrangement they have. This need not gainsay Moore's point, however, since it would be evidence that marriage is not doing what it is 'supposed' to do.

The family is also the 'cradle of our future society' (Wynn, *op. cit.*, p. 34). The reproduction, socialization and social control of immature members are essential activities in any society. Farmer observes that this 'is usually regarded as the central institutional function of the family' and that 'it can indeed be argued that the continued existence and influence of the family as a social institution is accounted for in terms of the functions it performs on behalf of society, and which contribute to the maintenance of society' (*op. cit.*, p. 14). Child-rearing is regarded, moreover, as a major source of emotional gratification: 'the successful rearing of a family provides the main sense of achievement for most people . . . . How often do those who have no children follow with generous interest and find satisfaction in the lives of nephews and nieces' (Wynn, *op. cit.*, p. 35).

The requirements of child-rearing may provide the context for defining the other 'needs' that the family meets (Farmer, *op. cit.*, p. 20):

> Stable and recognized sex relationships have psychological importance. Women need freedom from mental and material anxieties when they are engaged in producing and rearing children, and from this freedom follows the practical and socially important consequence of enhancing the chances of survival of a new life; for abortion and infanticide are commoner when the parental mating is an unacceptable one in the society. Stability in sex relationships also lessens the likelihood that men will dissipate their energies in sexual competition, and so indirectly increases their capacity to focus their effort towards the welfare of the family group.

The two functions of the contemporary family are then brought together in the rules constituting parenthood.

Parents do not reject their new-born babies because they are ugly or the wrong sex. In caring for any child his interests predominate. How they do this and how much they sacrifice on his behalf is more negotiable but they do not resent the costs incurred in terms of loss of freedom, income or ambitions, but rather define his well-being and progress as adequate reward. They do not leave the family group themselves, nor do they extrude any member except on certain special (negotiable) grounds, such as the welfare of other members, or when their situation becomes 'intolerable' (or if they are themselves 'psychologically disturbed', 'immature', drunken, or otherwise identifiable as incompetent). A good parent, with the help of other agents as necessary, attempts to counter all threats to the continued unity of his family.

THE FAMILY AND SOCIAL REALITY

So defined, how might this conception of the family correspond with members' experience? Does it, as Moore says, constitute 'projecting certain middle-class hopes and ideals onto a refractory reality' (*op. cit.*, p. 456)? Moore argues that, in general, advanced industrial conditions *prevent* the family from performing such social-psychological functions as are presently attributed to it, as compared with a strong kinship society such as Italy, where Stryker (1968) suggests there is a higher probability that any conflicting behavioural expectations will be resolved in the direction of kinship-linked expectations.

First, the obligation to give affection because of biological relations, an expedient when the division of labour was organized through real or imagined kinship bonds, is obsolete now that both are ascribed on the basis of an individual's qualities and capacities and this receives some degree of recognition in the popular saying 'you can choose your friends but you can't choose your relatives' (*ibid.*, p. 459). Second, the performance of economic tasks outside the home and the development of the mass media destroy the basis of paternal authority and provide models of behaviour for children which are not constructed in the privacy of the home. Third, the daily isolation of educated women from adult company, while performing menial tasks, makes it more or less impossible for them to live up to the prescribed ideal of homemaker, centre of the family, companion, confidante and youthful mistress of her husband.

This is not to say that many women would not be happy if they could 'live up' to this ideal. Le Masters (1957) finds that mothers with professional training and extensive professional work experience felt 'bitter' about their training when on bearing a first child they were forced to give up an occupation which had deep significance for them, but they also felt guilt at not being a 'better' mother. He argues that parenthood, rather than marriage, is the 'romantic complex' in American culture. It is the performance of these activities that is more likely to conflict

with other socio-economic commitments. Eventually, all but a
few of his couples studied made a 'successful' adjustment to
parenthood. However, Le Masters offers no explanation of how
this was achieved. As Moore observes, the question of what would
be a better arrangement is itself a moral judgment but 'any
social institution is a bad one that imposes more suffering on
people than is necessary when they have sufficient material
resources and scientific knowledge to do away with this suffering'
(*op. cit.*, p. 462). This is not, however, to say that the conception
of the family does not constrain members' actions and even their
beliefs. One can equally identify possible bases of correspondence
between the sociological conception of family life and members'
experience.

The first, and perhaps the most 'basic', of these derives from
the conception of a person as someone who is responsible for his
actions. Parents who are regarded as adult members of society
are generally assumed to acquire child dependants voluntarily,
the more so with the increased availability of contraception and
abortion, and, we may expect in the future, control of a child's
sex, and therefore can 'reasonably' be held responsible for their
actions as parents. Hence, whatever the particular conception of
family life held, it may be widely legitimated. Second, knowledge
of the constitutive activities of parenthood is such a basic element
of normal socialization that no competent adult could legitimately
claim ignorance, although parents who were themselves reared in
orphanages might 'have some excuse' for unparental activities.
As Garfinkel (1967) observes, it is part of members' commonsense
knowledge of social structures. Third, most parents may in fact
find child-rearing rewarding whatever their reasons, e.g. it is
good to feel essential to someone else's survival and to have a
purpose in life. Fourth, as Douglas (1971a) says of 'motherhood'
in particular, the family and parenthood is probably still seen as
so fundamental to our society that any public attacks on it incur
the risk of widespread disorder, and therefore public expressions
of any private disagreement is itself wrong. Fifth, there may still
exist greater private agreement in this area than over other
aspects of behaviour, such that the activities of parents are often
seen as 'right' and even 'natural'. Finally, parenthood receives constant reaffirmation in interaction with others outside the home. It
is in public that parents' 'good identity' is most at stake, and their
practices most likely therefore to accord with ideal prescriptions.
These last two points will be elaborated in chapters 5 and 6.

Hence, one might conclude that the actions of the majority of
parents are likely to be recognized and identified by themselves

in the same terms as our expert conceptions. However, despite Moore's (*op. cit.*) argument, the family is in many respects, both physically and symbolically, a private place within which many 'deviations' may remain secret, or known but tolerated by wider social groups. The well-documented wide variation in child-rearing practices noted earlier can be interpreted as evidence of the great 'freedom' that parents enjoy in bringing up their children. Moreover, it does not necessarily follow that, having produced a child, parents will want to continue his rearing, and if most *do* enjoy this activity, whatever the reason, this does not mean that all do. As those who choose not to have children may discover, there are other ways of 'fulfilling oneself' and if these are never discovered by the majority of adults, this may reflect more on other social institutions. It is, however, to such grounds that current defences of the necessity of the family essentially appeal.

Hence, even if one observed persons engaged in what they regard as family-related activities, one could not attribute any identifiable uniformities to an underlying cognitive consensus, to a widespread private agreement, or to the family's strength as an institution. Rather, one should view any apparent orderly properties as members' practical accomplishments, and examine how it is that they manage to make 'the family' visible in and through their actions.

Bittner (1965) analyses members' 'methodical uses' of the concept of 'organization' and suggests three possible types of use. Illustrative parallels can be drawn in the case of the family.

First, through the 'gambit of compliance' members may extend to a particular rule the respect of compliance 'whilst finding in the rule the means for doing whatever needs to be done' (*op. cit.*, p. 251). Thus, mothers who go out to work argue that it is to better the family's standard of living, or if they admit that they are bored, they may further argue that this is itself detrimental to family relationships. Second, 'the family' may be used as a model of 'stylistic unity' to give the appearance of coherence to actions which otherwise would not constitute or be regulated by membership. A man may drink heavily for a variety of reasons, but his wife may interpret it as improper conduct for a 'husband'.

Third, the concept may be used as a 'corroborative reference' to identify activities to which membership commits an actor, but which in themselves might appear irrelevant to and even undesirable in that status. Thus the 'drudgery' of washing nappies is symbolically transformed into a demonstration of proper maternal love. Finally, it should be apparent that such uses are

not restricted to members but may be those by which others
manage to assimilate parents' performances within the concept
of the family (see chapter 7).

THE FAMILY AS OFFICIAL MORALITY

If one focuses on the observable actions of parents, it is evident
that only a small proportion of them are publicly labelled as
'cruel', 'selfish' or 'inadequate' and formally sanctioned. Their
identification and subsequent treatment is of course likely to be
as problematic and subject to similar contingencies as in the case
of any other deviants. How then is this public conformity maintained? Following Douglas (1971a), adequate explanation will be
provided if the conception of family life that has been identified is
also what is implemented by agents of control officially empowered
to legitimate family behaviour, so that it is objectivated into an
absolute morality for the whole society. That this is the case may
be suggested by various forms of expression.

First, agents accredited with official responsibility for the care
and control of children often attempt to involve parents in the
process of intervention: hospitals institute 'mother and baby'
units and longer visiting hours; social work and psychiatric
agencies adopt a 'family orientation'. In the absence of adequate
parental control, orphanages may be organized on a basis of
'family units', or courts replaced by 'Children's Hearings', staffed
by lay members of the community to deal with criminal offences
of children under sixteen (Social Work (Scotland) Act, 1968).

Second, research in sociology and psychology commonly
stresses the crucial significance of early socialization for a child's
development, pointing to, for example, the effects of 'maternal
deprivation', and this has received increasing popular discussion,
so that attention is focused on the family as a major source of
social evils. 'Inadequate socialization' or a 'broken home' is
frequently invoked as adequate explanation of an individual's
delinquency, mental illness, drug addiction, and so on. Musgrove
(op. cit.) traces similar arguments in terms of the 'defective
family' or 'defective discipline' to the mid-nineteenth century.
The logical development of this has been recently expressed:
'Parents of delinquent teenagers should be punished as well as
their sons and daughters for the crimes they commit, a legal
expert told a conference on violence in London today' (Evening
Standard, Tuesday 21 November 1972).

Third, in our literature and other media children, as Coveney
shows, are commonly portrayed according to a predominantly

Romantic conception. The child symbolizes all those 'essentially good' qualities associated with spontaneity and creativity which worldly adults have lost. Musgrove (*op. cit.*) observes a similar phenomenon in the last century, when, influenced by the ideas of Rousseau, who thought society outside the family to be a source of vice and contamination, the pupils of 'public' schools and apprentices away from home boarded with local and often lower-class families.

This last point might be interpreted as evidence of a belief that we should therefore put the child's interests first, and perhaps this is what informs most of the other expressions noted. Sartre sees the imputation of innocence to children rather as 'an alibi . . . a ready-made refuge for times of misfortune, a way of asserting that one was better than one's life . . .. It is the function of children from the age of one to ten to represent for grown-ups the original state of grace' (1964, p. 57). In any case, the child's 'interests' or 'needs' cannot be defined independently of some conception of desirable child behaviour.

Schottland notes that 'frequently expressed by the United Nations are such convictions as . . . investment in . . . families, children and youth is . . . essential for long-term economic and social development' (1969, p. 135), and he shows how, though American policy relating to the family is not as formally organized as that of other countries, 'increasing consideration is being given to the role of government in assisting families to discharge many of their agreed upon responsibilities' (*ibid.*, p. 135), this being implemented through such programmes as industrial pensions, life and health insurance, sickness benefits, medical care and social services. Wynn cites the American Commission on the Year 2000, which argued that if children are 'a nation's most crucial resource, then one has to pay much more attention to what happens to children and to families with children, and where and why a society loses its resources' (*op. cit.*, p. 21). She points out that this has received increasing recognition in education policy.

She goes on to argue that in so far as they are presently inadequate, the whole range of social and insurance services which affect children and young persons should be revised, in order to spread the economic cost of family responsibility across all the country's adults, but also in order to meet the families' needs. That such policies and their suggested extensions are intended to maintain the unity of the family is suggested by the fact that they focus on the discontinuities between what is socially practised and what is biologically required. Thus: the sickness of the mother, because this may affect 'the bread-winning, child-caring and house-keeping roles of the parent' (*ibid.*, p. 230); the death of the father and especially the desertion of the father, because 'it is highly undesirable for a child . . . to feel that his father has been replaced by a Post Office book, entitling his mother to a small fixed allowance and that this is the full extent of the state's interest in his begetting' (*ibid.*, p. 241). All of these recommendations are predicted on the 'final misfortune for a child [which] is to be deprived of all parental care and of home life' (*ibid.*, p. 245). This may be compared with Harris's view that 'men are usually present but not absolutely necessary. From the child's point of view, the presence of the genetic father is not necessary at all' (*op. cit.*, p. 92), or Musgrove's that the danger is that children have no respite from 'the driving demanding home . . . [which] appears to be the "good home" ' (*op. cit.*, p. 73).

That there is official concern to maintain the family, and that this informs social policy may be explicit. In this country the Department of Health and Social Security has authorized a two-year survey of child-development and parenthood to be carried out by the National Children's Bureau. Its Director, Dr Mia Kellmer Pringle, gives its major focus as 'what we know of children's emotional, social and intellectual needs, how we satisfy them and what happens when we fail' (*Guardian*, Tuesday 29 August 1972). She says that 'we know with shame' that working-class children lose out from the beginning, but amongst the 'many forms of neglect, deprivation and cruelty' she specifies the professional man who is ambitious for his children but spends little time with them, and the mother whose social commitments lead her to entrust her children to a succession of au pairs. In other words, there appears to be increasing recognition that the official morality of child-rearing is not even constraining the actions of those middle-class parents which it might most be supposed to reflect, but the conclusion is not that we should therefore consider alternative methods of child-rearing. The strategy is rather to concentrate on the fifteens to eighteens 'in the hope that their attitude to personal relationships, marriage and the needs of babies and young children may be amenable to change'. Young parents with a first baby are also 'promising targets'.

Any parents, whether or not they have a disabled child, may be held accountable to the official morality for those of their actions which are public or held to have consequences for the public realm. The above quotation suggests that this may include any or all of the constitutive activities of parenthood. Not that this means that parents have no 'freedom' in conducting family affairs, that their actions are determined by others; rather, that they must make appropriate use of 'the family' in accounting for their actions and thus maintain a respectable appearance. Their situational appearances, then, are so organized or constituted by the official morality that others may see in them the persistence of the normal order of family life. As my extension of Bittner's (*op. cit.*) analysis suggested, parents may find in the rules the means for 'doing whatever needs to be done'. Ball (1970) observes that 'respectability' constitutes a 'bridge' between labelling theory's focus on societal definitions and Goffman's on impression management.

Goffman's (1968) demonstration of the possible situational variability of secondary deviation was presented earlier. Elsewhere, he analyses many of the tactics and strategies by which actors control embarrassment, honour each other's claims and protect their identities; in short, maintain interaction (see especially 1956; 1959; 1961b). Ball (*op. cit.*) points to two dimensions of truth/falsity and presenting/concealing and discusses several strategies that actors may adopt in constructing a respectable appearance. These concern: (1) the presentation of virtues; (2) concealing vices; and (3) the creation of the appearance of virtue where other circumstances 'really' pertain.

The verbal aspects of such constitutive and restitutive work are analysed by Scott and Lyman in the giving and receiving of 'accounts'. An account is (1968a, p. 46):

> a linguistic device employed whenever an action is subjected to valuative enquiry. Such devices are a crucial element in the social order since they prevent conflicts from arising by verbally bridging the gap between action and expectation . . . . By an account then, we mean a statement made by a social actor to explain unanticipated or untoward behaviour.

Scott and Lyman identify two general types of account: actors give 'justifications' when they accept responsibility for the act in question, but deny its pejorative implications and 'excuses' when they deny responsibility or appeal to mitigating circumstances by scapegoating, invoking biological drives, accident or unintentionality.

Evidently, what will count as an account depends on the order it is intended to restore. 'I was drunk at the time' is unlikely to be honoured as a father's excuse for injuring his child, though 'my wife had just died' might be. Blum and McHugh criticize

Scott and Lyman, arguing that they simply make the actor the privatized and exclusive source of information on his motives, shifting the emphasis to his talk without explicating the methodical ways in which such statements are generated in the first place: how the actor is constrained to *give* a reason; how the hearer accepts that it is an answer. They see the proper analytic focus as 'the deeper conditions of knowledge' or 'the organized and sanctionable conditions that would regularly produce the giving of a reason by a competent member in the first place' (1971, pp. 101–2). 'Motive' is seen as an observer's rule by which an event is connected with a 'biography' to produce a generally intelligible social action from an otherwise fragmentary series of performances. A biography is the observer's version of a set of experiences typically 'owned' by a given member which can be used as a normative order for the observed phenomena. In formulating this order, or showing the possible relevance of the biography for the event, they argue that one is formulating a type-of-person. One prerequisite of this is that the object of motive ascription knows that there are motive ascribing rules, or can be assumed to know what he is doing. It can be noted that these were the formal rules defining the concept of a person in Puccetti's (*op. cit.*) analysis.

My analysis of parents' responses to questions about what it is like to have a disabled child is informed by all of these authors. My eventual aim is to show that the meaning of having a disabled child to his parents is constructed by them from the variously expressed meanings of their situation that are culturally available to them. The general method of analysis is to treat parents' statements as the topic of investigation: to see the uses that they make of such meanings in these statements, rather than in unexamined intervening psychological processes and states, whether 'pathological' or otherwise. In general, I attempt to demonstrate that family life does not appear to be undesirably disrupted by the advent of a disabled child because of the ways in which parents construct their talk about this experience. They maintain a normal respectable appearance because they make situationally appropriate use of the normal family in formulating particular accounts of their activities. 'The family' defines the situations in which the giving of an account is appropriate; the possible grounds or motives to which an account can appeal; what will count as a 'vice' or a 'virtue' and what therefore must be presented or concealed if respectability as defined in the official morality is to be maintained.

Particular aspects of these analyses are taken up and extended in chapters 5–8, where I examine parents' statements in relation to the three topics of (1) the child's disability (chapter 5); (2) their own relationships and activities with others inside and outside the home (chapters 6 and 7); and (3) differences between their situation and that of parents who do not have a disabled child (chapter 8). In chapter 5 my main aim is to show that parents' definitions of their disabled child's behaviour are methodical constructions despite acknowledged discrepancies with normal spatial and temporal parameters of parent–child interaction. As I have already said, I assume that parents' statements can be taken as indicators of their actual judgmental processes when in interaction with the child; and I am less concerned with substantive characteristics of their definitions than with the methods by which they are constructed. However, I also show that these methods are, from what the parents themselves say, principally informed by the objective meanings of the child's condition as these are made available to them by others, primarily doctors. Therefore, in practice, parents' accomplishment cannot be understood without reference to moral considerations and it has moral implications.

Definitions of the disabled child are constructed in interaction with others where a normal appearance depends on an ability to make sense of his behaviour but where that appearance is placed at risk. In chapter 6, I examine the problems that parents say they face in such encounters and the tactics and strategies they adopt according to whether they wish to reveal or conceal their deviance, elicit or control others' definitions by managing the impression that their own and the child's appearance makes upon them. These then include the ways in which parents can attempt to avoid being held accountable as the parents of a disabled child. In the second part of the chapter, I examine what parents say when, as in the interview, they are so held to account, and questioned about the effects of the disabled child on family relations and activities. I show that the particular accounts which they give make evident otherwise unobservable aspects of their activities, invoke their own, or impute to other members motives which claim that others should see their 'abnormal' actions as understandable within normal terms, as continuing to maintain a family life which does honour the official morality. Typical differences in the ways in which parents do this constitute differences in the ways in which they appear presently unable, or previously to have failed, to perform the constitutive activities of parenthood.

In chapters 7 and 8, I take up the question of how parents accomplish this, that is, how they manage to appeal to normal motives in what no one regards as anything but an abnormal situation. I argue that, just as the public appearance of normal parents can be adequately understood as constructed in the face of official agencies empowered to control family-related activities, so the appearances of parents with a disabled child are informed by the activities of agencies specifically concerned with the problems incurred by having a disabled child. These effectively deny discrepancies between the official morality of normal family life and the situation of families which include a disabled child, by asserting more general or basic moral meanings of parents' experience as an example of the general phenomenon of suffering. They make available to parents objective meanings, the constructive use of which by parents serves to transform their situated appearances into congruity with the official morality and thus make claims to normal motivation understandable to others.

Parents continue to display the relevance of normal parenthood to interpretation of their actions by appealing to other more basic grounds for those actions. In the second part of chapter 8, I discuss the possible relationships between their statements as expressions of other-given meanings of their situation and their own experience. There seem to be few situations in which they might present a different appearance and in any case few other available meanings with which they might construct their experience. I suggest why this is at present so in some examination of the 'organized and sanctionable conditions of knowledge', or the prevailing moral order, of which the meanings of parents' situations are an important expression. I conclude that parents say what they say because the alternative is not to be regarded as parents at all, and that in our society this is more or less equivalent to not being regarded as a competent person.

First, however, I discuss in chapter 3 the stages through which I accomplished this formulation of the phenomena of having a disabled child, and, in chapter 4, present a summary of what parents said about this experience.

3 Methodology: some autobiography

'Methodology' is a more or less systematic or organized way of acting. An account of one's methodology must therefore include a statement of one's intentions or aims. Aims, however, can only be defined in the context of some conception of the nature of the problem at hand, or of some 'theory'. Method, then, embodies theory, and doing 'research' is not discovering new phenomena, but recovering 'what one had all along' (Blum, 1970, p. 305). It is an occasion for addressing one's 'mind' to, or 'bringing it to bear' on the problem at hand. In so doing, a theorist shows the form in which the world has meaning for him; he formulates a possible society. In doing this, he displays himself – how his intentions as a theorist are organized.

However, this side of an ideal society method is not only theory. It has already been argued that there is no necessary or unique relation between intentions and actions; that the same intention can be expressed in different actions; the same action may express different intentions. Further, that intentions can conflict both within and between actors, and the more institutionalized an intention the more powerful it is likely to be in constraining the expression, if not the recognition, of competing interests. A concrete theorist then, like any other actor, has many conflicting interests, not all of which he may recognize at any one point in time, and the appropriate expression of which may not be evident to him.

O'Neill (1972) argues that it is the task of a 'reflexive sociology' to 'unpack' the relationships between interests and theory or 'knowledge'. The following chapters culminate in an attempt to do this, as it relates to the 'facts' of having a disabled child, albeit in a sketchy and naïve way. If one supposes that my prevailing interest throughout has been to produce the 'correct form' of these phenomena, to give expression to my way of seeing the world, one can then see that, compared with the other constitutive activities of research, writing is the least constrained by competing interests, whether the writer's own or others'. One can act more consistently as a theorist within at least the minimal constraints of biological survival – one has to eat and sleep. In fact, however, I talked to friends and colleagues who expressed their ways of seeing the phenomena in question, and I continued to read and reread those of other writers on the same and 'related' topics. To the extent that I was influenced by these, I 'changed my mind' – perhaps this is why some writers shut themselves away from books or human contact. I was aware as I wrote the first draft that each chapter was 'informed by' its successor (i.e. written within the form that I intended for the next), but this is not to say that I was aware of an overall form. In a sense, I did not know what I was doing (though I thought I did). To the extent that it appears as though I did, this is because of subsequent 'revisions' on my part, but undoubtedly inconsistencies remain, including attempts to see too much or too little similarity in the expressions of other writers.

What I could not change is how I addressed the phenomena when in face-to-face contact with them in the 'field' – this was institutionalized in the interview transcriptions. Also, I felt I could not go on changing much in the detailed ways in which I organized what I saw – or the 'analysis' – though I did throw out quite a lot. In the interests of finishing the project I was committed to that organization – in one way and another I was engaged in the project for six years. In the following discussion I attempt to recover some of the interests which produced different formulations at different points in time, and which identify me as different kinds of theorist. I see this as occurring in three stages, which roughly correspond to the three substantively different activities of the project.

A   THE REPORTER: VOICE OF THE UNDERDOG

I did not choose the project, then defined as 'Parental Perception of Handicap'; it came with the job. When I started it I had just finished a three-year course in psychology, most of which I rejected, informed, if not very coherently, by some reading of phenomenology, Laing (*The Divided Self*, 1960), Goffman (*Asylums*, 1961), and Winch (*The Idea of a Social Science*, 1963). I thought that since behaviour is rule-governed, I could not discover any 'laws' or generalizations linking it to any antecedent conditions: people do things for reasons and different people have different reasons. Other interests, however, informed me that some people have more opportunity than others to state their reasons, and my job then was to give parents with disabled children a chance to make themselves heard. Though I would have denied it then, I was a journalist, moreover a truthful one: the 'voice of the people'. This kind of position is available in Becker: 'Whose side are we on?' (1967). (Actually, I rather think that I doubted whether people concerned with the parents, notably doctors, were 'reasonable men' – they were either misguided or wilfully putting their own interests first.)

Of course I knew that others had done this before me, notably Davis (1963) and, in my reading, Goffman (*Stigma*, 1968). Having 'reviewed' what they and others said, I decided that: the type of handicap was not of prime importance in differentiating parents' experience, and that having a handicapped child was not necessarily a 'tragedy', but rather resolved into a number of specific problems. Since it was not my responsibility to solve those problems, I should simply attempt to find out what they were. Further, since problems change, and people forget, it was necessary to look at them as they occurred – from the onset of having a handicapped child and for a period following this. The remaining questions then were: how to find parents who had just had a disabled child; how to decide which were 'suitable cases'; how to make and keep contact with them; how many to do this with and where, and finally, of course, what to find out and how. At this point, however, other interests had to be considered, so that I thought the last was the least of my worries.

1 FINDING CASES

Evidently, short of a house-to-house search, one would not know if parents were worried about their child unless they had approached some outside agency. GPs were considered as a possible source of referrals, but had to be rejected because of their professional responsibility of maintaining confidentiality. A predictive register was also investigated, but this was regarded (by its constructor, Younie) as too unreliable – many children 'at risk' would later develop normally.

Hence, I attended out-patient and paediatric clinics, and made frequent rounds of the appropriate wards of the local children's and maternity hospitals for a period of six months. Sometimes it was sufficient to check notes concerning cases expected at a clinic on a particular day; on other occasions it was necessary to be present throughout the clinic in order to find out what diagnosis was made by the doctor in charge.

This method of obtaining cases was very time-consuming, but necessary, primarily for practical reasons. Good contacts were established with doctors and some nurses in the hospitals. A meeting was held with staff to explain the nature and purpose of the project, and notices were put up in prominent positions requesting the referral to me of cases of children with 'any condition that is likely to be permanent, will prevent the child from leading a normal life, and where its existence has been recently suspected or diagnosed'. But, given that the other responsibilities of medical staff could be expected to assume priority, it was felt that I could not rely exclusively on these sources. In addition, though a small number of cases were obtained in this way, some referrals indicated that different criteria might be used by medical staff from those decided upon by the investigator, especially in relation to the length of time elapsed since diagnosis.

2   CHOOSING CASES

I decided that 'disabled' referred to some impairment of intellectual or physical functioning that was 'relatively serious' and 'perhaps permanent', but not terminal. Children suffering from such conditions were identified in consultation with the doctors concerned. Additional selection criteria were that it be the first referral to the hospital for the particular complaint or that the child be newly-born in the case of congenital disability; that the child be a member of a family with two parents living at home; and that the family be resident in one city. The latter two were included because, since I was interested in how families 'react' to a disabled child, I thought it necessary that the child be a member of a family with both parents still living together. The residential criterion was imposed partly for reason of easy access, and partly since it was assumed that doctors and other agencies were likely to be important influences on the way that parents cope with a disabled child. Hence it was important that the availability of such services be as similar as possible for all families.

Further constraints were not imposed, almost solely for the reason that the number of possible cases would have been too restricted. Thus, type of disability; size of family; age of child (child was defined according to the hospital's administrative categorization of up to twelve years); social class of family, etc., were recognized as possible influences on the processes with which the study was concerned, but priority was accorded to the above criteria.

Even if all the above criteria were satisfied, selection of cases for study was based on a decision as to whether the intervention of a research worker was 'appropriate' at that point in time, or in that family. This decision was largely constrained by the opinions of the doctors concerned. This was partly to maintain the necessary good relations with the hospital, but also since no other sources of information about the family were available. The research area is obviously one of great potential stress and, ethical considerations apart, even if initial contact was to be established, it was perhaps unlikely that a family which was greatly distressed at that time would maintain co-operation. This expectation was confirmed in the case of family R, as will be seen later.

Such considerations did not, so far as I know, cause the loss of more than three or four cases. It is, however, likely that families who made a 'good adjustment' to the disabled child were over-represented. Further, in cases of gradual onset of disability, a varying amount of retrospection was unavoidable. Finally, I had some evidence (a conversation in my presence) that a doctor's decision as to whether research was appropriate in a particular case was not based solely on a judgment of the parents' emotional state. In two cases, doctors' unwillingness that I should visit was based on a personal or professional acquaintance with the family concerned. This may have contributed to a bias against the inclusion of middle-class cases, of which there were only two out of the thirteen fully studied (see section 5 below).

3 NUMBER OF CASES SELECTED

I originally decided that the first twenty-five families satisfying the above criteria to come to my attention in the six-month period allocated for this phase of the study would be included in the study. This was felt to be the maximum number of cases that one worker could deal with, given the time-consuming nature of the chosen methods of research (see below, p. 67). However, this figure was never reached.

4 ESTABLISHING CONTACT WITH FAMILIES

Initial contact was made with twenty-two families by one of two methods. One was by letter, which was sent from the research worker requesting a visit to the family's home, suggesting a date and explaining its purpose in the following terms: 'I am working for the Nuffield Provincial Hospitals Trust on a study of families who have a child that has some kind of illness or other difficulty, to find out what problems arise, so that better services and help may be provided in the future.'

Evidently, this did structure the parents' expectations but some justification for requesting a visit is obviously necessary. Definition of the child's condition was intentionally vague to avoid causing anxiety to parents where either they were not aware, or it was not known to what extent they were aware, of the severity of the child's condition. Further, where it was known that parents knew the nature and extent of their child's condition, as medically defined, I thought that placing it in the general context of 'other difficulties' and 'illness' would make parents less likely to feel singled out, and perhaps 'defensive'.

The letter attempted to stress the 'research' nature of the visit, and was sent from the Medical Sociology Research Unit. This was to avoid the possible, though probably unfounded, disadvantages of an immediate association with the university. Later, if asked, I did explain that I was attached to both institutions. I did not know how to evaluate the effects of the apparent link with the hospital (both this and the Unit share the same address) – which link was made even more strongly where the second (though less frequent) method of contact was used: a face-to-face encounter in the hospital, where the introductions were generally made by a doctor. Perhaps over all the initial para-medical presentation of the study and the investigator was an advantage in that parents, in so far as they did define the situation in this way, were more likely to agree to being visited. Once contact was established, however, I attempted to stress that I was not formally connected with the hospital; that therefore complaints could be freely expressed, and that the information obtained was of course confidential. I also said that I was interested in finding out the kinds of problems facing families in general, and could not myself do anything about specific complaints.

5   LOSS OF CASES

One of the twenty-two families contacted directly refused an interview. All the others were visited as arranged at least once. Two of these were then found to be unsuitable. In one case (not reported) the baby was illegitimate, but this had not been entered in the hospital records; in the other (Q) the mother had heard the day before the interview that her child's condition was in fact terminal. Four more cases could not be visited a second time.

Two of these were refusals on the grounds of 'nothing more to report' (my impression that the mother in this case, R, was extremely upset was subsequently confirmed by Mrs A, whose child was in the same ward), and 'too busy' (U). One (S) did not open the door, though obviously at home, on three separate occasions, and the fourth (P) emigrated to Canada. In two further cases (T and F) the disabled child died after the second and third interviews respectively.

Thus the intended number of interviews was finally obtained in thirteen cases. Table 3 gives the twenty-two original cases, classified by type of disability and the number of interviews completed with each.

TABLE 3 *Type of disability and number of interviews*

Disability	Number of interviews completed	Number of cases
Epilepsy	0	1
Renal hypoplasm		
Absence of biliary system		
Retardation		
Hole in heart	1	6
Coeliac disease		
Galactocaemia		
Meningitis and hydrocephalus	2	1
Spina bifida	3	1
Mongol (3 cases)		
Epilepsy (2 cases)		
Diabetes (2 cases)		
Retardation (2 cases)		
Hyper-pituitary gland dysfunction with subnormality	4	13
Absence of gullet		
Asthma		
Obesity		
Total	63	22

6 RESEARCH LOCATION

Practical constraints account sufficiently for the choice of the families' homes as the location for research. Families with disabled children may not be able to travel easily, and if there is no direct advantage to them from the research, have no reason to make any special effort to do so. In addition, I thought that this would best enable respondents to speak for themselves, since they could exert greater control over interaction if it were in their own home. They could decide both the date and duration of the encounter, and it was thus more apparent that they were doing me a favour. Also, there was the opportunity of observing the respondent interacting with other family members, where these were present – though, of course, I recognized that my presence probably influenced this.

There were disadvantages, however, in that depending on who else was present, and given that I had no control over this, particular areas of questioning were sometimes impossible. For example, those concerning agreement between husband and wife, if both were present; or the definition of the child if he were there and presumed able to understand. On the other hand, occasions when one respondent left the room provided unplanned checks on validity and additional information that was not available from that respondent. Second, the family had control over who should act as their representative and, as is common in 'family' research, this was generally the mother. In some cases the father was away from home for long periods of time, or during the week; in others it was perhaps a reflection of the usual division of labour in that the mother usually took responsibility for such matters. I discuss some of the implications of this further in chapter 8.

7 CHOICE OF METHOD

I rejected standardized questionnaires from the outset, on the grounds that they 'do violence' to respondents' statements. I now use Cicourel (1964) to express such intentions. Questionnaires in effect filter the social processes under study through a pre-defined 'grid' of categories assumed to represent the range of possible alternative responses appropriate to the area of research. Fixed-choice (yes/no) questions represent the extreme in this respect, but scaling techniques may be no less inappropriate. It is meaningless to produce measurements or quantifications of phenomena whose dynamics are not yet understood.

Furthermore, the advantages claimed for questionnaires would rarely stand up to close scrutiny. They are supposed to eliminate 'observer biases', to provide a routine method of investigation and analysis which presents the same 'stimuli' to all respondents. Rather, at every stage of the investigation, a host of assumptions and interpretations are made by everyone employed on a project, which are commonly unacknowledged and uninvestigated in the presentation of results. Of course, questionnaires are an efficient means of collecting a lot of information, and are suitable where that required is routine and 'factual' – for instance, age, occupation and so on – but quite inadequate for most sociological investigation, and certainly in this area.

I decided that the 'obvious' method was to go and talk to parents about what it was like to have a disabled child. What it might be like, and therefore what kinds of things we should talk about, was informed by my reading and by my commonsense conception of family life.

Four 'interviews' were to be conducted with each family – the first as soon after selection as possible, the others at more or less equal intervals over the following twelve months. This was in order to obtain information on changes through time in parents' perceptions of having a disabled child. Evidently, such changes would still have to be inferred from parents' statements at four separate points in time, and these statements would be necessarily partly retrospective. However, it was felt that more frequent interviewing would not only have created too much work for a single interviewer, but would have greatly reduced the likelihood of continued co-operation from the families concerned.

Most of the interviews, which lasted an average of one and a half hours, were tape-recorded. I presented the recorder as merely a convenient labour-saving device, which point I myself appreciated on the occasions when it broke down. No parents indicated that they would prefer it not to be used. Any embarrassment was brief and several parents said that they had forgotten the recorder's presence. Only one asked me who would listen to the recording, and responses did not appear to be qualitatively different when the recorder was switched off.

Had I been left to myself, I should probably have continued in this fashion. However, after ten 'pilot' interviews, I was persuaded that at the very least I should make explicit the topics about which I talked to parents, and cover the same topics with each. Hence, the interviews became 'semi-structured' according to Richardson's (1965) definition. That is, I carried a schedule of the topics and issues to be covered, with some suggested 'probes', but no standardized form of questions, nor was their order held constant. This method allows the interviewer to phrase and rephrase his questions as he thinks necessary; to introduce topics as they appear appropriate; and to capitalize on 'leads' offered by the respondent. This is especially useful when the topics to be discussed may be highly stressful or very personal to the respondent. In theory, this method favours the creation of a situation which also allows the respondent to define what is significant to him in the area of questioning, how much time should be devoted to particular issues and so on.

8 AREAS OF QUESTIONING

Onset of child's disability:
If gradual: Birth details and subsequent development; what made parents think something might be wrong; what they did and why.
If sudden: How parents found out that something was wrong with the child, who told them what, whether they think they were told enough, soon enough.

Encounters with medical agencies:
Previous experience of hospitals and medical matters, and at subsequent interviews changes in such knowledge.
Details of all family contacts with medical agencies: GP, Health Visitor and hospital in preceding months.
Help (advice; information; special services) offered, accepted, sought.
Whether more could be done; who most help and why.

The disability:
Knowledge of causation and prognosis, its sources and adequacy. Where husband not present, wife's perception of husband's opinions on these matters. Subsequent changes in child's condition and prognosis, and parents' knowledge of it.

Family life:
a. Division of labour on a number of specified household tasks before onset of disability, and how decided upon; subsequent changes with reference to earlier responses; reasons for and how decided upon.
b. Family plans: whether child's condition had affected any plans in such areas as children's education; holidays; work. What new arrangements made and 'satisfaction' or whether 'happy' about these.
c. Family visiting patterns: frequency and reasons for, and satisfaction with, subsequent inferred changes. Other activities of family members; subsequent changes, etc. Visitors to the home: changes.
d. Child care and control: division of activities between parents; differences between children and between the disabled

child and others at the same age. How having the child affects treatment of other children; how they treat the child and their knowledge of his condition.

e. Husband–wife relations: with reference to specific decisions and changes made. At first and last interviews: how far like marriage of relatives and friends, and what changes since first married. At last interview: extent to which changed because of having the disabled child; how would wish it to be different.

Encounters with others:

a. With those with whom family visits: Whether discuss disabled child's condition; what help offered and accepted; whether would expect more and why. Attitude of these to parents and the child.

b. With non-visitors: Including agencies such as social workers and priests. Whether discussed child; help offered, etc.

c. Chance encounters: In street, shops, clinic. Comments made, advice offered, attitudes to parents and child.

Own and husband's responses to such encounters, what said, how felt and why. Whether have avoided places or people where might have to discuss disabled child.

I did then recognize that the interviewer does structure the situation, in so far as he has some idea of what areas may be important and does attempt to cover these with all respondents. Further, that one could not enter the situation without some such pre-conceptions, and the respondent moreover expects some degree of structuring – that the interviewer has some particular purpose in mind. Also, I saw that, as with fixed-choice questions, it is possible that respondents may 'discover' attitudes and opinions in areas about which they had not previously thought, or at least that such thoughts will become more systematized through the process of questioning.

The only clear demonstration of this was when Mrs C said she had not previously thought that their child's asthma might be responsible for his reported lack of progress at school, and subsequently she developed this explanation to a considerable extent. In a few other cases, I was aware that I was avoiding certain topics, either because of the presence of others, or because I could not see how to present the questions as 'relevant' to the respondent. The areas most difficult in this respect were those concerned with the effects of the child on his parents' marriage and changes in family life. I wished to avoid direct questioning, since I thought it likely to produce a blanket negative response, but simple repetition of the same questions at each interview may be interpreted by the respondent as wasting their time, if its purpose is not in any case transparent to them.

Over all, I hoped that since questioning covered all or most areas of family life, and since I did not fix the responses available to parents, artificial structuring of their experience was kept to a minimum.

B   THE ANALYST: AUTONOMOUS PROFESSIONAL

The tape-recorded interviews were transcribed in full, and the transcripts indexed by page and line to enable easy reference. I was then faced with the central problem of analysis: how to move from the particular statements by respondents to generalizations about those statements. My aim by then was not merely the redescription or presentation of the material in the commonsense terms used by respondents. I saw myself as a symbolic inter-actionist who should attempt to discover the underlying categories with which parents made sense of the experience of having a disabled child, so that I might understand their behaviour in that situation.

Having recognized that an analyst should not assume that his own categories are held by or represent similar distinctions to his respondents, I now saw that, reading Schutz (especially 'Concept and Theory Formation in the Social Sciences', 1962), the generalized categories or 'second-order constructs' that are produced may not necessarily be consciously held by any respondent. Besides, the analyst does start off with some idea of what categories might be important and useful in organizing his material. How, then, is the method used different from those which have already been criticized as inadequate and, in some cases, producing meaningless results? I then looked to others with similar intentions to see how they resolved this dilemma. First, I read Glaser and Strauss (1967) on 'grounded theory'. They say that particular items of data must not be treated in isolation from, but examined within, the context of their utterance, in order that their meaning to the speaker may be determined. Thus the 'essential' elements of a category of phenomena produced by the analyst are those which are similarly important to the persons experiencing those phenomena (see also Znaniecki, 1965). The categories of everyday life are rarely well-ordered or explicit, so that respondents may never have systematized such elements, produced and recognized the general category. But analysis is *grounded* in the respondents' definitions and the analyst's pre-conceptions are constantly tested against the data to determine their adequacy for understanding the phenomena.

The method does not aim at prediction, but at 'generation'. 'Causes' cannot be specified as distinct from 'effects' – the former are inferred from the latter, i.e. the data. The aim is to produce homogeneous categories of phenomena which then provide a basis for organization and interpretation of observed behaviour regularities or statistical correlations (see also Turner, 1953).

Lofland (1971) has attempted a systematic presentation of what these categories might be. Though others might be added according to one's particular concerns, he suggests:

1 Acts. Action in a situation that is temporarily brief.

2 Activities. Action in a setting of more major duration – constituting significant elements of persons' involvements.

3 Meanings. The verbal productions of participants that define and direct action.

4 Participation. Persons' involvement in, or adaptation to, a situation or setting under study.

5 Relationships. Inter-relationships among several persons considered simultaneously.

6 Settings. The entire setting under study conceived as the unit of analysis.

One then asks: what are the characteristics of these categories, the forms they assume, the variations they display?

He describes the production of such categories as the attempt to: (1) assemble all the materials on a given topic; (2) identify the variations among this range of instances; (3) classify them into types or sets of categories; and eventually (4) present them to the reader in some orderly form, preferably named and numbered.

Robinson's (1951) description of the conceptual processes involved in what he calls 'analytic induction' is similar:

1 Rough definition of the phenomena.

2 Hypothetical explanation of the phenomena (i.e. a 'working hypothesis' derived from knowledge of the field and the theoretical perspective held by the analyst).

3 Study of one case in the light of this hypothesis.

4 If the two do not 'fit', reformulation of the hypothesis; or redefinition of the phenomena in such a way that the particular case is excluded (i.e. the range of applicability of the hypothesis is limited).

5 After a number of cases have been examined 'practical certainty' that the explanation is adequate is attained (however, any negative instances will require reformulation or redefinition).

What all such accounts 'gloss' is the fact that, as I had read in Znaniecki (op. cit.), categories embody theory. As such they are analytically indistinguishable from the everyday 'documentary method' of interpretation, as presented in chapter 5. Statements made by respondents are taken as pointing to some underlying pattern, but these statements are interpreted on the basis of what is known about that pattern. Moreover, I did not recognize that what applied to my actions applied equally to those of my 'subjects'. I was a symbolic interactionist but they were not. That is, I was still taking parents' statements at 'face value', though I did know, for example, that some adopted standard English rather than the local Scottish dialect when talking to me.

Any research situation is a social encounter; equally, every social encounter is potentially an interviewing situation (Cicourel, *op. cit.*). The same analysis of behaviour therefore must apply to both. Hence, in attempting to explain parents' reactions to the fact of a disabled child by eliciting their definitions of that situation, one must also take account of the fact that these 'definitions' or statements by parents are behaviour towards the investigator in the research situation. Thus one must attempt to discover how they define that situation.

Evidently, the interview is not an 'ordinary' social encounter. I presented myself as a 'disinterested research worker' and I thought that carrying a schedule of questions helped manage this impression. In most cases, the respondents did not challenge the purpose of the interview. In two cases (G and U) it was the father of the child who wanted to know 'what it was all about'. Neither of these had been present at the start of the interview, nor perhaps played any part in the agreement to co-operate. One mother, Mrs O, (who was then in training as a psychiatric nurse, and thus perhaps more knowledgeable of, and even interested in, research in the area) asked to know in greater detail about the project. Two others expressed doubts that what they were saying would be of any use to me.

However, 'acceptance' of the interviewer's definition of the situation implies that there is some clearly defined 'respondent role' with which parents could have had experience. Having once agreed to an interview, respondents are more or less constrained by the 'normal' demands of courtesy to provide some kind of answers to questions. How they decide to present their replies depends partly on their conception of a 'research worker'.

The available alternatives in this study appeared to be: 'student' who has to produce a piece of work for an examination; the kind of questioner who administers opinion polls and market research surveys, of which most people have at least heard, and a kind of social worker (Mrs B revealed that she thought I actually was a social worker, in spite of attempts to rule out this possibility).

The kind of behaviour adopted by the respondent to each of these appeared to be: 'I'll help you all I can'; 'Ask me what you want to know (but get it over with)'; and 'No, I haven't any specific problems but I don't mind chatting to you'.

The most common definition of the interviewer seemed to be in this last category. In several cases an implicit comparison was made between myself and the health visitor who 'never helps you much', but is very welcome as someone to talk to. I later decided that if this was so, it meant that most parents treated me as a representative of an official agency to whom the official morality concerning family life with a disabled child should be expressed. Only Mrs N, whom I consider in chapter 8 as the one case of 'deviance', seemed to regard me as a 'stranger' to whom one is traditionally supposed to unburden one's sorrows, who yet actually *wants* to listen and with whom, therefore, one runs less risk of losing face. She said: 'It doesn't matter what you think.'

C THE WRITER RE-FORMS SOCIETY

However, having seen this, I did not know what to do about it, and continued with the analysis and started to write, treating parents' statements as more or less unproblematic indicators of their 'true feelings'. With this attitude I even managed to apply the ethnomethodological paradigm (much as in chapter 5 though more positivistically; see Horobin and Voysey, forthcoming), produced the 'elements of ideology' and analysis of the agencies' activities (as in chapters 7 and 8) and recognized the categories of 'responsibility' and 'power'.

Then I saw in parents' statements an expression of what I then called the 'official ideology' of family life – as presented in chapter 2 – but still did not relate this to other aspects of the analysis. I could see how definitions of responsibility and power influenced interaction between parents and others, but not why. I treated them as 'factors' rather than as constitutive properties of inter-action (see Voysey, 1972a).

The next change in formulation came when I was asked to write a paper on 'The Politics of Stigma', to which I agreed against my better judgment of myself as a professional sociologist (it was a chance of publication and money – it was rejected). I was then able to see both the 'ideology' and the agents' activities in the wider context of historical changes in the nature of morality and legitimation in western society (see Voysey, 1972b). Writing chapter 2 made me see the official morality of the family as an instance of this phenomenon, the more convincing since I had evidence of the public statements of some official agencies.

I then could not consistently treat any parents' statements to me as 'given'. I did decide that those in chapter 5 could still be so taken, since I had concentrated on differentiating methods of interpretation, rather than on what informed these. But I revised the paper on impression management, trying to make it consistent with how I now saw what parents said about relationships within the home. In the case of the latter I was confronted with previous selves in analyses which, filed away and forgotten, showed, like those of the writers criticized in chapter 1, that there were few effects of a disabled child on his family.

However, it has been some time since I would publicly defend The Reporter as a way of life. Committed to semi-structured interviewing, I ought still to have made myself consider other possible interpretations by making more effort to talk to other family members, especially fathers, and to the agencies with whom they came into contact. I did start to make notes on observations in the clinics, but was easily persuaded that this would involve too much work. I obtained, but have not used, the hospital records of the children in the study. Finally, a colleague suggested that I might live for a period of time in the homes of one or more families. There are several advantages to this method. 'Participant observation' reduces the dangers of inappropriate generalization through time and space – the longer a worker stays in the 'field' the more he is likely to revise his interpretation of the phenomena. The categories are not pre-fixed, but can arise from and be modified in the course of investigation. It is easier to discuss members' behaviour with other participants in the situation and any one may be observed in interaction with others besides the research worker.

On the other hand, the worker in the field is obviously a participant in the production of his data, and hence has to face the problems that were discussed above. He has to decide how to present himself or what role to adopt; to discover how his subjects define his presence in the situation, and hence what influence his intervention has on behaviour in that situation. In addition, he faces the same dangers of misapplication of his own categories to the phenomena under study (see Becker and Geer, 1970, for further discussion of these points).

I decided against such observation, partly because I thought it would be difficult to find families willing and able to assume the additional burden of a stranger living with them. In addition, I felt that within the confines of a home, whatever role was adopted by the investigator would influence interaction patterns in that situation, and the effects of such intervention. However, the evident success of the team who filmed family life in the BBC series on 'The Space Between Words' made me remember my major interest at the time. I was not prepared to commit myself that much to the project: I preferred to stay at home.

However, in chapter 8 I argue that even at home parents may present themselves as they do in such encounters as the interview, and that they may yet not always believe in what they say. Perhaps I should not have reached this conclusion had I approached the topic in other ways, but it would, I think, have been possible to do so without ever going to talk to parents at all and without any special sociological expertise. There are plenty of precedents, as the pamphlets and books cited in chapter 8 indicate. From my point of view it was worth it since, other considerations apart, I can thereby 'identify and understand myself independent of present social conditions' (Macintyre, 1964, p. 4).

Blum (*op. cit.*) argues that it is only by not wishing to convince others that theirs was the correct way of seeing the world that 'positivists' could 'live with' their formulations. I take him to mean that they thereby exclude themselves from their theories. All of the theories based on the interpretive paradigm implicitly include themselves in so far as they call for a subjective interpretation of social phenomena, and put man back into the world acting upon it. As I have already indicated, consistent recognition of this does not automatically follow. Also in chapter 8 I cite Light (1969) who points out that everyday actors can be as aware of the precarious nature of social reality as Berger and Luckmann (1967). I would add: was the commonsense world ever the same for Garfinkel's (1967) subjects after their incongruity experiences?

However, self-understanding is not my only interest, nor is it likely to concern the reader. I am not just asserting that I 'like' to see society in this way, that it makes me happy, but that it is how it is, and I am trying to convince the reader, although of course if he agrees it will be his accomplishment. Most of all, I hope that the following chapters would make sense to parents who themselves have a disabled child. First, however, let us see something of what they had to say.

4 The families with a disabled child

Over a period of eighteen months, I visited twenty-one families, each of which contained a child who had recently been identified at the local children's hospital as suffering from one of a range of disabilities. The child's mother was always present, sometimes the father or other child members and occasionally relatives and friends. In response to my questions, parents talked to me about such matters as: events concerning the disabled child's diagnosis and treatment; their encounters with medical and other agencies; their activities within and without the home; their relationships with relatives and friends.

In this chapter I attempt to summarize some of what parents said to me in order that the reader may later judge my interpretations of their statements. Evidently, I have had to be selective in condensing approximately 2,000 pages of transcription. However, I include many direct quotations from parents' responses and where I 'describe' them, I attempt to exclude interpretation on my part unless otherwise indicated. Thus I may say 'Mrs A *appeared* very cheerful', meaning appeared to me, but 'Mr and Mrs B *were* quite satisfied', that is according to their own account, though it may of course have been I who initially suggested that category in my questioning.

I have also, for reasons of space, had to cut down the original presentation which included summaries of all interviews with all twenty-one families. For all but four – A, B, K and O – I now give only the diagnosis and age at first interview of the disabled child, the age of other members, and occupations of equivalent status to those actually pursued: this is to preserve the families' anonymity. The families are identified alphabetically for future reference and the interviews numbered I to IV.

A GIRL, THREE MONTHS. CONGENITAL BREACH OF THE
OESOPHAGUS

Father: Clerical officer, Department of the Environment,
thirty-six.
Mother: Housewife, twenty-nine.
Other children: Boy, four.

I

This child was still in hospital, having been born a month pre-
maturely. Labour had been induced because of rhesus incompat-
ibility, and Mrs A had expected her to be taken straight away
for a transfusion. Since the child was also born with a breach in
the gullet, the hospital had wanted to attempt immediate surgery.
They sought the father's permission, 'explained exactly' what
was involved and asked if he minded informing his wife: 'I don't
think they wanted to tell me'. Next morning, when she asked
about the transfusion, he told her about the child's condition:
'I think it was better; I wanted to know exactly what was happening. Some people don't but I did'. She said, 'I wasn't surprised
and took it terribly calmly', and attributed this to the fact that
she was still under sedation for high blood-pressure. The surgeon
warned the parents that the join might break, and when it did
after four days he performed another operation inserting a tube
for direct feeding through the stomach. Another operation to
direct the oesophagus through the neck so that saliva need not
be sucked out was postponed several times because the child
developed minor infections. It was finally performed at two
months. Definitive surgery was postponed for a year until the
child reached fifteen to twenty pounds in weight.

The family was organized around the child's condition but no
'problems' were reported in any sphere. The major source of
information was the hospital, with which Mrs A reported herself
as more than satisfied. One or both parents visited the child
every day and telephoned the hospital in between 'which we
find is a great help', the ward sister being 'the best contact for
the day-to-day stuff'. They had been told that they could ask to
see the surgeon at any time: 'we have never found anyone un-
willing, they have always been very frank and told us exactly
what was going on . . . of course, I think it's up to the individual,
they find that we ask and absorb what they tell us.' Mrs A found
that feeding the child was not only easier than they had expected
but than it had been with her normal baby, since there could be
no 'wind'. She planned to face management problems as they
arose, but expected no serious setbacks. Meantime, she was

hoping that difficulties discovered with other such children in establishing normal feeding after the operation ('a minor problem anyway compared with the present') would be mitigated by her present practice, advised by the hospital, of putting food and drink into the child's mouth so that she could taste them. Other special techniques such as changing the stomach tube were acquired in the hospital before she was discharged.

Visiting the child was no problem since her four-year-old brother was left with a set of grandparents. A widowed neighbour was always willing to baby-sit and to do any shopping that could not be ordered by telephone. Mrs A found that she could visit friends and relatives in the afternoons or at the weekends, taking her son with her, or they could visit her. Both activities were, however, less frequent. Neither parent went out in the evening singly or together as they had done before but 'We've not got the inclination at the moment, if we did . . . I'd feel we were taking an awful advantage. If anybody can look after him . . . I'd like to nip off to the hospital . . . it's really ourselves that don't want to go, I think, more than anything.' They had decided not to go away on holiday partly because it would be difficult to carry sterilization equipment, but also so that they could be near the hospital. If they did not offer help, other friends and neighbours were always very interested in the child's progress. 'Everyone is asking when we are getting her home (though we are more concerned with getting her established)'.

Over all Mrs A appeared very cheerful, regarded the child's condition as 'temporary troubles to go through' (the hospital was not so confident), and thought that they were very lucky to live in a city with such good medical facilities. She had heard that many such babies in other parts of the country die before reaching a hospital which can perform the necessary operations.

II   Child: six months

Her reported competence was even greater at the second interview. The child had been discharged after Mrs A had spent some time in the mother and baby unit. Here she had not only gained practical experience in feeding the child, but 'had got to know all her little noises – if she cried a bit there was nothing wrong with her. If I'd been at home I'd have been in a flat panic'. At home she had discovered such 'tricks' as placing a towel under the child's neck to soak up the saliva. Although she had to be especially careful that the child did not catch cold, said they had had some 'ups and downs' and 'a bit of trouble' when a lung collapsed, and expected that she might have to telephone the hospital if the tube came out, she felt that the child was 'more or less treated normally . . . she's terribly good, I thought she'd be really awful'. Mrs A did take advantage of the health visitor's offer of attending the local clinic at a special time so that 'everyone doesn't look at her . . . [though] they mean it kindly and it doesn't really bother me'. She was glad to keep in touch with the hospital so that they could keep a check on the child's weight increase, and still felt they had 'no secrets' from her. She was even more optimistic about the future. Although recognizing that medical knowledge was as yet not very great, she had been introduced to the mother of a child who had had the operation and at age six was 'just normal'.

Visiting friends and relations was more restricted than before because of the three-hourly feeds, but 'it was worse going up and down every day. I feel better now she's upstairs'. Mrs A's mother was visiting more often and bringing in shopping, and her father drove them to the hospital and clinic when necessary. Apart from this, 'I would say everyone is very kind and that . . . they would watch [the other child] but we really haven't needed any special kind of help. And he accepted the fact that he would have to wait in the waiting room so we took him up with us'.

Mr and Mrs A still did not go out: 'I haven't asked anyone to baby-sit because I feel that it wouldn't be fair yet while she's so little and I don't think I would like to ask anyone really . . . to be responsible, but my neighbour would baby-sit for him while I go to the hospital or anything'. Asked if she saw herself and her husband as 'unfortunate' she said, 'I don't think so – you see some really ill children up there, children they can't do anything for, some don't even survive'. When asked if she had ever thought differently: 'No, not really, certainly not now.'

III   Child: nine months
The child was sitting with support, had been taken out in the car in her carrycot and been pushed around in her push-chair: 'She's delighted to get out and doesn't like lying so much now.' Mrs A thought the child would be crawling by now but she had been found to have a dislocated hip which was still in plaster. Mrs A was 'disappointed' that the hospital had not discovered this before – 'I did tell them I was' – but also said 'it was probably just one of those things – they were probably more busy – I'm glad they found it before she started walking'. The GP who now visited weekly said he felt 'a bit guilty' about this, but Mrs A told him that she would not have expected him to give the child

an examination. He had helped her by advising when and by how much to increase the child's food intake and therefore the size of the tube, about which Mrs A reported herself as having been 'awful scared'. Now she was happy to go to the hospital every two months: 'I've gained confidence. If I get her checked at the clinic I'm quite happy . . . if I had any problems I could just phone him up.' There was a new health visitor who was 'very interested' but 'I've really no problems – there's nothing that's bothering me'.

Mr and Mrs A had been out once: 'Because we were on holiday my neighbour said "go and get theatre tickets".' Mrs A still would not ask grandparents to baby-sit because 'I feel they wouldn't know what to do if she cried – it's probably silly really'. Others had offered so that 'I think it's up to ourselves to take advantage'. She would not ask anyone else to feed the child but Mr A did quite often: 'He'll do anything if I can catch him before he goes out to the garage.' He also did more of the gardening than previously: 'I find that's the one thing I haven't got time to spend on.' All decisions about family matters were discussed between them, which she felt to be like the marriages of their friends and not affected by having the child. The other child was quite delighted to have his sister at home and was 'always looking in the pram' and only 'apprehensive' at the thought of starting school shortly. Mrs A expected to be more restricted then since she would have to take and fetch him, but 'just as I would have done before'. She hoped still to fit in a cup of coffee with her friend on the way.

IV   Child: fourteen months

The last interview took place a week before the child was due to go into hospital for the operation to repair the breach in the gullet. She had not reached the intended weight for this but had stopped gaining. Mrs A was to go into hospital for two weeks before the operation, and Mr A to have mornings off work so that he could visit his wife and child in hospital while the other child was at school. Mrs A's mother would collect the child from school, give him and his father lunch and tea, 'so everybody's really organized – they're all very helpful'. After the operation Mrs A would come home for a week, when the child would receive intravenous feeding, and then go back in to try and get her used to normal feeding. She planned to give her two weeks and after that 'leave it to them [the hospital authorities], she might just take advantage of me'. The child was out of plaster but still wearing a splint at night, and this was Mrs A's one source of dissatisfaction, though she also said that the child might not have crawled yet anyway 'being so small'. As to the future: 'She's bound to be slow, but she's very alert mentally.'

Life was far less restricted than previously because the child now had three meals a day and 'she mixes into the household', and less than Mrs A had expected it to be. Another parent gave the other child a lift to school and he insisted on coming home alone. One of her friends often came in the car and collected her and the child and took them shopping. She said: 'Have pram will travel.' Friends visited as before and the grandparents 'just accept it now' so that the child did not make any difference one way or the other. The other child was more 'obstreperous' but 'he's just turning into a schoolboy I would say – he's taken it very well I would say. He's quite happy for me to go into hospital.' In general: 'We try not to make too much of it, we just go along in the same way as we did before, the only difference being, I would say, that it's probably drawn us closer together.' Mrs A said that they had always wanted two children and that they should be closer in age, but now: 'I doubt if I could have managed if there had been just two years between . . . so it's maybe all turned out.'

B   GIRL, THREE MONTHS. MONGOL

Father: Manager, grocer's shop, twenty-five.
Mother: Housewife, twenty-five.
Other children: Girl, four.

I

Mrs B said that 'Mr B noticed right away' that their baby had 'mongolic' features and asked the sister who told the doctor who told Mrs B six days after birth. Mrs B said that from the third day 'I kept looking at her and my husband was worried about her, but he didna' want to worry me. And I said to everyone who came in, "Do you think she's O.K.?" They said, "Of course she's all right." But of course they didna' want to hurt me . . . they canna' see it now.' But she still got 'such a shock' because 'I thought they would have told me' and felt that someone should have, although she was quite happy with the way in which she was told: 'It was my own doctor, funnily enough . . . he was awfu' nice . . . though he had to be firm.'

The first interview was after an out-patient clinic appointment when the child was one month old. The doctor concerned could not tell from the case notes whether the parents knew of their

child's condition and only discovered that they did from the
sister on duty, who in turn found out from a hospital
porter who knew the parents. At this encounter, at which I
was present, Mrs B asked only 'how bad it is'. In the interview Mrs B said: 'We're feart to ask questions – what we might
learn' and said 'we knew what it was so what else was there?',
although Mr B had taken out some library books on handicapped
children.

She turned rather to her extensive family for help: 'It seems to
be that way in a large family.' Mr B's father lived downstairs, her
parents locally, and four sisters and four brothers with their
families in the same city. Mrs B said: 'We've all had a broken
heart.' After leaving hospital with the baby she spent a week
with her parents: 'I just felt I should be wi' my own people – I
think that's how you feel.' The GP had visited her and 'he was
awfu' nice' but 'people would speak to me and I couldn't hear
them, I had a kind of block'. She was sedated for two weeks, as
was one of her sisters: 'We're awfu' close ye ken . . . she still
canna' believe it really – she upsets me and I canna' speak to her
because I ken she's upset . . . some days I am awfu' depressed
ye ken.'

Managing the child at home presented no difficulties: 'It calmed
me right down.' Mrs B could not think about the future at this
stage (although she asked me why a doctor had said that mongol
babies did not live very long) and asserted: 'As long as I can cope
I'm nae worrying.' There had been no problems in relations with
others outside the family: 'They all know round here, they've all
been awfu' nice . . . but I'm nae rushing round to tell everybody.'
Mr and Mrs B had been out twice for a meal, while her sister
minded the baby, and her mother their four-year-old daughter.
Most Sundays they went to her mother's for the day. Her mother
could not visit very much because she worked in the mornings,
but her sister came several times a week. Mr B's family might
have come but when the child was two weeks old, his sister-in-law
gave birth to a spina bifida baby (F).

Compared with them: 'I dinna' ken who's going to be worst
off – if he's going to be in a wheelchair it's going to be a lot of
work . . . but I think they can do so much for his kind as I see it,
but we've no hope.' Mr B had said 'Why should it happen to us?'
but Mrs B said she thought the child was 'the next in line and we
got her'. Her major worry was for the other child. She thought
she might 'take out' her worry on her and that the elder child
might suffer when other children found out: 'Ye ken how cruel
children can be.'

II Child: six months

The child now smiled, recognized the immediate family and required less support when sitting. Mrs B said: 'I'm just settled into a routine now' and that she felt less depressed but very 'nervy'. She said she wished more people would visit her. Her sister now only came one morning a week because she was very busy: 'They think I'm all right and I am really.' Her mother could not come more because she had to work. Mrs B had been out once, one evening with her husband, while a twelve-year-old niece baby-sat, but the girl's father had since said she was too young and could not do it again. When she did go out during the day, Mrs B said that now either 'people rush past and won't look into the pram', or they 'give advice when they don't really know at all'.

Her husband always helped bath the children, but worked very long hours, so that when he came in he wanted to sleep and 'can't understand why I get bored'. They were hoping to get a different house as the present one was too small, but she thought they would have to wait at least a year. The other child was reported as being very bored through staying in all day, and Mrs B had just returned from a walk which was just 'for her sake' and had seen a social worker who had promised to get the child into nursery school. Over all, she did report far more problems than before having the child, but did not think anyone could really help her: thus, of the health visitor, 'you know as well as she does'. Nor, after the results of a chromosome test could anyone be blamed: 'It's just the two of us together.' She concluded that, despite their own financial difficulties, which meant that there were few biscuits to offer me and that she had holes in her stockings, 'money's not everything – I've realized that now'.

III Child: ten months

Mrs B reported her second visit to the out-patient clinic. She still felt that 'they can't do much – it would be the Welfare' and other medical contacts were of little help. The GP 'says "you mothers worry about anything" so you just feel silly going'. The health visitor said: ' "You're taking this very well" – she makes you feel depressed.' In any case she did not want advice, 'I don't want to know – I'll bring her up.' She was very happy with the child's progress which, since she was sitting at eight months, appeared not much slower than the other child.

Mrs B appeared generally more cheerful. The other child had started nursery school and had asked if her sister could sleep in the same room with her. She herself went out more (partly because

it was better weather), walking far enough to visit a friend. She
now visited once a week with a girl in the upstairs flat, and her
husband had taken up golf once a week, for which she said she
was glad as he had never gone out before. She talked of many
things he did to help, such as cleaning the windows, looking
after the children, or cooking the dinner in order to let her go out.
They had been out on a family picnic, where everybody wanted
to nurse the baby, and away for a week in a cottage.

Most people now were 'kind really' and asked to see the baby
and, of those who ignored her, she said, 'I don't worry about
them – if I did I'd be a nervous wreck . . . I don't want sympathy
really – I'm just not that type . . . I usually take everything in
my stride but that was a big knock, though I'm getting over it
now. I wouldn't know what to do wi' myself without her now . . .
she's healthy, that's the main thing.'

IV   Child: fourteen months

The child's progress had been maintained. She could stand and
though she could not walk, 'we'll get her there some way . . . and,
of course, she's nae so much work for me not walking'. Mrs B
now seemed more impressed by medical opinion. She said, 'To
me, it's good but I didn't really know' and reported that the
clinic doctor had been pleased and the health visitor had said
that some mongol babies take much longer. She was considering
sending the child to a day centre: 'We must let her get any
chance to learn more than I can learn her . . . I suppose they can,
they've had them all before.' The other child was happy and doing
well at nursery school.

All the family now 'accept her', and Mrs B's mother looked
after her in order to let Mrs B out more. Mrs B felt that having
the child had made a difference to her marriage, 'I do think a
shock or something brings you closer together.' At the clinic
one girl had upset her saying that mongols are 'awfu' wild . . . I
said my one's nae' and asking what caused it 'as though it was
my fault'.

When something like that happens you feel right sorry for
yourself – you think you're the only one, but then when you
think about it . . . maybe we've got her, but we're both healthy,
we've got a lot to be thankful for . . . they say that time heals
everything – it certainly has with me . . . if I'd been told a
year ago that it was going to happen I'd have been horrified.
But I wouldn't be without her now – my husband says the same.
Love conquers all – that's true too.

C   BOY, SIX YEARS. ASTHMA
   Father: Plumber, forty-five.
   Mother: Housewife, thirty-nine.
   Other children: Boy, eight; girl, four.

D   BOY, TWO YEARS, TEN MONTHS. RETARDATION
   Father: Driver, forty.
   Mother: Occasional part-time cleaner, thirty-three.
   Other children: Girl, twelve; girl, nine.

E   BOY, FOUR YEARS, TEN MONTHS. DIABETES
   Father: Nurse, twenty-eight.
   Mother: Housewife, twenty-seven.
   Other children: Girl, two years, six months; girl, three months.

F   BOY, TWO MONTHS. SPINA BIFIDA AND HYDROCEPHALUS
   Father: Foreman in corn mill, thirty-four.
   Mother: Housewife, thirty-one.
   Other children: Girl, five years, six months.

G   BOY, ELEVEN MONTHS. RETARDATION
   Father: Ship's officer, thirty-one.
   Mother: Housewife, twenty-three.
   Other children: Girl, two.

H   BOY, TWO WEEKS. MONGOL
   Father: Driver, forty-three.
   Mother: Housewife, forty-two.
   Other children: Boy, seventeen; girl, fourteen.

J   BOY, FOUR YEARS, SEVEN MONTHS. OBESITY
   Father: Police officer, thirty-three.
   Mother: Housewife, twenty-eight.
   No other children.

K   GIRL, THREE YEARS, NINE MONTHS. DIABETES
   Father: Window dresser, twenty-six.
   Mother: Housewife, twenty-five.
   No other children.

I

Mrs K said: 'It was just a miracle we found out she was diabetic.'
She had been worried about her daughter's tantrums and loss
of weight for several months, but at first attributed these to a
two-year history of tonsillitis, and then to their having moved to
their own house. Finally, 'I had just about prepared myself it
was leukaemia – it was the way she wasted away in a matter of
months' and when the child cried and slept all over Christmas and
New Year she knew there must be something wrong. It was,
however, Mr K who said she should take the child to the doctor,
'rather than worry myself sick – or else I'd be sitting here yet'.
There, after asking whether she had put sugar in the bottle, the
GP diagnosed diabetes. They had to wait two weeks before the
child could be admitted to hospital, where she was joined after
two days by her mother. Mrs K said she was never shown how to
do injections until two days before they went home, and she had
been hoping that the district nurse would come in.

Mrs K was still very nervous about doing the injections, finding
that the child screamed and kicked so much that she often tore
the skin. She had had sedatives 'but they didn't really help . . . .
From Mondays to Fridays I don't sleep, I'm up the whole night
thinking about something . . . . I've never believed it, I mean
I still don't believe it, though it's in the back of my mind that
it's true.' The hospital doctor had recommended that she join
the Diabetic Association, which, he told her, was against his
usual practice. He told me that he attributed her 'near hysteria'
to the fact that her thirteen-year-old brother-in-law had also
recently been found to have diabetes, and had taken six months
to become stabilized. A more immediate reason seemed to be
that her husband was away all week, and although Mrs K went
out visiting her mother or mother-in-law most afternoons, she was
alone every evening. She said she could get baby-sitters, but did
not bother. She did not like sleeping alone, but was reluctant
to let the child start sleeping with her. Her main fear was that
the child would have a reaction: 'I know what happens . . . but
I'd rather I had seen it, because I think I'd go into a state of
panic. I'm terrified about it; I'm dreading it.'

Controlling the child's diet appeared to be no problem, as she
had never given her many sweet things. She had stopped baking
for two weeks 'to give a chance to her' but now let her help 'but
told her not to put it in her mouth'. She thought that the worst
problem from the child's point of view was that she lacked children
to play with: 'That's what I told the doctor, she has fits of
depression quite a lot . . . [it's] since we came here, so I can't

really tell if it's due to this.' She had taken K to dancing classes, but the child would not stay as she felt everyone was looking at her. Mrs K was not worried that other children would tease her, 'there's nothing they can tease her about as it doesn't show', but she was hoping that K would not need injections all her life as she had had a friend whose legs were 'a mess'. The hospital doctor had however told her that tablets did not work for children and that it was likely that she would: 'I wouldn't like that.'

II Child: four years, one month

K now had two children to play with, either at her own or their home, and her mother thought she was better for it and having less hysterics. She also now attended dancing classes and had been in a show. She had had a few 'turns' but only one bad one. Mr K was at home which was 'a good job' and he telephoned the doctor at seven in the morning, who told them to give the child biscuits and sugar. 'There wasna' much he could do about it as she wasna' unconscious.' The child recovered in half an hour and went to sleep: 'I was terrified to put her through, so I just put her with us . . . . I didn't eat for two days [and] every night when [my husband] is away I never get a decent night's sleep.' Mrs K took her to the hospital two days later and they reduced her insulin, told her she could ring straight through to them if ever she needed advice. On another occasion K was ill and had not eaten for six hours when the doctor came in: 'Another panic station . . . . I had a sore back and a sore head, everything was wrong, but I got my mother to come out . . . . I got an awful scare.'

She thought the doctor nice, but found she never remembered to ask all the questions she wanted and relied on books and magazines for information: 'There's quite a lot to find out yet . . . always something you learn every day . . . . I'm trying to find out about child psychology.' She was due to see the dietician, but thought she knew enough about the diet now, the main problem being that other people, in particular a girl of thirteen who took K to the park, had been buying the child sweets. Mrs K had only explained to her daughter's friend's mother what she could eat. However, she agreed with her mother-in-law (who had come in) that at least K would not help herself to, or buy food, as did her thirteen-year-old uncle.

Although Mrs K was much happier when her husband was at home, and he was trying to learn more about diabetes, K would not let her father or anyone else give the injections. Despite her fear of reactions, Mrs K did now say: 'I think it's something that works into your daily routine. You can't get nervy. Although your mind's always at it thinking about where she is ... but you're saying "Don't panic, don't panic" ... so I've more or less got myself settled. Of course I've got my knitting – it helps you to work it off, or reading books ... marvellous how you can just settle yourself down without tablets.'

III   Child: four years, four months

K was now at a play-school, about which Mrs K had been told by the district nurse, one morning a week. She herself enjoyed meeting the other mothers and helping with the children: 'It keeps her happy and it does me because I'm out mixing.' She had been scared the first week that another child would take K's biscuits as K would never say anything, and was glad she was in a different class from her daily playmates. K had had another reaction, again when her father was at home. Mrs K again was 'passed out' – 'I was shaking', and she had also fainted on another occasion. She was therefore going to the doctor for a tonic. Giving the injection was not so bad since they had bought a Hypoguard and she also used ice-cubes to deaden the pain. K's general behaviour was better, although she was very active and talkative: 'She's got nobody else to speak to I suppose.' Mrs K tried to amuse her when she could not go out and play, by letting her sew buttons on dusters, wash her dolls' clothes and so on: 'It keeps her happy for hours. You've just got to make amends with things like that.'

Mrs K seemed fully competent in managing the child's diet and urine testing, but found that her mother-in-law tended to give the child extra when she was there playing: 'She doesn't think she's doing any harm.' She thought that this was because her brother-in-law looked after his own diet, and she really talked to no one about the child's condition: 'They always ask how she's getting on ... but they always ask "will she ever get better" and it's a funny thing to ask. They don't understand but they're interested.' She thought that her husband had 'got to the stage where he's accepted it and just takes it as it comes. He's the sort of person ... that keeps worries to himself, but we haven't discussed it much ... but me I plan away ahead and I worry too much. There's nothing you can do about it. I think you do have to take it as it comes.'

IV   Child: four years, eight months

Mrs K had found a morning job doing a little light housework and taking a dog out. This was so that the three of them could save enough money to go to the Isle of Man for a holiday, but

she said it was good for K and for her to be out of the house. At
the last out-patient visit the doctor had been very pleased with
the child, and told Mrs K she was controlling the diet well. Mrs K
was of course pleased, and herself thought K was 'just healthy
now, just like a normal child . . . in fact, I think she's healthier
than before'. K had had one reaction at home and another one
in town shopping. Mrs K had gone into a shop and asked for sugar
and the child had quickly recovered, but Mrs K thought herself
no more confident: 'I'm still the same really. [My husband] said
"I don't know what you've got to worry about. You've got to
live with it." . . . when everything's O.K. I feel fine . . . when
she's got a setback it just puts me right back again. It makes
you feel as though your insides have been turned out.' She was
also worried when K went out to play lest she did not come back
promptly for meals: 'It's sorta in the back of my mind all the
time [but] there's no sense in keeping her in – she sits and cries.
I treat her like any child and I give her a hiding I suppose you'd
say.'

K was due to start school, about which Mrs K was glad, and
she had been to see the teacher to explain about the diabetes.
She had also started to teach the child how much food she should
have, and let her practice injections on her teddy bear. She
thought: 'What I know I can't really go much further about
knowledge', and no one could help her any more: 'It's just up to
myself now to put up with it'. Asked if she saw other people as
worse off, she said: 'Oh yes, you always feel sorry for yourself
rather than someone else, don't you? But like you see on TV
there's always somebody worse off. Even those polio victims,
there's someone worse off than them, though you've got to feel
sorry for them.'

L   GIRL, FOUR YEARS, FOUR MONTHS. HYPER-PITUITARY DWARF.
? MENTAL SUBNORMALITY

   Father: Ship's mate, twenty-eight.
   Mother: Housewife, twenty-eight.
   Other children: Girl, nine; girl, eight; boy, eight; girl, seven;
   girl, six; boy, six; girl, three.

M   BOY, TEN YEARS, THREE MONTHS. ? EPILEPSY

   Father: Higher Executive Officer, Department of Trade and
   Industry, forty-eight.
   Mother: Part-time clerk, forty-seven.
   Other children: Boy, eighteen.

N   BOY, ONE MONTH. MONGOL

   Father: Hotelier, forty-two.
   Mother: Housewife, thirty-seven.
   Other children: Boy, three.

O   BOY, NINE YEARS, TEN MONTHS. EPILEPSY

   Father: Staff nurse, forty.
   Mother: Student nurse, thirty-three.
   Other children: Boy, thirteen; boy, twelve; boy, seven.

I

This child had some history of epileptic seizures. At six, he had
been found lying in front of the fire with a burn on his arm;
a year later Mrs O saw him have 'a typical grand mal seizure'
and retrospectively defined the first occasion similarly. Although
her GP said 'don't worry', she insisted on having an EEG
performed. For a few months he had been on phenobarbitone.
'I think the doctor thought to settle me down.' Then two weeks
before the interview the police arrived, saying that O had been
found in the street with his brother and taken to hospital. Her
first reaction was that he had been fighting and maybe broken a
window. Then 'something just dawned on me . . . and I said
"This is the thing I've been dreading more than anything – don't
tell me he's had another fit" . . . it must have been at the back
of my mind'.

   I included this case, however, because Mrs O said that she
had insisted on further examinations, not because of the seizure,
but because two days later O had had a 'blinding headache' and
since her husband's brother had just been taken ill with a brain
tumour (and had died that day), she thought O might be the same.
She said of herself that she was 'slightly hysterical' but blamed
her GP for seeming so 'disinterested', although she recognized his
argument that 'if you make more of it the child will make more
of it . . . but at the same time what am I supposed to do if . . . he
gets knocked down because he's had a seizure? From O's point of
view, that's how I look at it.' The child was due to have another
EEG, but had meantime been put back on to phenobarbitone, and
the hospital doctor had advised that he should not go swimming
or cycling.

   Mrs O said the child seemed to understand and not to mind,
and had not asked to go swimming, but she had long been worried
about him. He had been enuretic since the age of two-and-a-half
and now, though bright at school, was 'very aggressive – he likes

to fight and knock everybody around . . . and just instigate trouble. I think he's a psychopath, the way he's going.' Primarily, she traced all his troubles back to his birth: 'I don't think I've had the same emotional tie with him. Maybe I'm over-compensating now. I probably feel a lot of guilt now, because I've never been as close to him. When he was very small he wouldn't breast-feed. This led to a lot of frustration in myself.' More recently she had been very unhappy with her husband, and had one particularly bad argument the weekend of the child's seizure: 'I wouldn't like to think this had anything to do with O . . . . I said to the GP, could mental stress bring it on? He said: "Oh, I don't think so", but he may just have been reassuring me.'

Her other worry was about the future. Her husband was far more worried about the child's condition: 'Although he's had these lectures on the stigma of mental illness, he still feels there's a stigma on it. And now it's happened to him.' Neither of them, however, treated O any differently, and when she discovered that his teacher had stopped him doing gymnastics, she went to school and complained. The children at the school had started calling him 'fainter' but his own brothers were very good, especially the youngest who would keep an eye on O whenever they went to Life-Boys. Mrs O described them all as 'very independent' and able to take themselves off for walks all day. Mr O's father was a doctor and had encouraged Mrs O to get the child investigated. She said she did not see much of either family – 'We're not a close-knit family' – although her brother and sister and her husband's other brother all lived in the city. Her own mother had always had more to do with her other daughter's child. She had been 'disappointed but very realistic'.

II Child: ten years, one month

Having had an EEG, the child's epilepsy was diagnosed as 'idiopathic'. He had no signs of a tumour, but was still on phenobarbitone. Mrs O again said 'More for my sake the doctor said', but this might only be for a year. Mrs O did not seem very concerned about the fact that O often forgot to take the drug, but was still worried about his aggression and psycho-pathic tendencies. She was very preoccupied with her recent separation from her husband and apparently eager to talk about this, suggesting that we might meet sometime for coffee (we never did). She had had to take her husband to court to get him to pay maintenance, and had also discovered many debts.

III   Child: ten years, six months

Mrs O had taken the child back to the out-patient clinic, and insisted on his seeing a psychiatrist, thinking that his fits might be hysterical. 'He's a bed-wetter as well, and I thought it might all be tied up. I'd rather get it all straightened out, you know, if there was anything mentally ill . . . before he's really growing up. And the psychiatrist said "There's nothing wrong with him, he's a very normal little boy". (The psychiatrist's report said: 'O had a very strong façade of not letting things concern him, and one cannot deny that he needs it. Within these overall limitations one felt that his overall adjustment was reasonable. I discussed the situation in these terms with Mrs O . . . and tried to reassure her that it is not an aggressive act directed against her.') Mrs O now attributed the enuresis to 'attention seeking', but said he had been dry the last week 'under the threat that he doesn't go on holiday on Saturday, so it is workable with him'. He was still aggressive: 'I think there's maybe a time when he does work himself up to a seizure, so I make an intensive watch on him and make sure he takes his pills.' She was fairly optimistic about the future, still expecting him to be off drugs in two years. 'It means he could drive a car and do all the things that any other child could do', but meanwhile 'there'll still be a little doubt in my mind'.

Mrs O was still having difficulty getting maintenance from her husband and discussed this with me at some length. A man whom she had known for about a year, a stone-mason, was now living with her. O had been swimming once with his brothers, but Mrs O was doubtful whether she would allow him to again: 'I've really spent hours of anguish thinking of him in the water and that you know . . . I don't think I'm an over-protective mother. He [her friend] might argue this point . . . I just get terribly responsible . . . . I think it would be my fault if he did go in the water and this happened, because it would be by my permission that he went.' She thought, however, that other children had now stopped teasing him, and his brothers 'have really forgotten all about it'. The only effect was 'inasmuch as I tried to make them a bit responsible for him when he was out'.

IV   Child: ten years, ten months

O had not been back to out-patients and had had no further fits, but he got 'very excitable and silly when anybody comes in'. Mrs O again let him go swimming because the second eldest boy had become more of a 'loner' and Mrs O felt she could trust him to watch O. Mrs O had passed her final examination and was

financially better off, although she had still received no maintenance from her husband. She was mostly happy with her friend,
who looked after the boys when she was on duty. She had found
herself 'terribly short-tempered with the children and bursting
into tears at the slightest thing . . .. I think everything caught up
with me', and she was to have an examination for a suspected
ovarian cyst with which she was in pain.

O still suffered from enuresis most nights: 'I could go mad,
but I don't roar and shout at him . . .. I'm quite prepared to go
along with it, hoping it won't last long'. As regards his epilepsy,
she said: 'I've been a bit more confident as regards the future . . . .
It's in the background now, but if he was to have another fit,
it'd be right to the fore again.' Of his general behaviour she said:
'He'll do anything for anybody if you ask him in the right way
[but] though he gets equal shares he gives me the impression he
gets missed out. Say I was giving out the cake now, O would be
the first there with his hands shaking, really shaking.' She was
still worried about his aggressiveness: 'It's maybe a bit early to
say, but I think he's inclined to psychopathic . . .. I know it's a
shame to say, perhaps he shouldn't get married – oh, I'm looking
away forward now . . . but we wouldn't like any woman to go
through what we've had to go through with his father.'

P   BOY, TWO MONTHS. GALACTOCAEMIA
Father: Shipwright, twenty-one.
Mother: Housewife, twenty-one.
No other children.

Q   BOY, TWO MONTHS. CONGENITAL ABSENCE OF BILE DUCT
Father: Research physicist, thirty-six.
Mother: Housewife, thirty-one.
Other children: Boy, eight; girl, six; girl, two years, six months.

R   GIRL, TWO MONTHS. HOLE IN HEART
Father: Clerk, twenty-eight.
Mother: Housewife, twenty-seven.
No other children.

S   BOY, THREE YEARS. COELIAC DISEASE
Father: Labourer, thirty-two.
Mother: Housewife, thirty-two.
Other children: Boy, eleven; boy, ten; girl, six; boy, five;
girl, six months.

T   GIRL, THREE MONTHS. MENINGITIS WITH HYDROCEPHALUS
      Father: Works manager in flour mill, twenty-seven.
      Mother: Housewife, twenty-one.
      Other children: Boy, two.

U   BOY, TWENTY MONTHS. RETARDATION
      Father: Driver, thirty-seven.
      Mother: Cleaner, thirty-three.
      Other children: Boy, twelve; girl, nine; girl, six.

These are the parents I interviewed and some of the things they said to me. In the next four chapters I present my interpretations of their statements, as they relate to the following topics: (1) the disabled child's condition; (2) encounters with others outside the home and relationships within it; (3) their situation as compared with that of parents of normal children.

Definitions of the disabled child as rational constructions: social contexts and common sense

'Something was wrong' with all the children selected for the study. A major task for all parents was to discover what was wrong with their child, to see in his appearance and behaviour an underlying condition that could account for observed discrepancies between his behaviour and that of a normal child.

This task is essential both to the private performance and to the public appearance of normal parenthood. If parents are to fulfil their normal responsibilities towards the child, act effectively as his custodians and socializing agents, they must be able to understand his behaviour. Failure to achieve this may constitute grounds for extrusion of the child as another means of ordering the situation. Only one father, Mr W, was reported by his wife as having considered this during the time of interviewing, and Mrs T said, after the death of her child, that she had wanted to put her in an institution partly because of her fears that she would not be able to cope with her.

Again, if parents are to appear to be coping adequately with and caring for the child, they must be able to present an orderly definition of his behaviour to others. Chapter 1 showed that those studies which ignored parents' attempts to do so concluded that family life was uniquely disrupted by the advent of a disabled child; whilst in those which examined the processes through which parents came to define their child as disabled, family life appeared to be continuous with its existing style and structure. These latter authors examined the problems that parents faced in constructing an orderly definition of the child in interaction with doctors and other professional agents (Hewett, 1970; Meadow, 1968) and the strategies they adopted to sustain a given definition. Davis (1963) suggests 'normalization' where parents seek validation from others, and 'disassociation' where they avoid audiences which might invalidate their definition.

My focus in this chapter is closest to Davis. I shall examine what parents said about their attempts to discover what was wrong with their child in interaction with him and with others concerned with him. I am, however, concerned less with the substantive nature of the parents' definitions of their child and their social psychological implications than with the interpretive processes through which those definitions are constructed. Examination of these processes is essential to an adequate account of parents' apparent normality; the alternative, as I showed in chapter 1, is to invoke variables which are identified not in parents' responses but in unobservable intervening psychological processes. The general method of documentation through which a sense of order is constructed in and through a particular item, whether behavioural or otherwise, was outlined in chapter 2. Here I extend this presentation and attempt to characterize different methods adopted by parents in judging items of the child's behaviour in terms of typical differences in the dimensions on which such judgments are made. All of these methods are shown to be orderly or rational according to commonsense standards. I present first the principal ideas of Schutz's (1964) analysis of common sense.

Schutz argues that the everyday actor experiences the social world primarily as a field of actual and possible acts, and only secondarily as an object of thinking. His knowledge of the world is organized not in terms of a scientific system but in terms of degrees of relevance to his actions. Schutz distinguishes roughly between four such degrees or zones of relevance. The 'primary' zone, or that part of the world which is within our reach, immediately observable and at least partly dominated or controlled by us, is the realm of knowledge of acquaintance. Here an optimum of clear and distinct understanding of its structure is required. Second, there is a 'halo' of what seems to be sufficient knowledge *about* a particular phenomenon. Third, there is a region in which it is sufficient to 'put one's trust', and, fourth, the realm of unwarranted hopes and assumptions. The contours of relevance, or what is problematic and what taken for granted, are determined partly by an actor's biography or his unique stock of knowledge, the accumulation of his past experience, and partly by his choice at any one point in time among various interests. They shift according to his prevailing interests in a particular here-and-now context or to his definition of the situation.

At all times commonsense knowledge is, first, incoherent because interests are themselves not integrated into coherent systems but organized under 'plans' which change with the situation. Second, it is partially clear. The actor does not search for truth and certainty, but 'all he wants is information on likelihood and insight into the choices or risks which the situation at hand entails for the outcome of his actions' (*ibid.*, p. 94). Third, commonsense knowledge is inconsistent because an actor may consider as equally valid statements which are in fact incompatible; for example, as a father, citizen, employee, etc. His thinking is distributed over subject-matters located within different and differently relevant levels. However, within any one group the system of knowledge takes on the appearance of a sufficient coherence, clarity and consistency 'to give anybody a reasonable chance of understanding and of being understood' (*ibid.*, p. 95).

Knowledge is derived partly from the individual's own experience but mainly from that which others have and pass on to him. Such 'socially derived' knowledge has four typical sources. First, the 'eye-witness' who communicates his direct experience to an actor and who is believed on the basis of two idealizations: (i) the interchangeability of standpoints, and (ii) the congruency of the systems of relevance of the actors concerned, by which it is assumed that biographical differences are irrelevant for the purposes at hand. Heeren (1971) points out that it is these idealizations which are at the core of Garfinkel's (1967) work which, in violating them, shows them to be integral parts of the commonsense world. However, they must be altered for the other typical sources of knowledge. The second source of knowledge is the 'insider' for whom the observed event in question has its place in a system of relevancies substantially different from the actor's. He is believed on the basis of the assumption that 'because he experiences the reported events in a unique or typical context of relevance [he] "knows it better" than I would if I observed the same event but was unaware of its intrinsic significance' (Schutz, *op. cit.*, p. 132). The 'analyst's' opinion is based on a system of relevancies similar to the actor's and is more influential the more the actor is convinced of its congruity with his own relevancies. The 'commentator's' opinion is based on a system of relevancies considerably different from the actor's, but it is trusted if it enables the actor to form a sufficiently clear and precise knowledge of the underlying deviating system of relevancies.

Schutz makes a further distinction between two types of systems of relevancies. The 'intrinsic' relevancies are those which are 'the outcome of our chosen interests established by our spontaneous decision to solve the problem by our thinking' (*ibid.*, p. 126).

They remain to a certain extent within our control. However, there are also situations and events which are not connected with our chosen interests but which have to be taken as they are. Such events as sickness, bereavement, acts of God, or the metaphysical problems of fate are 'imposed' upon us and we have no power to modify them except by transforming them into intrinsic relevancies. So long as this is not achieved they remain unclarified and rather incomprehensible. Schutz observes that we are less and less able to define what is and what is not relevant to us. Politically, economically and socially imposed relevancies have to be taken into account, but the 'man in the street' treats these merely as data or conditions for his course of action: 'it does not pay to try to understand their origin and structure' (*ibid.*, p. 130).

For parents of normal children child-rearing is relatively unproblematic. The fact that in performing this activity the child's interests should predominate may, as I argued in chapter 2, constitute an imposed system of relevancies, and having a first baby be a 'crisis'. However, beyond this any competent adult has a ready-made stock of knowledge handed down from ancestors, or acquired in 'anticipatory socialization', which provides a guide to the kinds of situations likely to occur and trustworthy 'recipes' for interpreting his behaviour and handling him in such a way as to attain the desired consequences. Thus, most children start to teethe in their first year; so this is the normal explanation of increased crying and changes in sleep patterns. Parents with previous direct experience are more likely to know about specific practices for dealing with such events, but other routinely available sources are relatives, neighbours and friends with children of a similar age. Their opinions can be more or less trusted as those of 'eye witnesses', especially given direct experience of their normal honesty, reliability and so on. Of course, parents may also seek the opinions of others such as doctors, or child-rearing manuals, but even those who attempt to rear their child 'according to Dr Spock' do so from choice, and since 'all children vary' can always discount such knowledge as not relevant to their unique child for whom their direct experience in interaction with him constitutes the best guide.

This attitude of 'thinking-as-usual' is maintained so long as certain basic assumptions hold true. Schutz gives these as, first, that life will continue to be the same as it has been so far; that is, the same problems requiring the same solutions will recur, and former experience will suffice for mastering future situations. Second, that one may rely on the knowledge handed down by parents, teachers, tradition, habit, etc., even if one does not understand its origin and real meaning; third, that in the ordinary course of affairs it is sufficient to know something about the general type or style of events one may encounter in order to manage and control them; and fourth, that neither the systems of recipes nor schemes of interpretation and explanation are our private affair, but that they are likely to be accepted and applied by our fellow men. If only one of these ceases to stand the test, thinking as usual is unworkable.

For parents of a disabled child one or more of these assumptions is untenable. Having a disabled child is an experience of which, at most, parents usually have knowledge about rather than direct acquaintance. At the birth of a child many mothers may fear that something might go wrong, but in the absence of ante-natal difficulties this is unwarranted by any specific evidence. They know that the majority of babies are born normal and are more likely to seek out such assurance as 'is he all right?' than demand the exclusion of all possible evidence to the contrary. Moreover, this is itself 'normal' parental behaviour since the good parent would not want his child to have anything wrong with him. The discovery or suspicion that there is something wrong reveals the inadequacy of parents' existing knowledge as a reliable guide to the situations that can occur. The appropriate-ness of normally taken-for-granted recipes for child-rearing is called into question and parents may not know how to interpret the child's behaviour, nor therefore what action they should take towards him. New zones of knowledge become immediately relevant to the parents' situation and eye-witness opinions are no longer necessarily trustworthy.

At the start of the study, whether because the disabled child had been born in or referred to hospital, medical knowledge constituted the appropriate system of relevancies, and parents sought the opinions of doctors as insiders who were expected to know the meaning of the child's appearances better than they. In chapter 2, I said that parents' experience of incongruity were produced not necessarily through their own evaluations of the child's appearances as discrepant with those of the normal child, but that definitions of his condition might be initially and ultimately those of doctors. In Schutz's terms, his disability constitutes an imposed system of relevancies. However, this applies only when the disability was initially identified in hospital at his birth. In cases which I shall typify as having a 'gradual onset', discrepancies were perceived by parents in terms of their own experiences of him and of normal children, or that of others such as relatives or friends who shared a substantially similar stock of knowledge. Differences in onset do, I shall show, constitute typically different methods of making sense of the child's behaviour, but in all cases the parents' task is the same: to construct a unique, situated definition of the child's behaviour as disabled, from the objective meanings available to them, and in all cases at particular points in time, as parents attempt to do this, similar problems may arise.

A doctor's knowledge of disability is that of the 'expert' which 'is restricted to a limited field but therein it is clear and distinct. His opinions are based on warranted assertions; his judgments are not mere guesswork or loose suppositions' (*ibid.*, p. 122). Clinical practice is based on a system of 'typical cases' (Scheff, 1964) organized by a doctor's immediate and derived knowledge of things that can be 'wrong' with children in whom certain characteristics or symptoms are evident. Medical categories and interpretations then, as Richardson (1969) argues, tend to turn attention away from a child's unaffected abilities. Of course, doctors know and tell parents that even within a given category great variations in severity of impact may be found and in an individual case rarely commit themselves to a specifically definite prognosis which predicts the precise ways in which the child's functioning may be affected. However, doctors lack direct knowledge of a particular child's, and even any disabled child's, behaviour in an everyday face-to-face situation and, as chapter 1 suggested, behaviour in a clinical setting is not necessarily a reliable guide to that in others. Hence, doctors cannot provide parents with specific recipes for action in interaction with their child.

In many of the cases studied doctors never did provide parents with clear definitions of their child's present and future condition. This again crucially influences the methods that parents adopt in attempting to make sense of his behaviour. Neither, however, did they give an unqualified normal prognosis. Hence, parents continued to seek a definition which would constitute the child's behaviour as either disabled or normal, and, as I showed in chapter 2, such definitions, whether commonsense or medical, are grounded in polarized moral categories. Hence, the order which they seek in his behaviour is absolute. Although he may be more or less seriously affected, either the child 'is' disabled or he is not. Whether parents attempt to transform imposed into intrinsic relevancies, or seek a definition which transforms or reveals the underlying order of intrinsic incongruities, their task of making sense of the child's behaviour is in this sense similarly structured.

As will be seen, from what most parents said, by the end of the study medical definitions, whether or not clearly presented, were a primary constraint on their own. If doctors said that the child was disabled, then this was treated as a fact of life independent of parents' own observations of him; if doctors did not say definitely that the child was or was not disabled, then parents said that they similarly suspended judgment.

I said in chapter 2 that I would treat parents' statements as public accounts which are so formulated that they appear to satisfy the facts of the child's condition as medically defined, and that these accounts may bear no relation to their practices of making sense of his behaviour when in interaction with him. At the end of this chapter I discuss the possible implications of parents' definitions for their child's subsequent development, and similarly conclude that one cannot make such predictions on theoretical grounds alone. None the less, there are several reasons why one might expect what parents say about how they see their child's behaviour to be an adequate representation of how they do in practice see it.

First, some parents had sought medical opinion as the relevant source of inside knowledge on what was really wrong with their child. Second, even those for whom such knowledge had been imposed are likely to see it, at least initially, as superior to their own, whether because they lack direct experience of the child in question, or because medical matters constitute the realm in which lay opinions are least likely to be seen as relevant. Young (1954) shows that where a problem is defined as medical the help of such outside agencies is most likely to be sought; indeed, such a definition often entails such a course of action especially for physical illnesses where there is no evidence of individual incompetence. Third, parents must construct some order for the purposes of interaction with the child, and it is this interpretive, cognitive activity rather than the specific normative practices adopted that is in question. Perhaps parents were constrained in questioning to present more order than they actually experienced, but it seems unlikely that they would have a private method of making sense of the child's behaviour that is entirely different to that which they make publicly apparent. Hence, I shall treat their statements as adequate indicators of their perceptual and interpretive processes.

In examining such processes I shall use analyses which extend Schutz's work. He uses the concept of 'typifications' to refer to the constitutive units of the domains of relevance. Our knowledge of the social world is to some extent always in the form of ideal types, whether of persons or of courses of action. Heeren gives the two most important examples of these: the 'personal ideal type' which is formed of 'another person who is expressing himself or has expressed himself in a certain way', and the 'course of action type' which refers to 'the expressive process itself, or to the product of that process on the basis of which we can make inferences about the process' (*op. cit.*, p. 53). Such types provide an actor with knowledge of the subjective meaning typically intended by a certain type of person as he performs a given action and the possible objective meanings of observed actions respectively. Evidently, in a specific situated interpretation both kinds of types are invoked. Parents' interpretations of a given instance of their child's behaviour depend upon their conception of the kinds of things that children in general and this child in particular might be expected to be doing, which actions are differentiated according to the range of intentions that it is possible for a child to have. The constructive use of such types, however, involves complex processes of perception and judgment.

Garfinkel (1963) analyses the various dimensions on which particular items of behaviour or of a setting are evaluated in creating and sustaining a sense of order, or what he calls 'perceived normality'. He gives these as: (1) *Typicality:* that is, the perceived formal features which enable identifying an event as an instance of a certain class or category. Child crying 'in pain' might be distinguished from 'wants attention' when it is accompanied by 'clenched fists' or on the basis of pitch. (2) *Likelihood:* that is, the chances of occurrence of an event. An instance of crying if a child cries frequently may 'mean nothing at all'; if rarely, he 'must', for example, be in pain. (3) *Comparability* with past or future events. Evidently comparability is the basis for making judgments on the other dimensions. (4) *Causal texture* is the commonsense version of cause and effect, involving the identification of some phenomena as the conditions under which the behavioural item in question will occur. 'Hunger' or 'teething' constitute causal textures for 'baby crying'. (5) *Instrumental efficacy:* some means are more efficient than others in achieving desired ends; behaviour is therefore characterized as appropriate or inappropriate depending on how it facilitates an objective. A child who continues to cry when all his 'possible needs' have been satisfied may be told to 'stop it – you'll only make yourself sick'. (6) *Moral requiredness*, its necessity according to a natural or moral order: anything morally required is a prerequisite to

membership within a given definition of the situation. If the child
is normal, then he must smile when he sees his mother, but if he
cries it might mean a number of other things too. To the extent
that parents reconstitute perceived normality, items of the child's
behaviour become 'displays' or can be taken as 'pointing to' its
underlying pattern. At the same time that pattern is constituted
out of, or may be modified on the basis of observed items of
behaviour.

In my analysis I draw more heavily on McHugh (1968) than on
Garfinkel. Some elaboration of his ideas is therefore necessary.
McHugh adopts most of Garfinkel's components of perceived
normality, only replacing 'comparability' with *congruity*, which
refers to whether judgments of events (in terms of the other
dimensions) are accurate rather than normatively correct. He
uses these, however, to specify what, following Mead, he regards
as one of the two bases of knowledge – 'relativity' – the other
being 'emergence'. This seems to amount to a great extension of
'comparability', though he does not say so.
  'Knowledge' includes anything that gives meaning to an
observation, regardless of its 'truth' or empirical status, and is
essential for *human*, i.e. social, action. Knowledge, or the ordering
of experience, is based on comparisons of observations at a point
in time and through time. The concept of relativity points to the
lack of an ultimate reality, that though there may be substantial
agreement as to what can count as comparable instances of the
'same' phenomenon in characterizing an event in its relationship
to other events, any given instance is potentially categorizable
on the basis of some other quality unknown to an actor at this
point in time and space. Since this is determined on the basis of
existing knowledge, in this sense, as McHugh says, relativity and
emergence both create *and* limit the possibility of knowledge.
  The process of 'emergence' locates any given definition in the
present but as informed by, and informing, constructions of past
events and future programmes. The creation of temporal continuity
is a process in which an actor searches for the 'underlying' meaning
of discretely occurring instances. McHugh conceptualizes its
several components. (1) *Theme:* actors adopt a more or less
provisional definition of 'what is going on' in a given situation
at the moment. This involves the prior assumption that there is
some pattern, and it is future- and past-orientated in that it is
taken for granted that it will be possible to make sense of what is
yet to occur, and that what has occurred can be used to inform
future definitions. (2) *Elaboration:* once defined, individual

instances of the appearance of a theme are located, and the theme is substantiated. 'What would be a mere happenstance without a theme comes instead as an exemplar' (*op. cit.*, p. 38). (3) *Fit:* instances do not always substantiate a given theme, but may test its applicability. Depending on the relationship between the two, the theme may be modified or abandoned, or the instance discounted in some way. (4) *Revelation:* some instances, however, cannot stand alone and may only be judged as substantiating a theme, are only understandable in terms of some other immediately preceding or following instance. Actors know that in some cases they must 'wait and see'. Revelation may consist in the reduction of surprise when one event makes intelligible or gives insight into the meaning of an earlier event, or the creation of surprise when an event transforms the meaning of an earlier one – making for 'comedy and worse' (*ibid.*, p. 41).

My interest in this chapter is not in *which* items parents perceive as evidence of *what* underlying pattern, thus displaying their normative order or values. Rather, it is in *whether* items are taken as displays on which dimension or dimensions. Thus, I largely exclude what McHugh includes – a description of the operation of preferential rules which would require a consideration of individual parents' knowledge of the disability. Any illustrations provided are of course substantive in origin, but description of them is partial. Hence characterization of different types of perceptual, judgmental processes made is 'metaphorical' (*ibid.*, p. 18). Finding differences in such phenomena, I attempt to locate these systematically in terms of three identifiable parameters – those of speed of onset, clarity of diagnosis and certainty of prognosis. These constitute the definitional context. Evidently, these are not definable in terms of characteristics of the disability alone, but rather are negotiated products of interaction between parents and others concerning the disabled child, and I indicate briefly the typical patterns of negotiation concerned. The substantive characteristics of interaction between parents, family members and non-members, and their substantive implications for parents' experience of having a disabled child, will be examined in chapters 6, 7 and 8. Here I attempt to show that in different contexts the process of definition of the child's behaviour is typically organized in a specifiable way, that there are typical differences in the ways in which items of behaviour are recognized and identified (or not, as the case may be) as evidence of an underlying order, and in terms of which that order is constituted.

THE DEFINITIONAL CONTEXTS

The contexts within which typical differences in the construction of the meaning of the child's condition are shown are identified in terms of whether parents define (1) *onset* as sudden or gradual; (2) *diagnosis* as clear or unclear; (3) *prognosis* as certain or uncertain. Such identification was grounded in parents' statements. Interpretation of these statements was, however, informed by studies of analogous phenomena – mainly those of family adaptation to an event unexpected according to some natural or moral order, such that, following W. I. Thomas's definition of 'crisis', it 'interrupts the flow of habit and gives rise to changed conditions of consciousness and practice' (Schutz, *op. cit.*, p. 96).

These included 'disasters', i.e. events which affect a whole community or wider area (see for example Drabek and Boggs, 1968; Wallace, 1956) and those limited in impact to a family unit or kin network: for example, bereavement (Parkes, 1970); alcoholism (Jackson, 1954) and mental illness (Sampson *et al.*, 1962; Yarrow *et al.*, 1955). Primarily, these suggested the significance for participants of the speed of onset of an event, its historical background, the existence of 'warning cues' and their relative ambiguity or clarity. The importance of prognosis was derived from studies in this area, to which I have already referred, viz. Davis (1963) and Meadow (1968). Some explanation of how these categories were used is necessary.

1 *Onset* This is defined as sudden by parents where discovery of disability is not preceded by any specific awareness that this might occur, i.e. as distinct from any general fear at childbirth or later that 'something might go wrong'. That is, parents have no 'reasons' to expect that the child is *disabled* and though they may retrospectively discover them, the initial suddenness of the event, as will be shown, continues to inform subsequent interpretations. Or, though parents suspect or are certain that 'something' is wrong, this is not in the same category as the actual outcome. This does not relate to 'severity'; for example, in two cases the expected diagnosis was of leukaemia, i.e. a terminal condition, and those given were diabetes (K) and obesity (J).

Onset is defined as gradual where a period of ambiguity concerning the nature of the child's condition (as normal/not normal) is ended by the parents seeking or being referred to expert opinion.

2 *Diagnosis* A 'clear' diagnosis is one which is perceived as establishing the child as unquestionably normal or not normal. In the latter case no specific (medical) category need have been imputed; rather, whatever is wrong with the child excludes him

from 'normality'. In the former there may be some items of behaviour which are incompatible with a normal definition, but parents do not perceive any other definition to be appropriate.

Where diagnosis is 'unclear', competing definitions of the child's condition appear more or less equally plausible in the light of observed evidence.

3 *Prognosis* In a situation of 'certain' prognosis, parents 'know' that whatever their present definitions of the child, whatever their clarity, in the future he will be disabled or normal. This does not exclude such questioning as 'what will he be like?'.

Prognosis is 'uncertain' where alternative predictions are more or less equally plausible.

Parents' definitions of the character of onset, diagnosis and prognosis are constructed in interaction with others concerning the child, and informed by the kind of relationship between the participants; parents' attribution of competence to the other; their own knowledge of disabilities, expectations of normal child development and so on. Evidently, any changes in such patterns of negotiation may be associated with changes in parents' definition. For example, an encounter with a hospital specialist may be a turning point in parents' perception of diagnosis; increased knowledge of the specific characteristics of a disability may decrease the certainty of prognosis which may again become more certain after the failure of remedial measures. There are many possible patterns of change. See, for example, Figure 1.

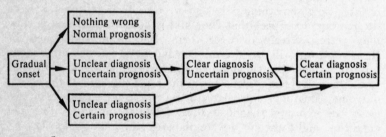

FIGURE 1

In line with my focus on typical processes rather than substantive differences, I do not present the pattern that occurred in each case, nor, therefore, do I attempt to account for particular changes. I do however present two case examples which illustrate the polar career types as identified by the three definitional features of onset, diagnosis and prognosis. These give some idea of the shifts in definition that may occur through time, presented as 'b', and I summarize the patterns of negotiation associated with such changes, presented as 'a'. I then generalize these findings, drawing on the other case material, and characterize the typically different processes of perception and judgment which may be evident in parents' statements at any one point in time. These are related to the eight logically possible contexts produced by different combinations of the definitional parameters.

TWO CASE EXAMPLES

I   SUDDEN ONSET – CLEAR DIAGNOSIS – CERTAIN PROGNOSIS: CASE H

1   *Sudden onset*

a. Though defined eventually as sudden, onset of the child's mongolism was delayed for the parents since earlier potential cues, e.g. that the child was taken to the 'special nursery', were normalized. This was because Mrs H knew from other mothers' experiences that the special nursery cared for babies with 'routine' problems such as slight jaundice or feeding difficulties. To hospital authorities the condition was immediately evident, but their apparent intention was to adopt a gradualist strategy in communicating the fact to the parents. Mr and Mrs H were provoked into demanding what was wrong, on being told that the doctors were 'worried', but they were not expecting any serious outcome. However, the full diagnosis was then given to the parents in a single encounter with the doctor concerned. He perhaps assumed that the disability was equally evident to the parents, and that they were therefore asking for confirmation and would not have accepted any normal explanation as adequate.

b. The sudden occurrence of mongolism in their child is atypical – that is, not an instance of a category normally associated with childbirth – and there are no past events with which to compare it. Although 'I'd heard people say "mongol" ', there was no likelihood of it occurring – 'you don't look for that kind of baby coming to yourself'. Therefore it appears arbitrary or causally indeterminate – it 'just happened'. The fact of mongolism may be 'true', but it is incongruent with actual experience of the child: 'He doesna' look to me – but there it is.' Nothing, then, in the parents' experience legitimates the event, so that 'you can't even imagine you've got one'. The only 'reality' of the fact of the child's mongolism is wholly other-given.

The parents' expressions of meaninglessness at the sudden onset of disability are addressed partly at the event itself, as well as its concrete appearances in the child. That is, even had diagnosis been perceived to be congruent with the child's behaviour, the likelihood of mongolism and its causation cannot be discovered in that behaviour, but requires other symbolic resources or meanings. It should be noted that Mrs H did not say that they questioned the moral requiredness of the child's condition; she did not say 'Why did it have to happen to us?'. Nor did any parent, though some reported having done so in the past. This, I argue in chapters 7 and 8, is a product of the use of other moral meanings which may provide some order to parents' experience in these three (and other) respects, and all of which may be derived from medical knowledge as it is made available to parents in interaction with doctors.

The lack of congruence in this case is contingent – had the child's condition been evident to his parents, the diagnosis would have 'made some sense'. Shortly, it will be seen that it is only to the degree that Mrs H perceived some congruence between the diagnosis of mongolism and the child's behaviour that construction and maintenance of a definition of the child as a mongol is possible.

2 *Clear diagnosis*

a. The initial source of information was of course the hospital, whose reasons for so diagnosing the child were not contested by the parents. However, through time Mrs H constructed a more favourable definition. This seemed to be a product of: increasing direct experience of the child; information about other similar cases from other sources such as the media, where impact had been relatively mild; comparison with 'normal' children whose development is slow; and the favourable definitions of others such as family friends, and especially strangers who have no commitment to parents. Thus, for example, 'they canna' see it in him, they dinna' notice any difference to a normal baby'. The validation of medical authority, however, continues to be necessary, and though Mrs H challenged the adequacy of a doctor's definition at an assessment encounter, the structure of which she felt to disfavour the child, she never rejected the appropriateness of the overall diagnosis. When relatives said that 'nothing's wrong with him' she discounted this as but a normal strategy of 'our family, they dinna' let you get down in the dumps'.

b. A clear diagnosis 'objectively' locates the child as a typical member of a known category, that of mongolism. It thus provides an 'underlying pattern' as a theme for parents to pursue in interaction with him. However, so long as there is imperfect perceived congruence between the known characteristics of the category of mongolism, and of its particular appearances in the child, parents may be said to have two ongoing definitional tasks: the construction of the meaning of the category, and that of the child's behaviour. Obviously, the two are interrelated: the parents learn what mongol means partly from the child's behaviour; but, more importantly, the former is more 'powerful', it constrains the latter process in typical ways, both:

(i) in general, because it is 'there underneath', and

(ii) in particulars, i.e. according to the specific characteristics that the parents impute to mongolism.

The theme of mongolism cannot be abandoned, whether or not instances which elaborate it can be located in the child. 'I dinna' notice any difference to a normal baby' but 'it's definitely there'. The problem is not to test the fit of the diagnosis, but rather of making it fit too well, because 'I dinna' ken what to look for in him'. However, the undisputed fact of mongolism acts to reveal the meaning of instances of perceived behaviour anomalies, which are therefore 'no surprise' – 'You know just what he is, whereas you'd have been saying "Oh, he's not doing such-and-such" '.

Such anomalies, then, form the basis for constructing a definition of the child as mongol, in terms of the components of relativity. This does not preclude perception of normality, however, nor need this be an 'autistic' construction; that is, one which no one else could be expected to see. Individuation of the concept of the child can be congruent with, indeed is partially contingent on, (ii); that is, differentiation of the meaning of the objective category. When it only has meaning in terms of, for example, visible stigma, if 'he's got the whole lot', then that is what he is, and 'you're just as well knowing to start with'. But as the parents 'learn more' about the particular disability, so previous perceptions of the child – 'I knew he was coming on fine, you could tell' – can be made congruent with the present knowledge that: 'It's very slight, they said.' By this token one's own authorship of the definition becomes less suspect.

If 'different kiddies have different things' then this fits the observation that 'he doesna' look by features', which then can be seen as an instance which elaborates the hope that 'it's not going to be too much'. Moreover, lack of it may be accounted for, e.g. although the child is not walking, which is known to be an indicator of the condition, 'when I saw his foot, I wondered if it was maybe that'. Finally, when the child's present behaviour is juxtaposed with past remembered definitions, the parents realize how 'good' his development is: 'we just thought he wouldna' be moving at all from what we knew about these babies'.

3   *Certain prognosis*

a. Medical authorities were again the most important influence on the parents' definition, and in this case they did not delay communication of the fact that the disability was permanent. Neither parents nor non-medical others presented any evidence or belief to effectively counter this definition. Non-medical sources of information were important, however, in the parents' discovery of the varying severity of prognosis. Mrs H met a neighbour's five-year-old mongol niece who favourably impressed her with her ability to play games independent of adult supervision. Medical authorities validated this in so far as they did not commit themselves to an explicit prognosis, but they countered what they saw as attempts by the parents to hope that the child may turn out to be normal. Mrs H said she told one doctor that the child seemed to be developing as quickly as had her other children, and that he had replied 'But he definitely is mongol'.

b. Meanings are so constructed that they make sense of past events and future programmes. Expectations of the future are seen as *following* from, and reasonable in terms of, the way that things are at present. But where the future is 'known' independently of present appearances, as is the case with permanent disability, then the process of inference is reversed. That is, knowledge of the future informs present interpretations: the child appears normal at present, but 'is not' because disability provides a permanent underlying order. Definition of his condition must therefore account for this 'fact', the nature of which of course varies according to the objective meaning which the disability has for the parents.

When this is congruent with the child's appearance 'he is what he is' (and always will be). Given adequate categorization in terms of the components of typicality, likelihood and causal texture, it is easy to make sense of the situation, and 'there's nothing anyone can do about it'. The child's behaviour is appropriate (instrumentally efficacious), given lower expectations of him, and even necessitated (morally required) by his membership in the category. But, as the meaning of the disability is differentiated, so the future becomes less determinate in terms of the *specific* implications of the condition. As the parents discover in what ways the category applies to *their* child, so they can attempt to infer what he may be like in the future.

Thus they *do* make predictions, but it is not a 'normal' planning process. They are highly aware of the probability of falsification by later events; they are expecting incongruity because of the underlying disability. Thus 'every day you think about it, how he's going to come on'. A stated solution is the attempt to 'live only in the present' and 'just take him from day to day'. 'I don't know what he's going to be, I'm just waiting' indicates a suspension of the commonsense belief that people with whom we are in constant contact do not and should not change, which, as will be seen in chapter 8, is one element of parents' special ideology. If their actions are incompatible with our conceptions of them, then 'that is what he's really like'. Even in situations where change could be expected and predicted, it is not uncommon to hear a surprised 'my, you've grown'.

Parents of the permanently disabled child cannot take normatively expected age and status development for granted. 'He's only a baby' may now adequately explain behaviour which, if persistent, must take on a very different meaning. Thus 'now he's just a normal baby' but 'we're looking for it that there'll be nothing wrong'. The knowledge that 'they can't tell till he's older' encourages inferences from present definitions. If 'it can be very slight', then the belief that 'he doesn't seem as though he's going to be awfu' backward' may be temporally consistent. Subsequent events will of course be the test of this, but if, for example, doctors say that the child's progress is 'amazing', then this is 'reasonable' substantiation of the theme.

Nevertheless, it still can never be assumed that the child will attain the next normal stage of development. Parents can say only 'I'd like to hear him speak' when they know that 'these babies usually have something wrong'. Parents cannot perceive normality in their child's behaviour: their definitions must be consistent with the permanent fact of disability. Their particular expectations of him will be principally constrained according to their conceptions of the 'objective' meaning of the disability. Over all, they remain unusually aware of their own authorship of their definition and of its inherent contradictions: 'I look at him and I'm looking for things and they're maybe not there at all', or, on another occasion, 'you're seeing him as you want to'.

II   GRADUAL ONSET – UNCLEAR DIAGNOSIS – UNCERTAIN PROGNOSIS:
      CASE D

1   *Gradual onset*
a. There was considerable disagreement in this family as to which cues first led to their questioning the child's normality. As he eventually attained the abilities of sitting and walking, so a normal definition was sustained. The fact that this was supported

by the husband's parents, who were in more frequent and generally 'closer' contact with the family, outweighed the dissent of Mrs D's mother and her own doubts, for whom her nephew was a constant source of comparison. Referral to the clinic for speech assessment finally occurred with the health visitor's intervention: 'She really started it all.'

b. Where onset is seen as gradual, there are no world-shattering consequences. The parents' definition is emergent: redefinitions take account of perceived discrepancies between the child's behaviour and/or other cues; therefore, they know how it has 'come about'. It also makes sense across space; it is precisely because of cues 'out there' that they have become aware of discrepancies. They themselves have constructed the meaning of their child's behaviour, such that they maintain the perceived normality of events. Typicality is based on comparisons with classes of phenomena, which, given the ambiguity of the condition, can be selected for characteristics which support any desired definition. Thus, he's one of these kiddies who [are slow at sitting, walking, talking] and it is therefore possible to have some idea of what is likely to happen in the future. In this case the outcome of 'disabled' has increasing likelihood; it is very much something that 'can' happen. This constitutes an underlying pattern against which the appropriateness of the child's behaviour, his status as normal, are continually reassessed.

Where disability can be typified as an instance of comparable 'normal' phenomena, the question of purpose with reference to this particular instance becomes less relevant. It is intrinsically part of things that can happen, i.e. the normal moral order, and though still regrettable it is 'just one of those things'. Parents may be uncertain and concerned about the cause of the child's condition, but the lack of known cause alone does not render their knowledge inappropriate and inadequate for coping with the child (though it may have implications for their inter-personal relations, see chapter 6).

In summary, where onset of disability is perceived as gradual, its meaning is very much the parents' own creation. As such it *maintains* the perceived normality of events and is constructed in congruence with what is perceived 'out there'.

2   Unclear diagnosis

a. The diagnosis made by the clinic was 'slow', and though it confounded the parents' expectations of a more specific diagnosis, was unchallenged by them. Rather, clearly unfavourable definitions from others (for example, Mrs D's mother) were discounted, since 'they [the clinic] said there's nothing wrong'. Any source of information (relatives, the nursery school, the health visitor) which suggested a favourable explanation of the child's behaviour was therefore plausible. When some standards of comparison cast the child in an unfavourable light, more 'appropriate' audiences were sought out, on the argument that, for example, if 'they [siblings] were ever so quick' he is not necessarily slow. But the child's status as normal remained in question when the child's fellow pupils, who were seen as a more representative group, demonstrated the extent of the child's backwardness, and when less progress was made than had been expected. The failure of the hospital's predictions that 'it'll all come together' meant that the possibility of disability could not be abandoned.

b. The parents' growing awareness of disability in their child is met with no clear confirmation. Mrs D said that the doctor at the hospital told her 'we can't find anything, he's just bound to be slow'. Therefore, subsequent definition of the child has no different basis on which to proceed and is an essentially similar process to that which led to identification of the 'problem' in the first place. Nor does it invalidate earlier definitions; there can be no insight as to what was 'really' wrong all along. 'Slow' is consistent with the commonsense belief that 'children vary' and does not set the child apart as an instance of the category the meaning of which is discoverable by the parents. It does not therefore constitute an underlying 'fact' with which experience of the child must be made congruent, since 'he's not mental'.

The main source of information for the parents in constructing the meaning of the child's behaviour is his behaviour as it appears to them. They do not need to search out evidence of abnormality, having already identified the dimensions significant to assessment of the child's development. As such, the process of definition is similar to that used by parents who have never questioned their child's normality. But it is not the *same*. The child's development has been questioned, cannot now be taken for granted, and the parents are aware of the process: 'I didna' notice much [with the other two], it was all coming natural for the first time'. Moreover, there are objective other-given meanings attached to phenomena, such as 'destructiveness', inability to speak, etc., which may be or become available to parents and therefore act as typifications of the child; 'I've heard that many old mother's tales about if he doesn't do this and that', though parents do not have to see these as appropriate in this particular instance.

In the situation of uncertainty created by concern over the child's behaviour with no clear diagnosis as to what is 'really wrong', parents continue to search for ways to make adequate sense of his behaviour. They can order his appearances in terms of typicality, likelihood and even causal texture, but so long as there are perceived incongruencies with any given definition, inferences as to what is 'going on underneath' or to what pattern these point remain problematic. Thus, any ordering is inherently unstable on any dimensions. They are therefore uncertain as to what it is appropriate to expect of the child, what he ought to be doing, if he must be expected to be slow. What appears to happen is that parents adopt a provisional theme of 'normal' (given that it is the more desirable alternative) and in order to make this congruent with the child's evident abnormality, successive 'but' clauses are proposed. As these fail to account for the discrepancies and/or as other possible meanings are made available to the parents, so different sub-themes can be substituted, given that there is nothing 'really' wrong with the child. These may appeal to things 'in' the child, or 'in' the situation, e.g. it is because 'he had a difficult birth' or 'he can't get out to play here'. Each new explanation makes sense of the child's present behaviour, past events are seen 'in a new light' and future expectations are accordingly revised. Each, therefore, prolongs the possibility of a normal outcome.

The sub-theme that 'he was a small baby (so we must expect him to be slow)' is elaborated by the eventual achievement of walking, since substantiating instances can be taken at their face value. When the child fails to talk in the expected time, and therefore this explanation no longer fits, 'he had difficulty in breathing and needs a tonsillitis operation' is a substitute which provides insight into the meaning of past discrepancies and, since rectifiable, is consistent with 'underlying normalcy'. Again, it is a nasty surprise when the operation fails to have the expected result, but then the child is to enter a nursery and 'being with the other kiddies will bring him on': that is what has been lacking.

The very fact that parents are highly aware of their own authorship of the definition 'I'm seeing him every day, maybe I'm not noticing the difference' and 'I'm just taking it for granted that there should be more [progress]' acts in this situation to provide a further explanation. Past anxiety perhaps was groundless for this reason. There is nothing really wrong with him, and maybe 'he just needs longer'.

3 Uncertain prognosis

a. The hospital authorities presented no definite prognosis, nor did they suggest what points in the future might be taken as decisive in defining the nature of the child's condition. Mr and Mrs D therefore used other sources of information to construct a definition of the child in the present, from which they could make predictions about the future. Given that their present diagnosis remained uncertain, prognosis was equally indeterminate. Favourable predictions were preferred and could be retained so long as turning points were seen to remain. Both medical and non-medical others provided such possibilities; e.g. the nursery school matron suggested that 'another six months and you'll know a difference in him'.

b. Where the future development of the child is seen as indeterminate, and where the nature of his condition is unclear, no meaning of his behaviour is *a priori* untenable. Therefore, it is entirely rational to see the future as predictable from present reality. If he is not speaking now, and if this continues, then 'he won't get into normal school, I know that for a fact'. But since he *can* be expected to be normal, then it is consistent to believe that he is really normal now. Any evidence which appears to elaborate this theme can be accepted as such, e.g. 'he can say other kiddies' names, it's only his sisters' he can't manage'.

Lack of fit between current behaviour and such a conception can be accounted for. He needs more attention, therefore 'it would definitely help him if he was left with the children he's with now'. The congruity of present appearances can be discounted: 'he may start to speak all of a sudden like he started to walk, and I'm expecting this', that is, the present does not *necessarily* imply anything about the future, if alternative predictions are preferred. If subsequent events are inconsistent with previous expectations, then the discrepancy can be reconciled. 'I'm always waiting for this what they used to say: "He'll come on all of a sudden" but now I know he's coming on in bits and pieces' removes the nasty surprise and even redefines the event as providing 'insight' into what can really be expected of him, and thereby redefines the present meaning of his behaviour.

'You never can tell' is a feature of commonsense rationality, but it does not express a real belief that '*anything* can happen'. My typifications embody and constrain the range of 'possible' futures. Mrs D knows that 'it is impossible to say how he'll come on' and is therefore aware that she cannot take the validity of her definition for granted. Thus, she tests out the theme of normality in an attempt to reduce uncertainty by imposing some order on to future events: 'I think if we give him three more months at the nursery we should see a difference in him.' Since these goals are the parents' own construction, they can be appropriately revised if they are not attained. Thus 'he really hasn't had a chance yet' reconstitutes the adequacy of the current definition of the child as 'not really backward'.

The ultimate test will be that goal set by another, which is seen as significant by the parents since it has 'inevitable' consequences for the child's subsequent career. Mrs D knows that if the child does not reach normal standards of development by school age, then he will be defined as backward, and accordingly treated by the educational authorities. This stage had not, however, been reached by the end of the period of study.

TYPICAL DIFFERENCES IN PERCEPTUAL/JUDGMENTAL PROCESSES

I   SUDDEN ONSET – CLEAR DIAGNOSIS – CERTAIN PROGNOSIS

There is nothing in parents' past experience which led them to expect the event, but they know that something definitely is wrong with the child and that there is nothing in the future that will change this. Hence, as McHugh finds, they have nowhere to look for meaning but to the here and now, and they focus on assessments on the components of relativity (*op. cit.*, p. 103). Since the underlying order is given, the issue is its congruence with the child's appearance. Where parents 'can't see it' in the immediate situation, they are close, like Mrs H, to 'meaninglessness' – 'it doesn't make sense'; where they can, it is more one of 'powerlessness' – 'I can't believe it'.

In the cases reported here, this situation was first constructed in a hospital setting, and it was doctors who gave the parents the 'bad news' that the child was disabled. Another possible situation might be an accident where the child is evidently severely injured or dead. Mrs M reported the death of another son in a road accident in terms of her disbelief that he could 'really' be dead despite the evidence, which she recognized, of blood coming from his mouth. Mrs K, in the first interview, had never seen a diabetic reaction. She said 'I'd rather I had seen it, because I think I'd go into a state of panic' and 'I've never believed it – I mean, I still don't believe it though it's in the back of my mind that it's true'. In subsequent interviews Mrs K had redefined onset as gradual, remembering a variety of past events which, together with greater knowledge of the typical onset of diabetes, made the child's condition an understandable outcome.

Most mothers reported their initial response to the sudden onset of disability in terms similar to those described by McHugh as 'meaninglessness'. They cried, were under sedation, and as

Mrs B put it 'people would speak to me and I didn't hear them'. Mrs A said that she 'wasn't surprised and took it terribly calmly' but attributed this to the fact that she was already under sedation for high blood-pressure. However, as McHugh says, any normative influence may be treated as a legitimate base for definition rather than having none, and for most parents this was the moral requirement of daily care for their child.[1] Mrs B said this 'calmed me right down' and Mrs N was worried so long as she was not sure that there were some special practices that she ought to adopt. Emergent definitions were, however, typically 'thin', being based mainly on typicality and causal texture. McHugh found that powerless subjects were preoccupied with cause. With reference to the occurrence of the disability, parents in this study did not say so explicitly, but chapter 6 shows how their actions and statements can be differentiated according to their own and others' imputations of causal responsibility. With reference to the conditions of occurrence of specific items of the child's behaviour, their definitions were precarious, since because of the known, underlying order of the disability they formed little basis for a prediction; 'taking it from day to day' and 'treating him as normal now' were typical responses.

The importance of such strategies is demonstrated in two cases where they were impossible since the children were kept in hospital and though visited daily were mainly available to visual contact only. Mrs R was reported by Mrs A as in a state of 'shock' eight months later. Mrs T appeared to reconstitute family life as though the child had never been a member (meningitis had occurred at three months), reported her fear of being unable to cope should the child be discharged and later relief 'in a sense' that the child had died. Similarly, so long as Mr N avoided contact with his mongol child he was determined that he would be 'put away', but in the third interview was reported by his wife as now willing to feed the child and as afraid that the hospital would 'take him away'. In the last example there was a substantive difference between the present and future orders. Mrs A expected total recovery of her child after an operation (though the hospital did not) and hence reported no difficulties in ordering the child's behaviour on the basis of the underlying condition, treating her rather as 'sick'.

II   SUDDEN ONSET – CLEAR DIAGNOSIS – UNCERTAIN PROGNOSIS

Uncertainty about the future, as was seen, furthers the prediction of likely outcomes from present definitions once these have been constructed in interaction with the child and others concerning him. Where there is a clear diagnosis these are primarily medical experts, though some parents doubt their reliability – 'How can they tell?' – as their own predictions seem equally likely on the basis of their ongoing experience with the child. This, together with the sudden onset of the condition, may be the basis of their uncertainty. That is, because the definition of the child as disabled was not initially their own construction but rather was imposed by others or events beyond their control, it remains an untrustworthy guide to prediction. In this situation, as compared to that where prognosis is certain, it is more the past which informs present interpretations.

Mrs F said in the first interview that she had 'been going into the future' because she had thought that once the child had had an operation for spina bifida he would start to recover. Such predictions were falsified when the child was readmitted to hospital having developed hydrocephalus and then 'it became a case of taking it from day to day'. This orientation continued throughout the time of study; by the third interview the child had had seven operations. Mrs F also said that they read all they could about spina bifida 'so that we can understand what's going on'. Since direct knowledge of the individual child was intrinsically unreliable, they focused rather on medical knowledge of such children in general.

Mrs M in the fourth interview, although she had been given a normal diagnosis and prognosis for her hitherto suspected epileptic son and could perceive no anomalies in the present, said 'you never can tell' and thought it might happen again. In all cases parents cannot simply assume normal emergence and are more than normally prepared for and 'half expect' later incongruities. This can be characterized as 'wait and see'. Future events should 'reveal' the true meaning of the child's condition and may confirm or allay previous fears.

III   SUDDEN ONSET – UNCLEAR DIAGNOSIS – UNCERTAIN PROGNOSIS

This situation is similar to that in the second case analysis except that 'something definitely happened' and, as in the last situation, may happen again. However, without a clear diagnosis with which to order present appearances, parents engage in assessment of the present situation on all components. In attempting to construct a definition rather than assume normality 'but for', or excepting certain present discrepancies, they may elaborate several themes, simultaneously looking for incongruencies in each. The 'best test' seems to be that of causal texture; it is once situations in which 'trouble' might be expected, given a particular definition of the possible association between such situations and the child's behaviour, had been successfully negotiated that some congruence is perceived.

In the first interview Mrs M thought her son's seizure might be related to the anniversary of his brother's death in a road accident; to his general nervousness, also manifested in a stammer, or that it was 'just one of those things'. Presumably adequate tests of the first would occur the next year; meanwhile Mr and Mrs M noted that he could read aloud fluently and win prizes at poetry recitals, that he became more excitable in the company of visitors, and eventually concluded that he was 'sensible' enough to be allowed out on his own. The perceptual orientation in this situation is a more active 'ongoing search'.

IV   SUDDEN ONSET – UNCLEAR DIAGNOSIS – CERTAIN PROGNOSIS

There were no cases in this category. This is probably a product of the medical nature of the events concerned. Given the typical unwillingness of doctors to present a definite prognosis, it is difficult to imagine a situation in which they would do so without any diagnosis. It can therefore only be suggested that an event such as the child's scream or crying might, though uncategorizable, sound so 'strange' that it 'must' mean something is wrong with him. Perceptually, this could be a 'sense of foreboding'.

Several parents, however, retrospectively reconstructed their experience prior to the diagnosis of their child's disability in terms of 'waiting for something to happen'. Mrs B said that she kept looking at the child, thinking her appearance odd, and asked all her visitors if they thought the child was 'O.K. – but of course they didna' want to hurt me'. For Mrs N it was others' appearances that were discrepant. She had thought that doctors and nurses avoided her or spoke to her evasively and 'knew really by their whole attitude' that something was wrong with her mongol son.

V   GRADUAL ONSET – UNCLEAR DIAGNOSIS – CERTAIN PROGNOSIS

This situation is similar to the last except that parents' fears are emergent, elaborated in concrete instances of the child's behaviour though not adequately defined in terms of relativity. Observed behaviour items are not perceived as typical of any specific category so much as inappropriate for certain other categories, in this case that of normality.

In the fourth interview Mrs L thought that, notwithstanding her child's intellectual progress and physical growth, some of her habits such as eating out of ashtrays were so 'odd' that 'I'm sure she's going to be backward' and she was not convinced by her mother's or doctor's assurances to the contrary. In a substantively different case, Mrs O perceived her son's present status as an epileptic to be doubtful but years of observation, now reinterpreted, with the aid of a recent psychiatric training, comparisons with her other children and her husband's own 'psychopathic' behaviour, fostered a growing suspicion that the child was going to be a psychopath when he was older. As in all situations where there is a certain prognosis, the future informs present and past definitions in such a way that, whether or not present evidence can be perceived, interpretation of the child's behaviour is typically constrained. In this situation parents 'distrust appearances'.

Some parents' accounts of the events preceding referral to the hospital suggest a similar feeling that 'something is going on'. Mrs J said 'I thought it was abnormal' when her child grew out of his clothes rapidly, yet was active so ought to have 'burned up his fat'. Mrs K had thought that something was wrong when her daughter, later diagnosed as diabetic, lost weight, became difficult to control and eventually refused to eat at Christmas. Both these mothers had feared leukaemia. In a second case of diabetes Mr E had, over a period of months, seen his son have several fainting fits, drink and pass urine excessively.

VI GRADUAL ONSET – CLEAR DIAGNOSIS – CERTAIN PROGNOSIS

In contrast to the last situation, a certain prognosis here consolidates present definitions which are in turn temporally consistent with past experience. The outcome may not be morally desirable if the child is defined as permanently disabled but perceptually it is more 'normal' than any of the other situations. Given adequate knowledge of the objective category of disability, emergence can be assumed allowing a more or less normal degree of 'open-texture' or 'world-openness'. Parents may of course be acutely anxious about certain aspects of the child's management, e.g. administering injections or the likelihood of his having a reaction, but, as in the case of mental illness (Yarrow *et al.*, 1955), diagnosis is typically experienced as a 'relief' after earlier ambiguity, even if, as in case L, in the first interview, it is only given as 'something in the brain'.

For Mr and Mrs J the diagnosis of obesity was such a relief that they subsequently defined and treated the child as normal, making little apparent effort to keep him to the prescribed diet despite reported medical warnings that 'a fat child becomes a fat adult'. Mr E said 'He is a diabetic; once a diabetic, always a diabetic. He will be getting injections all his life and that is that. Come time he'll be growing up and at seven he'll be doing his own injection and it shouldna' be nae problem.' The prevailing feeling here is that 'it all makes sense now that we know'.

VII GRADUAL ONSET – CLEAR DIAGNOSIS – UNCERTAIN PROGNOSIS

Here parents' definitions of the child are spatially located and consistent with past experience. Compared with the second situation discussed above, this knowledge of the child makes more predictions available. Perhaps informed by memories of past ambiguities rather than sudden shocks, these predictions appear more likely to be 'optimistic', but, as in the other situation, may counter medically given prognoses. Mrs K said in the first interview that she had briefly entertained the possibility that her diabetic daughter might get better, since she appeared so much more healthy than prior to diagnosis. In the second interview Mrs C said that she believed that, despite her asthmatic son's frequent absence from school at present, he would eventually get better – 'they say it takes seven years'. In the last interview she still did not think that the various doctors involved had 'got to the bottom' of the child's trouble, but she now thought they had done all they could in trying out different drugs and so 'if they canna' find out what it is, it's just as they say, and time will tell. So we're just sort o' resigned to that.'

As in II, the orientation is 'wait and see' in so far as later events will be the test of parents' expectations. But it might better be described as 'we shall have to see (of course)'. That is, although the future remains substantively uncertain, it informs present interpretations less than present appearances. If the child looks all right, then he probably will be. Parents do not have to simply 'take it from day to day' but can actively construct predictions whilst keeping open the possibility of other outcomes. This method, like the last, is also similar to that pertaining under 'normal' circumstances.

VIII GRADUAL ONSET – UNCLEAR DIAGNOSIS – UNCERTAIN PROGNOSIS

Here individual definitions of the child are normally emergent. However, as in the second case analysis, the continual reconstruction of incongruencies as they are perceived makes such definitions more or less equally plausible and therefore inherently unstable. Parents are constantly re-assessing the here-and-now situation, assessing the child's behaviour on the components of relativity. Were they not morally and situationally required to make such sense, the frequent questioning 'What's going on here?' might induce them to abandon the effort, as did some of McHugh's subjects in experimental conditions. Two sets of parents did so in so far as they defined the task as that of the hospital. In both cases they thought that the doctors concerned had not properly fulfilled their own responsibilities. Mr and Mrs U felt that their child's septic foot, and consequent difficulty in walking, was due to a rusty needle having been used to inject it, and said, when questioned about the child's condition, that doctors 'wouldn't answer'. Mr P was sure that his child had diabetes in addition to galactocaemia because he had direct knowledge of its symptoms in his nephew, but this was denied by doctors. He said that all his attempts to obtain information had been frustrated; when he had tried to look at the child's chart a Sister had threatened to take it away. Mr P said he was not worried about the child's condition because 'We've nae facts, you can only worry on facts'.

Parents' decisions to seek expert opinion might be interpreted as similarly shifting responsibility, were this not to risk judgment on themselves as good parents in that they might be held responsible for the child's condition. Some evidence that the latter was the case appears first in some mothers' accounts of the events constituting gradual onset, that it is a third party who often intervenes. In cases E, K and L husbands, in D the health visitor, and in J and G grandparents, were instrumental in referring the child to the hospital. Second, parents reported their dissatisfaction with the lack of definite outcome. Mrs L could see no relevance in the treatment prescribed, whilst Mr E carried out his own tests for diabetes, returned to the doctor and only then obtained a clear diagnosis.

Of course, parents are, as was seen, relatively 'free' to define the child as they wish, but it is not difficult to understand why, as in V above, diagnosis of any kind may eventually be experienced as a relief. It provides an answer to the common question here which is 'there *must* be some sense in it'.

I have attempted to describe the typically different ways in which, when discrepancies between expected and actual events occur in the experience of rearing a child, his parents engage in perceptual and judgmental work to normalize them. If situation

VI is perceptually the most 'normal', then it might be concluded that, as Hewett (*op. cit.*) found, doctors should present diagnosis and prognosis as clearly as possible and onset as gradual. Doctors do typically attempt to 'gradualize' onset, sedating mothers and so on, and of course diagnosis and effective treatment is also the medical ideal. The grounds for doctors' practices and their implications will be examined in subsequent chapters. Here I consider whether differences in parents' definitions of the child 'may so disturb the persons responsible for his socialization as to further jeopardize a child's chance of obtaining the varieties of experiences he needs for adequate socialization' (Richardson, 1969, p. 109). That is, to what extent may parents' definitions favour stigmatization of the child, to what extent may they be generalized to explain other areas of the child's behaviour, and how far may this constitute secondary deviation in that the child's disability becomes central to his experience?

I have no evidence of the child's own responses, but it can be argued that the younger the child the more his definition of his disability *will* be that imputed by his parents. In socializing the child, the family does not, or not only, give him a general preparedness for the 'world outside'. It is a very specific socialization into the world of the family and, until the child goes outside his immediate family, this *is* his world. It was there when he came into it, he has no conception of life before it was there, he had no part in its construction and it is therefore 'massively real' for him (Berger and Kellner, 1964). Therefore, if his parents say he is normal, he 'is'; if totally disabled, then this too is the way things are.

In general, where a medically clear diagnosis is given stigmatization is more likely to occur. Despite the typically presented uncertainty of prognosis, expert categories and interpretations are generally seen as more 'rational' and 'scientific', if only, as Douglas (1967) suggests, since such groups are expected to make good sense of the phenomena falling within their responsibility. Moreover, such objective meanings may previously have been meaningful to parents and may constrain their actions at least in so far as they expect to (and actually do) encounter them in others.

What then is the comparative likelihood of stigmatization by parents in the two situations illustrated by case examples earlier? The first situation is most likely to lead to stigmatization, since the appropriateness of the overall category can less easily be questioned and its permanence doubted. In so far as it constitutes an absolute moral category (see chapter 2) it may thus effect a total transformation in the child's identity for his parents. For the child, what might be one of a number of images of himself in interaction with his parents, becomes 'the real me'. Consequently, although increased knowledge of the disability, comparisons with normal children, etc., make more favourable definitions possible, the category can continue to be employed to explain/reveal the 'meaning' of undesirable characteristics of the child, to question appearances of normality, and to seek out those characteristics which persons of this same category are expected to share.

In the greater ambiguity of the second situation there is no underlying 'fact' with which to make congruent interpretations of the child's behaviour. If present appearances do suggest an unfavourable definition, that of 'normal' is still possible, given an uncertain prognosis. Though parents may seek standards against which to assess the child, they are free to define which should be considered as 'appropriate', and where necessary other audiences can be sought. More meanings are likely to be defined as culturally appropriate in an ambiguous situation, and though parents may share the same categories as others they can deny that their application is appropriate in the specific instance of their child.

Although distinctions of this kind can be made between meanings imputed to the child's disability by parents, it must be recognized that it is in parents' responses (as compared to those of other groups, whether professional or community) that evidence of stigmatization is least likely to be found. This is a consistent finding across all areas of deviance. Even in situations which 'favour' its development, normalizing tendencies are likely to persist; the pace of labelling within the family is generally slow (Rubington and Weinberg, 1968, pp. 1–12). Strictly speaking, this applies to 'public' labelling. Thus, Yarrow *et al.* (*op. cit.*) find that wives delay consulting outside agencies, such as psychiatrists, long after they have perceived abnormalities in their husband's conduct. Parents, especially those of large families, may typify family members in such terms as 'he's the baby', 'she's the clever one', which may have crucial implications for a child's self-conception. None the less, there are several conditions acting against this.

Following Garfinkel's (1956) analysis, families fail to provide the conditions of 'successful degradation' necessary to the imputation of a total identity. First, it is difficult to see the child as a 'type' when in continuous interaction with him; rather, this favours 'individuation' (Weinstein, 1969). Second, parents, as has been seen, often do not know what is *specifically* typical of the

disability; what may be 'symptoms' to others are unique characteristics to the parents. Third, the child cannot often be held
responsible for his condition (but where he is, it makes a difference,
see chapter 6). Fourth, the parents may be seen, or see themselves,
to be at least partially responsible for the occurrence of the
disability, and certainly for the child's subsequent care and
control. Fifth, extrusion of a family member is generally, as has
been argued, condemned in our society, and on both counts
parents would place at risk their *own* good identities. Finally,
parents constitute the 'wise' for the child (see chapter 6), and
may rather coach him in strategies which can mitigate the
stigmatization which he may experience outside the family.

By the end of the period of study most parents said that they
defined their child's condition in ways that were congruent with
the limitations entailed by medical definitions. Whether or not
such definitions were ambiguous, these constituted the basic
constraints upon parents' individual perceptions of the child's
behaviour even though this required that they engage in 'abnormal'
interpretive work. The major examples of such 'uncommonsense-
making' were: (1) that parents attempted simultaneously to
construct both the meaning of the disability in general and that
of the individual child's behaviour in particular (Case I and
Type I); (2) that they elaborated several themes simultaneously
which were presently equally plausible (Type III); (3) that they
focused on one meaning in spite of present evidence to the
contrary and which in the light of later developments required
continual reconstruction (Case II and Type VIII); and (4) in all
cases where the future was certain, made reverse inferences as
to present meanings, whilst, where it was uncertain, they were
unable to trust the present as a reliable guide to the future.
Finally, all parents were more than normally aware of the active
nature of their constructive work.

In Schutz's terms, doctors seem more likely to be treated as
'insiders' so long as and to the extent that parents have no
direct experience of the child which constitutes an alternative
framework of interpretation (Type I and Case F). They are
trusted as 'commentators' if parents manage to form some
knowledge of doctors' different framework of interpretation or
acquire some understanding of the general category of disability
so that at least they can understand how doctors arrive at their
definitions. Thus Mrs K came to see her daughter's apparent good
health as a sign of the good control rather than the disappearance
of diabetes. Mrs C and Mrs G recognized that doctors genuinely

could not tell them how their children would develop. Even then, however, the appropriateness of medical categories may be doubted where great discrepancies persist in the parents' immediate perceptions of the child's behaviour. Mrs H knew the typical characteristics of mongolism and that her son possessed many of them, but after six months he was still developing according to her expectations of a normal baby.

Disagreement with doctors at any one point in time occurred where parents' experience of the onset of the disability was such that they could not see how anyone could have foreseen the event and they cannot therefore reasonably assume that it will not happen again (Type II, Case M). Similarly, if parents' own past experience of the child had proved as reliable a guide to understanding his behaviour as that of doctors then they may not see why it should not continue to be so (Type VII, Case C). Such claims are strengthened where others offer opinions which are substantially similar to parents' own, or suggest alternative interpretations which appear more plausible than those of doctors. Mrs H reported doubting the diagnosis of mongolism in the third interview when she also reported that neighbours had commented on the child's 'lovely eyes' which for her had been one evident characteristic of the condition.

Parents who do not cite any other opinions which substantiate their own (Types IV and V) might be seen as the most 'irrational'. These include the cases of mothers who were at some point regarded by doctors as 'over-anxious' (e.g. Mrs G and Mrs K), or, as Mrs O described herself, 'hysterical'. Parents' fears may of course be or turn out to be unjustified and doctors know that in the majority of cases this is so. None the less, in any individual case, and whether they appear over-optimistic or over-pessimistic, parents can cite reasons for their assertions. Parents construct their definitions from the unique standpoint of day-to-day direct contact with their child; the evidence available to them is different from that available to others. Their tendency to assert the unique characteristics of their child is legitimated both by commonsense conceptions of great variation in normal child development and by expert diagnoses of disability which rarely leave no aspects of the future unprescribed and which are typically presented to parents in such terms. Finally, parents' perceptions of their child are organized by different interests to those of doctors and these may be more likely to produce 'distortions' in so far as parents do not wish their child to be disabled, or, on the other hand, fear that they may not properly fulfil their responsibilities towards him if they assume that he needs no special care.

When seen from their perspective, parents' definitions of their disabled child appear sensible and understandable. When a mother says 'I can't see it' this may be because *in her experience* her child has not yet appeared in ways which would have questioned her normal categories of interpretation. Far from indicating psychological disorder, parents' methods of making sense of their child's behaviour display an ingenuity and commitment that makes the fact that they manage to sustain such efforts seem as surprising as that some may at certain times disagree with expert opinions.

6 The presentation of normal parenthood: private activities and public performances

Parents' definitions of their disabled child's behaviour are rational, orderly constructions when seen in the context of their everyday experience of child-rearing. Their methods of interpretation are informed by the meanings that others impute to the child's behaviour, but such meanings must make sense of parents' own perceptions. By the end of the period of study most parents said that medical definitions did more or less constitute their methods of making sense of the child's behaviour. Those who doubted or discounted the adequacy of such definitions cited evidence from their past and present interaction with the child. Evidently, whether or not parents agreed with others' definitions, their decisions were grounded in substantive processes of interaction with others and with the child. Thus far, these and their implications have remained largely unexamined.

Presenting an orderly definition of the child's condition is necessary to parents' appearance as able to provide for his adequate care and control. The construction and maintenance of that definition, however, is accomplished in situations which place that competence in question. Moreover, in situations where it is known that they have a disabled child, other areas of their conduct may become subject to scrutiny as they are asked about his influence on their family life. Hence their own good identity as parents, and that of the family in general, may be at stake.

In the first part of this chapter, I examine the problems that parents may say they face and the strategies they adopt in obtaining and evaluating others' definitions of the child and in asserting their own. This shows that parents cannot assume that others necessarily say what they 'really' think, or judge their expressed opinions simply in terms of their knowledge of the disability and the individual child. Similarly, parents themselves may not always seek to present the child as he appears to them when in interaction with him, and when they do, their actions may be subject to misinterpretation with consequent implications for their own identities. In the second part of the chapter, I present parents' responses to questions about the effects of having a disabled child on various aspects of their family life, and show that these are so presented as to maintain a normal appearance. Typical differences in the styles that parents adopt in accounting for their actions are related to negotiated definitions of the ways in which their situation is different to that of normal parenthood.

In chapter 1, I argued that an unexplicated model of normal family life enabled many writers to identify certain deleterious consequences of the advent of a disabled child. Sustaining this assumption of pathology required that parents' statements be variously discounted. Others, wholly or partially rejecting the assumption of pathology, focused on the event as initiating new processes (Farber, 1964), to the management of which parents bring their existing knowledge and skills (Hewett, 1970) and the experience of which is phenomenologically continuous with family life prior to the existence of the disabled child (Davis, 1963). However, these writers were unable to account for structural similarities in such processes without similarly abandoning the parents' perspective. My argument is similar to that of Birenbaum (1970). Like Davis, Farber and Hewett, Birenbaum focuses on the ways in which an 'unmanageable' problem is made routine by mothers of retarded children, so that most such children 'remain in their communities, and relatively few . . . are placed in residential care' and families so affected do not appear on the evidence available to become 'downwardly mobile in the class structure of American society' (op. cit., p. 56). Unlike them, he identifies mothers' methods as attempts to construct a 'normal appearing life style' being concerned with the everyday impressions that the family makes in the local community.

Birenbaum takes his focus from Goffman (1968) who includes parents of the disabled as an instance of his second type of 'wise'. Wise persons are themselves normal but intimately acquainted with the lives of a particular category of the stigmatized. The first type is one who for some reason is particularly sympathetic towards the stigmatized, but must actively seek and often wait for his validation as a 'courtesy member' of the category with whom no shame need be felt nor special self-control exerted. The second type are those whose 'relationship through the social structure to a stigmatized individual . . . leads the wider society to treat both individuals in some respects as one' (1968, p. 43). Birenbaum considers three possible 'adaptations' by this second category. These include (1) total disaffiliation from the stigmatized, and (2) demonstrating a total 'acceptance' that entails the loss of one's own claims to a normal identity. He finds that mothers of retarded children adopt a third strategy: presenting a 'normal appearing round of life'. Successfully upholding this claim requires that they avoid situations in which their obligations to the child are obtrusive. Thus they discontinue relationships with those who do not show 'consideration', i.e. who 'indicate by their actions that the family [is] being re-evaluated as a result of having a retarded child' (*op. cit.*, p. 189).

As their child's wise, parents of the disabled 'provide a model of "normalization" showing how far normals could go in treating the stigmatized person as if he didn't have a stigma' (Goffman, 1968, p. 44). Others, uncertain how to treat the disabled child, can take their cue from his parents. However, parents are crucially different from most other persons with a courtesy stigma because they do not choose their position, and far from being expected to refuse, are encouraged to welcome its responsibilities (as will be seen in chapter 7). Hence they are less likely to create embarrassment by 'confronting everyone with too much morality' (Goffman, *op. cit.*, p. 44) though they may be accused of investing too many resources in the child if it is at the apparent expense of other family members. The relationship is different for the stigmatized, too, where he is a child. He does not choose his parents as his accredited representatives. Moreover, they do not adopt his standpoint; rather, the younger the child the more his perspective will be that of his parents.

This analysis suggests that Birenbaum's (*op. cit.*) findings may have limited applicability. The first adaptation, total disaffiliation, seems likely only in 'extreme circumstances' and the second, 'total acceptance', may rather be widely legitimated. Evidently it is necessary to examine the conditions under which parents adopt different methods of managing interaction with others, in such a way that, far from avoiding interaction, they may become more than normally competent performers.

First, however, it should be noted that though the model of interaction used is principally that developed by Goffman (especially 1959), I take into account two general criticisms advanced by Weinstein and Deutschberger (1964). They say first that Goffman never systematically pursues the question of individual purposes in interaction. For example, although he does not claim that the stigmatized always seeks to present himself as 'essentially normal', neither does he specify the conditions under which other intentions may predominate. Second, they point out that Goffman's model tends to be somewhat static;

once the 'working consensus' has been reached it either continues essentially unchanged, or breaks down irrevocably. Rather, both the tactics used and the very tasks themselves may change and be subject to continuous renegotiation in any one encounter.

In the rest of this chapter I first outline the specific activities in and through which parenthood is normally constituted inside and outside the home. On the basis of this a number of particular problems that parents with a disabled child might be expected to face are identified. I then discuss the interactional problems that such parents report and the strategies they adopt in managing the child's appearance with its implications for their own and the family's identity. The focus is on encounters between parents and others outside the immediate family, including professional agents, where the child is either present or constitutes a potential constraint on interaction; that is, not necessarily an explicit topic.

The problems and strategies are examined in four areas: (1) creating the desired impression; (2) 'breaking through'; (3) information control; and (4) obtaining information. I then give parents' accounts of the effects of having a disabled child on family relationships and activities, also presented in four areas: (1) their relationship with the disabled child, and the effects on (2) normal child members; (3) marital relations, and (4) non-member activities. This shows that parents do not deny any such effects, but that the ways in which they account for them sustains an appearance which is congruent with the normal order of family life. Four typical styles of managing this impression are suggested: (1) coping splendidly; (2) making amends; (3) stoic acceptance, and (4) avoidance. These are related to negotiated definitions of parents' 'responsibility' and 'power'. Finally, I suggest some of the ways in which parents develop a 'special' interactional competence, and its possible implications for the child's and their own identities.

THE EVERYDAY ACTIVITIES OF NORMAL PARENTS

To qualify as 'adequate' members of their category, parents must organize their activities so that they provide housing which has the properties of a home (though there may of course be disagreement over what these are) of which the inhabitants are in good health and appearance. They must attempt to allocate family resources of time and money, and distribute home work according to the 'needs' and capabilities of each member. Each of these must be so trained and supervised that they may be or become trusted to know and act in accordance with the rights and duties of their status.

Outside the home parents must ensure that members observe the standards of wider social groups, and maintain a balance between the competing claims of other groups and the family on the resources of individual members (Goode, 1960b). In any case, the public appearance of any member may be taken as evidence of the family's 'private' state. Given their common identification, the behaviour of any one member may reflect on the others. The sibling of a 'delinquent' may himself be the object of suspicion, for example, and it is 'common sense' that 'children reflect on their parents'.

As 'team-managers' parents should ensure that the proper impression of their individual and joint behaviour is sustained. Members who cannot themselves be trusted must be controlled. Young children 'are' incompetent performers; 'socialization' may be regarded as the teaching of social competence (Weinstein, 1969). Parents must therefore cast a child in situationally appropriate identities and provide him with the necessary documents of these; hence, strangers can feel just anger if they are led by cues of dress colour to mistake a baby's sex. They should not take him into 'adult' places at the wrong times nor allow him to intrude on others' privacy in public places. Whenever the child is present, parents must invigilate his performance and make proper restitution when it gives offence.

Ongoing family life may depend on the 'fulfilment of a thousand mutually anticipated acts' (Goffman, 1969, p. 382) but it is, of course, experienced as routine in most important respects. For the parents this derives from several sources. First, as has already been argued, no competent adult could legitimately claim ignorance of its basic constitution. Second, parents may tacitly agree on many of the appropriate regulative rules, though this depends partly on the similarity of their biographies (cf Berger and Kellner, 1964). Third, the family constitutes in many ways that situation most favourable to the institutionalization of conduct; it has many of the characteristics of a 'total institution'.[2]

The management of children in encounters with others is perhaps normally the most problematic areas for parents. Such encounters are important since, as indicated, they are places where definitions of parents' competence are constructed and further, given that children are not trustworthy participants, where that competence is most threatened. Children are unreliable 'props' and unpredictable 'equipment' and may always 'let the side down'. None the less, such management can be largely routine and others routinely discount (though they may recognize and laugh at) impressions created by young children to the extent that they are defined as 'non-persons'.[3] Further, such encounters may be as instructive and rewarding for parents as for others. For parents of the disabled, in contrast, all activities may become problematic.

In general, the advent of a disabled child may be seen as breaching the institutionalized order of family life. If the grounds for extrusion of the child are not now invoked, i.e. the child is not institutionalized, then the basic constitution of family life is not challenged. But to the extent that the appropriateness of the old rules and recipes for action is called into question, parents are uncertain both as to how they should best perform their everyday tasks and what new tasks may be necessary.

Thus they may not know whether or how to reallocate family resources (what sacrifices should be made and by whom); nor to what extent a redistribution of labour is necessary. They may wonder if activities outside the home should be curtailed and visitors discouraged. The care and control of the disabled child may not only be physically more arduous but parents may not know whether routine methods are applicable or what special techniques are required. They may be unsure what behaviour it is appropriate to expect of the child both at home and in public. Finally, they may be uncertain as to how relationships outside the family may be affected and whether new inter-personal tactics may be required.

In any one encounter, then, parents may have a variety of often conflicting aims. As regards the proper upbringing of their child, they may have to discover what is medically wrong with him and what action is therefore appropriate. Knowing this, they may be concerned with its implementation and getting 'help' of various kinds from others. They have the conflicting responsibilities of teaching the child to define himself as 'essentially' normal whilst guiding him in strategies for managing his stigma.

The performance of all these tasks is much aided by a knowledge of how the child appears to others which may then, of course, inform parents' attempts to constrain *alter*'s definition. Further, parents may be concerned with such matters even in encounters which 'really' focus on 'normal affairs'. Where parents are unsure of the child's 'real' condition, or their own general competence, they may be highly conscious of *alter*'s opinion as implied by his treatment of parent and child.

Parents' aims may conflict not only at any one point in time, but through time. The temporary relief of day-care may increase the likelihood of the permanent mortification of the special school.

Concealing the 'true' extent of the child's disability from over-anxious or over-sympathetic relatives may prevent their taking any part in his later management. Such conflicts may lead to changes in parents' aims, not only between, but within, any one encounter. What starts off as an attempt to gain validation for a normal definition of the disabled child may become a plea for help.

Finally, it is important to realize that although parents' general aims may be those of covering up or coping with the child's abnormality, minimizing embarrassment and maintaining the expressive order, particular situations may require stressing or even exaggerating the stigma. Obtaining help often requires this strategy.

TYPICAL PROBLEMS AND STRATEGIES IN IMPRESSION-MANAGEMENT

1   CREATING THE DESIRED IMPRESSION

For a variety of reasons, e.g. obtaining help or avoiding embarrassment, parents may wish to present a particular definition of their disabled child to others. However, they face problems in doing this. The child's disability may, of course, in fact discredit claims to a particular identity. But, even where this is not so, impression-management is difficult because both the child's and the parents' actions are open to misinterpretation.

Like normal children, the disabled child may lack the social skills to co-operate with his parents' attempts and sustain their projected definition of him. Thus, Mrs H's[4] claim that her mongol child was 'coming on as fast as his brother' was discredited when he made no attempt to hold the cup offered him by the paediatrician despite his previous ability in this skill. That is, the disabled child's 'normal' disobedience and mistakes are more likely to be taken seriously and interpreted as symptomatic of his condition. All children 'let you down' in front of visitors but the retarded child's tantrum was documentary evidence for his grandmother (D) of the aggression typically associated with backward children. This is especially so since expressive behaviour, such as muscular reflexes and eye movements, is generally seen as a spontaneous and therefore reliable indicator of underlying phenomena: reliable since young children are commonsensically held incapable of practising artificial 'spontaneity', they 'are' as they appear. In fact, children do learn to produce 'symptoms' that are rewarded by sympathetic adults, and the appropriate interpretation of such behaviour is, as will be seen shortly, a problem for parents.

Adults, of course, are assumed to produce such skills, and parents may commonly be suspected of 'misrepresenting' their child. However, this is often without basis. On the one hand, they may appear to overplay his normality, but even in such cases as that of Mrs K, whose hope that her daughter might 'get better' countered medical knowledge of the pathology of diabetes, what might normally be seen as the legitimate behaviour of a proud parent is here more readily defined as 'not facing up to reality' – a typical case in paediatrics. When, on the other hand, parents present the child as more disabled than he appears to others, their definition may be similarly discounted as 'over-protectiveness'. Mrs C herself retrospectively defined her behaviour in this way: 'I might have been too worried about him . . . feeling his head when he was sleeping and things like that . . . I think it was silly in a way.' Parents of the disabled have more opportunities for being so judged because they engage in more encounters where the child's identity is in question. Moreover, the costs and rewards involved are likely to be higher. The dismissal of their pleas may delay the offering of necessary help, as shown in Mr E's account of their difficulty in obtaining a diagnosis of their son's diabetes.

Success in constraining *alter* to accept their interpretations of the child's behaviour depends first on parents' own knowledge of the child's behaviour, the recognition of its distinctive normal and abnormal characteristics. They may be uncertain as to what (if anything) is wrong with him or how severe it is, and where 'expert' definitions are available these rarely provide an adequate guide to everyday management. Parents can only discover the extent to which the disability actually 'obtrudes' in interaction through their experience with the child in different situations. A speech defect is not apparent to others when conversation does not include the child, while answering for him is a readily normalizable strategy. Second, success depends on a knowledge of how the child appears to others in what kinds of situations. When in doubt, parents may assume that what is 'evident' to them is equally so to others. Mrs H discovered that most people did not recognize her baby's features as peculiarly mongol, hence letting the child 'pass' became a possibility. Parents may also find that others' perceptions of the 'focus' of the disability vary and then attempt to control them. When others expressed their definition of diabetes as disqualifying a child from all effective interaction, his parents counter-asserted that 'once he's had his injection he's just a normal little boy' (E).

Given such knowledge, parents may discover the extent to which back-stage work can produce a normal-appearing child. Mrs N found out that dry hair and skin were typical characteristics of mongols, and thenceforth made special efforts to use appropriate shampoos and cream. Mrs H demonstrated to me how they had taken photographs of their child 'sitting' on the sofa by surrounding him with cushions to prevent his falling over.

2 'BREAKING THROUGH'

Interaction between parents and others is often problematic because of mutual ignorance of the other's definition of the situation. Even if the participants have attained what Scheff (1967) terms the 'third-level of co-orientation' – that is, where *ego* knows that *alter* knows that *ego* knows that *alter* knows (that the child is disabled) – there remains the difficult problem of 'breaking-through' and openly recognizing the fact.

Participants generally lack expertise in managing such situations. Further, the act of mentioning the child's disability redefines the situation and imposes a new set of rules upon action within it. *Alter* may have to express sympathy, the parents their grief, too great poise is inappropriate for either.[5] Both may wish to avoid embarrassment and the possible reconstitution of their existing relationship. Even when the presence of disability has been acknowledged similar problems may persist in the negotiation of its severity, visibility, and so on.

In each case, as Davis (1961) finds for the adult stigmatized, it seems to be generally the task of the parents to indicate the appropriate definition of the situation and conduct within it. Of course, some complete strangers cannot restrain their curiosity, but more commonly it is only certain categories of others who, by virtue of their relationship with the parents, can give unsolicited opinions. Grandparents D and J suggested that the child should see a doctor since their motives must be assumed to be of the best. Even doctors, when they must break the news of the child's disability to parents, appear to manage a context of growing awareness in which parents experience a 'sense of foreboding' and may eventually ask what is wrong. Only when this and other direct strategies, such as using the child's father as a 'less-emotional' mediator (A and B), fail do they stage a showdown and insist that parents 'face facts'. For five days after the birth of his mongol son Mr N refused to inform his wife, and only did so when the child was discharged from the special nursery and his condition likely to become apparent to his mother.

3 INFORMATION CONTROL

Where parents know that their child is disabled they have to decide who to tell what. Often they may wish to conceal their child's stigma. Where the disability is not very evident, parents may be able to control its 'known-aboutness' so that they can act as if the child were normal, with all except the informed few. This is still problematic, however, since parents do not have objective knowledge of the meanings *alter* imputes to the disability. Thus, the doctor may only be fooled in so far as he is dependent on parents' admission of information (he need not know of the effects of the child on other members of the family). Moreover, parents often doubt the sincerity of, and therefore discount *alter*'s expressed opinions. Close relatives are especially suspect of employing 'protective practices' (Goffman, 1959, pp. 201–6), tactfully appearing to concur with the parents' definition. Mrs G[I] was no longer very convinced by her husband's mother's reassurance that there was nothing wrong with the child: 'I don't know if she's just saying it.' Mrs B retrospectively saw her visitors' denials that they could see anything wrong with her new baby as because 'of course they didna' want to hurt me'. Further, keeping secrets requires careful management. Parents must control the behaviour of the whole family and themselves maintain a united front in order to sustain the desired impression of the disabled child. The young brothers of children A and T were appropriately instructed about their sisters' conditions, even though they 'don't really understand'.

Sometimes, however, parents may wish to reveal rather than conceal. Letting others 'in' may have definite advantages in terms of emotional support or practical help and such considerations may influence the parents' decision as to whom to tell. Thus, they can only appropriately express feelings of grief and resentment with close family and friends who can be expected to share in their sorrow, and even so, as will be seen in chapter 8, this is for a limited period of time. They may train certain others to manage the child in their own absence, like Mrs E who told the child's teacher how to recognize the symptoms of a diabetic reaction, and supplied her with sugar to give to the child. But they are likely to weigh such advantages against the costs of involvement discussed in the previous section: too little help may be preferable to too much sympathy. Thus, parents A and G concealed the 'true' severity of or their worries about the child's condition from grandparents who 'will only get upset', and strangers are often the best confidants since both parties know that the involvement will go no further. Mrs N treated me in this way, saying 'it doesn't matter what you think'.

Such calculations are inappropriate in some cases since, whether or not they can help, certain people have a 'right' to know. These

persons are principally those relatives and friends who will share
the parents' grief, or who, like young siblings of the child, would
themselves be hurt were they to hear it from another source.
As in Sudnow's analysis of the communication of the news of
death (1967, pp. 153–68) they should be informed quickly and by
someone closely related to the parents – in fact, often by the
child's father. Mr B[I] visited his own and his wife's parents,
brothers and sisters to tell them that their baby was mongol.
Other parents reported daily telephone conversations or visits
with relatives immediately following the onset of the child's
condition, or during subsequent critical periods (A; M[I]; R[I]).
Other than for this select group, given the complexity of information control, and the discovery that 'bad news travels fast',
parents may simply opt for the strategy of 'letting it get around'
(B[I]; F[I]; N). This removes some of the uncertainty in interaction,
though it does not solve the problems of 'breaking-through'.

4 OBTAINING INFORMATION

Often parents want to find out *alter*'s 'real' opinion of the child,
despite the risks to their own identity. This may be a central aim
when they are themselves uncertain about the child's condition
or seek trustworthy advice on how best to help him. Others'
definitions are also important in order to inform parents' activities
as impression managers and suggest suitable strategies for
different audiences and, finally, in order to teach the child the
kinds of responses he will encounter should he become responsible
for managing his own performance.

Given such intentions, there are two main categories of persons
whose definitions of the child are important. First, those with
desirable resources: some people's opinions (e.g. doctors) are of
intrinsic value; those of others may constrain their willingness
to help. Friends may not baby-sit if they over-estimate the extent
of the child's disability; employers may be unsympathetic to
requests for time off work if they do not define the situation as
serious. Second, it is important for parents to discover the definitions of those who have power over the child and can make
important decisions about him, whether now or in the future. If
doctors and teachers between them largely control the child's entry
into and progress through school, parents are in a better position
to influence the child's future if they know to what extent he is
'officially' disabled.

How can parents find out *alter*'s opinion of the child? Direct
inquiry as an opening tactic is likely to be too threatening, both

to the parents themselves – it may give the game away unnecessarily – and to *alter* from whom, as Mrs B[I] discovered in
questioning her visitors, it may elicit only a vehement denial
which cannot be further pursued. A second tactic consists of
checking *alter*'s statements against his observable interaction
with the child. Doctors may belie their assertions of the child's
normality through, as Mrs G observed, their sustained testing of
the child's reflexes. Parents may conclude that *alter* is himself
uncertain: Mrs L said 'I don't think they know themselves'; or
'they never give you a straight answer' (Mr P). A more subtle
strategy is that of 'testing'[6]. Parents proceed by 'hinting' at the
object of their concern, whether it be the meaning of specific
symptoms or general anxiety at the child's condition. Mrs G[I]
repeatedly presented her child at the clinic ostensibly for severe
vomiting but 'by the way' attempted to elicit an evaluation of
the child's physical development.

Such tactics may be sustained over a number of encounters,
but if they do not succeed in resolving the uncertainty, parents
may then resort to 'outrage', i.e. challenging *alter* with a definition
of the situation that must be accepted or denied with at least a
convincing show of sincerity if he is not to lose face, the parents'
trust, or endanger his own and his profession's integrity. Thus,
parents J[I] and K[I] confronted their doctors with the assertion that
their children had leukaemia; another, Mr N[I], said: 'Are you
trying to tell me my child is a mongol?' Such definitions may be
seen by parents as 'too awful to be true' but are used by them to
define the boundaries of what is. Of course, sometimes such
assertions prove correct.

FAMILY LIFE AND THE NORMAL ORDER

In situations where it is known that they have a disabled child,
its effects on family life are potentially evident, and parents'
good character at stake. The research interview was one such
situation. Parents were asked directly: (1) what difficulties they
found in managing the disabled child, and whether having the
child had any effect on (2) their other normal children; (3) their
marital relationship; (4) their non-family activities inside and
outside the home. In effect, they were being asked to evaluate
their own performance of the constitutive activities of parenthood.

1   RELATIONSHIP WITH A DISABLED CHILD

In chapter 5, I examined differences in the processes of documentation by which parents manage to make sense of their child's

condition. Here I want to show how the *substantive* resolution of parents' doubts and difficulties concerning the child constitutes their relationship with him.

Parents report problems in interaction with a disabled child within the home in terms of doubts concerning the adequacy of their skills in managing him, and of more than normal difficulties in interpreting his behaviour. The cries of any young baby may be ambiguous, but where a child is known or suspected to be disabled, parents may further not know whether they constitute evidence of his condition, and if so what action they should take. A similar 'tantrum' in different cases indicated the onset of an insulin reaction (E), an epileptic fit (O), or a retarded child's attempt to communicate in the absence of verbal skill (D), and therefore required either chastisement, or the administration of sugar, or phenobarbitone, or an attempt to discover his desires. Hewett (1970) gives examples of mothers' anguish when, imputing 'naughtiness', they chastised their cerebral palsied children, only to be met with hurt surprise. One of the mothers in this study, Mrs G, said she had been content to let her child lie all day until she began to question whether his apparently 'good' behaviour was related to his slow development, and then described her efforts to give him more of her time.

So long as parents defined their child's behaviour as symptomatic of his condition they expressed their willingness to put his interests first and 'do anything' for him. For example, Mrs A and Mrs F were prepared to go into hospital to acquire special management techniques, even though it meant leaving their husbands and younger children. One of these, Mrs A, had decided to have no more children, so that she could devote herself to nursing the child; another, Mrs O, repeatedly visited specialists and demanded that they carry out further investigations on her epileptic son, whilst alternately forbidding and allowing the child to swim and ride his bicycle, as she calculated the risks involved. One set of parents, Mr and Mrs E, incurred what was to them the great cost of diabetic sweets, so as 'not to make a difference between them', and two families (C and M) postponed or curtailed their holidays, rather than risk a deterioration in the child's condition.

Such expressions of concern were modified with the ascription of motivational states. As the child thereby acquired an identity, or a moral character, he could be treated as a person with whom normal interactional skills might become appropriate. In several cases mothers decided that their children were now 'sensible' enough not to require their constant vigilance, but this was generally presented as being in the child's interests. 'You can't forever watch him' (Mrs M) and 'you've got to let her out and play' (Mrs K). Another mother, Mrs J, admitted her failure to keep her child to the prescribed diet, but accounted for it in terms of his uncontrollable desires: 'he just takes a roll', 'he's sick of eggs', or of his individual characteristics, 'he's never been a meat hand'.

However, where the characteristics described were 'bad', the child seen as 'lazy' (D), even a small baby as 'playing up' (A), or the doctor seen as ultimately right in thinking that a child used his asthma to avoid school (C), then parents might argue that 'you can't let him get away with it [tormenting his sisters]' (D). Or, recognizing that it might still help the retarded child to play with him constantly, Mrs D now said 'you just canna' do that all the time'. Finally, where parents could never regard their child as a person (a spina bifida child (F) never learned to recognize his mother), then given that she claimed adequate skills for his physical care, she said later that there was now no point in going into hospital simply to be with him.

Some parents, however, did not resolve their difficulties in either way. They did not regard the child as 'sick', nor were they sure that normal methods of handling him, if appropriate at present, would continue to be so. This seems to be the situation analysed by Birenbaum (1970). Parents in this study similarly claimed to follow the recipe of 'treating her as normally as possible' while acknowledging that the most they could hope for in the future was that the mongol child would be suitable for 'special' schooling. They asserted 'as long as I can manage her, I'm not worrying' (Mrs B). Indeed, on the discovery that normal handling works, 'I think it helped and calmed me right down'. Mrs H said that they were 'taking it from day to day'. Such expressions continued so long as the child made what were regarded as appropriate responses to his parents' efforts. Birenbaum found that the second most frequent rule cited by mothers of retarded children was 'give love, affection and attention', and he argues that its invocation was necessary as the child failed to benefit from *instrumental* teaching. The fact that mothers here did not use this account may be explained by the younger age of the children concerned, that they had not reached the stage at which further progress was not expected.

2   EFFECTS ON NORMAL CHILD MEMBERS

Parents generally denied any bad effects of having a disabled child on their other normal children. If they admitted it, it was defined as past, and action as having been taken to avoid its recurrence. When the sister of a spina bifida child (F) had mumps her father expressed his horror at discovering that 'you forget she can be ill as well', and subsequently the parents made special arrangements for the child to attend dancing classes. Another child (B) was reported as having been bored at home, but as now having a neighbour's grandson to play with, and her interests were cited as the only grounds on which the mother would risk having another child, which might also be a mongol. (Conversely, the desire not to have more children may equally be presented as in the normal child's interests.) Finally, even previously agreed on actions, such as sending the normal child to nursery school, may be temporarily reversed 'in case she thinks she's being put away' (Mrs B).

Parents may make it evident that such efforts might be contrary to their own interests. The same mother, having just returned from a walk, said 'it was for her sake really, I've had enough', another (Mrs N) said that she went out every day 'even if I have to make up messages' (i.e. invent an excuse to go out shopping). Parents may say that problems could arise in the *future*, but it is implicit in their recognition that therefore they will attempt to avoid them, and they may relate plans to, e.g. take the normal child out during the school holidays (F). As regards the present, they cite evidence that the other children do not mind. This may relate to other interests which occupy the child, or special treats that they have arranged for him. Mrs A said that the normal child was looking forward to sleeping with his father when she went into hospital to be with the disabled child; Mrs B produced evidence of her older daughter's progress in drawing since she had started at nursery school, asserting that 'she's a different person'.

Further, parents described the other children's responses to the disabled child. This is presented in a typical rhetoric. The normal child 'kills her with kindness' (B), is 'dying to have him home' (F), 'just dotes on him' (H), and may be 'always in and out of her room' (A), or asks to share the same room at night (B). If other children are presented by parents as suffering in any way, this may be defined as normal. There are no children round here for the child to go and play with anyway (C); he is slightly jealous 'but only like with any new baby'; or, he is getting difficult to handle but 'he's just at that age' (A). If older children are at home, and this allows their parents out, this is only because 'they would stay in anyway, and I wouldn't deprive them of going out for [the child]' (H).

Alternatively, parents may define their other children as 'unreasonable' in objecting to the disabled child's favoured treatment. This may be because they are 'old enough to know better' (D); too much bigger to allow them to fight with the disabled child without parental intervention (M); or where, in the case of the sister of a diabetic child, 'it doesn't really hurt her to go without [sugar on her corn flakes]' (E). Even here, parents made evident other ways in which they did not discriminate between the children: 'they both get told off' (M); 'she gets a little slap too' (L); and Mrs E still made puddings and cakes for the rest of the family.

The only situation in which parents stated that they did put the disabled child's interests before those of the sibling was where he was defined as sick. Thus one child (F) was reported as fed up with having to visit her brother in hospital every day, and when another (C) complained that his brother's wheezing kept him awake, his mother said she told him 'you ought to be glad you haven't got what he's got'.

3   EFFECT ON MARITAL RELATIONS

Mothers (I have the wife's perspective only here) admitted changes in their relationships with their husbands, but in all cases these were defined as desirable. Often this was expressed as 'it's brought us closer together' (A, B, T), or 'we've sort of come through it together' (H). With reference to specific household activities, either these were reported as unchanged, reflecting an earlier negotiated division of labour, and wives might affirm that 'I wouldn't want him to do more, he's had enough when he gets in' (B) or as fairly modified to suit special contingencies. Husbands might take time off work to enable their wives to go into hospital with the disabled child (A), or if the wife was herself ill, then even a man who normally did nothing in the house 'was sitting there sewing buttons on the kid's clothes' (L). Wives reported that their husbands did more than normal if a 'man's skills' were required, e.g. in controlling an epileptic child's excitability (M), or coping with the crisis of a diabetic child's insulin reaction (K). Husbands also did more where simultaneous demands were made on mothers' time (bathing two children at once – B), or where the extra time spent on a disabled child meant that the gardening had become entirely the husband's responsibility (A). If wives said that they wished their husband would do more to help, it was not so much for their own sakes as for the children's. Thus, even in the case (N: to be described more fully in chapter 8) where the husband wanted his mongol child institutionalized, threatened suicide and never even went to see why the child was crying, his wife reported her anger in terms of her concern for their other child.

Husbands were generally presented as caring, even if they did not show it: 'My husband doesn't show his worries' (L), 'he's the sort of person that keeps worries to himself' (K), and as sharing such additional activities as visiting the child in hospital (A; F; T), in so far as this was compatible with other considerations, notably their work and having meals. If they were absent from home, then they telephoned regularly if they could, and 'he always asks about [the child]' (G).

Most reported discords were approved by wives in terms of, or at least acknowledged as having, beneficial consequences. Thus 'he said I'd just have to get used to it', 'he made me go to the doctor rather than worrying myself sick, or I might be sitting here yet' (K), 'he said get a move on and contact the doctor before she starts school' (L). Mrs K said that, in an argument, she had blamed her husband for their child's diabetes, but she said 'I felt awful after . . . [it was] rather than blame myself, I suppose', and now said that 'we could never leave each other now because of her' since no one else would know how to cope with her, and 'you should have a responsibility for your children, we are responsible for it, you see'.

4 EFFECTS ON NON-MEMBER ACTIVITIES

Here I am concerned with the distribution of resources (mainly of time) between family members and non-members. That is, the family's use of outside resources, their involvement in outside 'non-member' activities, and the perceived effects of both on family relations.

Immediately after the identification of the child's disability many parents reported a great increase in interaction with relatives, friends and others from outside the home. As Farber (1964) found, this was because more people visited, telephoned or wrote to the parents than was usual. In one case the onset of disability was explicitly reported as 'like a death in the family' (B), and, like the bereaved, parents could not properly refuse such offers of sympathy, even if they did not want it (cf Sudnow, op. cit.).

They generally defined them as well-intentioned: 'everybody's been awfu' nice', and 'are kind really' (B); 'everyone's interested' (A); 'everybody asks after him' (N). Mrs T observed that 'some ask because they're nosey, but the others at least it's someone to talk to [otherwise] you'd go mad climbing up the wall'. Other mothers reported satisfying such inquiries even if it meant that 'I haven't managed to get into a routine yet' (H), or 'it takes me two hours to do my shopping' and 'the way some people round here go on they make you really depressed . . . "Oh, how awful, what a burden"' (F^I). Mrs B^I found her sister 'upsets me and I canna' speak to her because I ken she's upset . . . some days I am awfu' depressed ye ken'. In the next interview, however, she said of other people who avoided her that 'I don't worry about them – if I did I'd be a nervous wreck . . .. I don't want sympathy really . . .. I'm getting over it now'.

As has been seen, parents may report that they have to manage others' expressions of sympathy and advice, and acceptance of such offers depends partly on parents' existing relationships with *alter*. Beyond this, however, they reported accepting help first in time of 'crisis'. Thus neighbours might be asked to look after another child, do some shopping, or spin-dry laundry, if this facilitated mothers visiting their disabled children in hospital (A, G, F, L). Second, offers might be accepted in the interests of other children, to take them to the dentist (N), or to dancing classes (F). Third, others might of course baby-sit 'simply' to enable parents to go out together. In all cases, acceptance was premised on the assurance that the disabled child was safely left in another's care. So long as this was not the case, one or other parent remained with the child, mothers would not go out to work, even if it entailed financial hardship, holiday plans were revised or abandoned. Mrs N said that she had to be persuaded by her neighbour to leave her mongol child and take her other son Christmas shopping; Mrs B said that her sister had persuaded her that it would do her good and the child no harm to go away on holiday; another family (M) delayed their holiday a day longer than advised by the doctor; and the situations in which the outside activities of other members of the family might be reported as restricted have already been examined.

Parents who said they did not go out much, either singly or together, asserted that they did not 'really' mind. Mrs B said she would like to get out more, but 'I'm not really worried'; Mrs D said that she had given up taking her retarded child visiting because of his destructiveness, but defined this as a relief, because 'you couldn't sit still with him two minutes anyway'. (Though I categorize this mother's public behaviour as 'avoidance', see next section.) Whether they regarded it as possible or not, they claimed that they did not want to go out. Often the situation was defined as normal, either in terms of their previous leisure activities, or as expected with any new baby, lack of time being the most frequent account. Mr E said that 'we'd rather be at home' while their children were small. However, only one mother, Mrs H, claimed positive satisfaction with the reorganization of her own and her husband's time around their mongol child, asserting that 'this is our life now'. Their other two children were both about to start work and spending less time in joint family activities.

In general, we see that parents present themselves as fulfilling their responsibilities of care and control towards their disabled and normal children, maintaining a fair distribution of resources within and without the family, which does not discriminate amongst them and in which their own interests are secondary. The work involved is more or less fairly shared between husband and wife, taking advantage of certain offers of help from others, who are thereby successfully maintaining the unity of the family. Any problems that arise in the future will be met with the same consideration. Parents thereby claim that they should be regarded as 'good' members of the normal order of family life. This does not mean that they simply deny any discrepancies with their experience, whether past or present. Rather, that the ways in which they account for such discrepancies induce others to interpret their presentation of family life as congruent with the normal order. In Birenbaum's words, we can read their statements as 'an expression of an effort to get others to regard the family as more or less conventional' (1970, p. 60).

RESPONSIBILITY AND POWER

I, however, argue that there are typical differences in the ways in which parents seek to achieve this: that parents adopt different 'lines of action' (Weinstein, 1969), according to the prevailing definition of the situation. Two components seem to be involved: parents' 'responsibility' and their 'power'.

Imputed responsibility for his actions, as was seen in chapter 2, is a critical condition in the management and control of any deviant. Here it refers to whether parents or others define the parents as causally implicated in (a) the child's disability, either genetically, or through negligence of their duties as parents. Inadequate care and control may result in the child falling victim to illness or injury, be it physical or psychological. Mrs G thought that she had encouraged her child to make no effort to sit by only taking him from his cot when he cried for food; another mother

(O) thought that her son's epilepsy was partly a result of her inability to breast-feed him, and consequent failure ever to feel 'close' to him. Responsibility may further imply (b) any perceived 'suffering' on the part of other child members, and (c) any other ways in which family respectability is questioned.

'Power', like 'imputed prognosis' (Freidson, 1965), concerns the 'curability' of parents' position; that is, whether they are defined by themselves and others as able to 'do something' to change their situation. This depends on such considerations as (a) the nature of the disability, e.g. the management of diabetes requires the parents' co-operation with doctors; (b) the parents' knowledge of it – until they can recognize important symptoms, they may feel helpless and doubt their competence should problems arise; and (c) the parents' resources. Money can alleviate many problems. Paid nurses relieve the physical burden on parents, and thus minimize changes in the family division of labour and resultant stress; home tutors avoid the stigmatization of the special school. Commitment to caring for the child may be far less costly, because sacrifice is unnecessary. Holidays can still be afforded, the mother's earnings are less likely to be crucial to the family budget, other children need not be deprived. Middle-class parents may suffer more from the 'disgrace' of a mentally handicapped child (Farber, 1959), and be more isolated from kin and 'community' help, but they are likely to make greater use of routinely available formal agency services (Mercer, 1965) and obtain preferential treatment through professional and informal 'contacts'. Further, they are most likely to possess skills relevant to managing encounters with such agents (Schatzman and Strauss, 1955; Scheff, 1968).

It must be stressed that assessment of 'responsibility' and 'power' is based on actors' definitions. They are not objective facts to be 'faced up to', but are always open to negotiation. Parents and others may hold different definitions, and each may influence the other. Doctors provide parents with 'scientific' grounds for disavowing responsibility; parents may believe and convince others that their amateur physiotherapy is a help to the spina bifida child (F). These issues will be taken up in chapter 7.

If the two components are treated as dichotomous, their combination produces four possible permutations, which constitute different moral interpretations of parents' actions by themselves and others, and thus interaction between them. I want to suggest that for three of these situations there is a typical line or style which may be adopted by parents and proffered by others as an appropriate way of managing interaction while maintaining the good character of the parents. That is, by appealing to certain grounds, citing the relevant motives for their actions, parents may be formulated as adequate members of their category. In the fourth situation, since this is not possible, interaction may be highly circumspect.

1 'NOT RESPONSIBLE, HAVE POWER'

The predominant line here can be characterized as 'coping splendidly'. This is typical where the disability most approximates an 'illness', i.e. it is known to be of 'physical' and non-hereditary origin; treatment is possible; it can alleviate and even control (though not cure) the condition. As regards the disabled child, parents here have an important part to play, if it is only to ensure that the child keep his appointments with the specialist. 'Doing what the doctor says' is a ready defence against criticism, and an excuse for rejecting advice. Others may even be impressed by and express admiration for the parents' new competence in medical matters, and incompetence is usually evident only to knowledgeable others, e.g. doctors. Equally, it is a situation in which others' help can be accepted with less risk of appearing incompetent, though, as we saw, parents may claim that they require persuasion where this is in their own interests, that it is not contrary to those of other members.

Mrs A represents an extreme example of this style. Throughout she appeared calm and confident, regarding the child's breach of the oesophagus as a 'temporary trouble to go through'. Reported 'problems' were limited to practical matters of reorganizing family activities in order to visit the child in hospital and acquiring the special techniques necessary for feeding the child. She sought and accepted offers of as much help as she needed to fulfil these tasks. Her constant source of reference regarding the child's progress was the hospital: 'if they are pleased, we are', and when she said that 'everyone is asking when we are getting home' she added 'we are more concerned with getting her established'.

Parents can also appear to be coping well when they claim that the disabled or normal children are more or less responsible for their own actions, but that they themselves are still active in managing family relations. This is of course culturally legitimated; parents are supposed to accord children more independence as they grow older. Thus they report deciding to invest less resources in the disabled child (time spent in hospital, or playing with him), or requiring the normal child to make some sacrifice (because 'it doesn't hurt her' (E), or 'they should know better' (D)).

In fact, this style of presentation was the most common in the interviews. This may be evidence of how parents defined the interview situation, and of its inadequacies as a research strategy, in that little observation, nor therefore questioning of parents' activities, was possible. Parents may, as seen earlier, adopt this strategy as a way of avoiding unwanted involvement, or upsetting others. But it may also be because it is precisely this line that is actively promoted and fully legitimated by formal and informal agencies (see chapter 7).

2 'RESPONSIBLE, HAVE POWER'

In this situation parents typically appear to be 'making amends'. They can feel guilt despite others' efforts to discourage them from 'taking the blame'. This seems to produce greater efforts on behalf of the disabled child and an unwillingness to discuss him in routine encounters, except when challenged. They may then dramatize their concern for his welfare, and make evident their sacrifices on his behalf as the only way of neutralizing threats to their identity. This perhaps accounts for the 'shopping around' different agencies sometimes reported in the literature – within the National Health Service, this consists mainly of repeated visits to the same agency.

Mrs O[1] reported herself as 'slightly hysterical' but 'I don't think I've had the same emotional tie with him. Maybe I'm over-compensating now. I probably feel a lot of guilt now because I've never been as close to him.' She also cited marital problems as a possible cause of the child's epilepsy since a recent seizure had followed a particularly bad argument with her husband. So long as she held herself responsible, she discounted her GP's reassurance to the contrary: 'I said to the GP could mental stress bring it on? He said "Oh, I don't think so", but he may just have been reassuring me.' She recognized his argument that 'if you make more of it the child will make more of it . . . but at the same time, what am I supposed to do if . . . he gets knocked down because he's had a seizure? From O's point of view, that's how I look at it.' She had been to O's school and had an argument with his teacher when she discovered that they had stopped him doing gymnastics, and again before the third interview when she felt that the teacher had been unreasonably angry with the child for doing the wrong homework, especially since upsetting him might bring on another seizure. Mrs O had also demanded that her son see a psychiatrist who had said, 'there's nothing wrong with him, he's a very normal little boy'. She was somewhat reassured but still uncertain whether to allow the child to go swimming: 'I've really spent hours of anguish thinking of him in the water and that you know . . . I don't think I'm an over-protective mother . . . I just get terribly responsible . . ..' With regard to other members, if parents reported difficulties for which they held themselves responsible, it has been seen that this was *after* they occurred, and then parents similarly stressed corrective and preventive measures they had since taken. Again, if parents appeared to restrict their own activities outside the home 'unnecessarily', they may be seen as making restitution in terms of their own suffering.

3 'NOT RESPONSIBLE, NO POWER'

Here parents demonstrate 'stoic acceptance', which appearance is most common in cases of 'tragic' disability, e.g. congenital abnormalities. As with death, parents must learn to 'face the [medical] facts'. No one can offer any real consolation, neither can they accuse parents of negligence. It is here that parents claim to be 'taking it from day to day', once assured by doctors or through their own experience that their skills for managing the child's physical care are adequate. Their major interactional problem may be the control of others' expressions of sympathy and ignorant advice. Thus Mrs B said 'they give advice when really they don't know at all'; Mrs N that 'they say some funny things. One of the favourite questions is "Are you going to keep him?" '. She added 'I would never ask that'. Mrs T's rejection of others' advice was more vehement: 'There's a lot of them say "Oh, she'll be best away", why should people tell me what to do?'

As in the first situation, parents may repudiate responsibility by implicating the disabled child himself. For example, Mrs J legitimated her failure to keep her child to a diet in terms of his uncontrollable personal characteristics. Similarly, in later interviews Mrs O increasingly interpreted her son's behaviour in terms of his underlying psychopathic tendencies, and given her previous efforts on his behalf, might claim if challenged, 'I've done all I can'. Normalizing accounts of the jealousy or 'obstreperous' behaviour of other members ('he's just at that age'; 'only like with any new baby' (A)) similarly invokes factors and conditions over which parents can exert no control.

4 'RESPONSIBLE, NO POWER'

These conditions typically apply in cases of 'undifferentiated' mental subnormality, and parents' behaviour in this situation seems to be that described by Birenbaum (1970) as 'avoidance'.

Since there is no known physical cause, parents seek it in their own management of the child, but there are no 'special' techniques that they can acquire to correct their mistakes, i.e. make amends. They cannot do what 'any normal' parent would do, having been responsible for their child's condition. Hence, parents may try to keep the disability a guilty secret, and restrict interaction to those who share in the responsibility, or whose condemnation is mitigated by their knowledge of the parents' good character in other spheres, such as the proper care and control of other children. It can be noted again that parents avoided mentioning any inadequacies in such spheres, until they had made appropriate restitution, and in this situation this seems more likely to take the form of self-imposed retribution. One effect of this strategy is that they may therefore avoid going to professional agents, who might in fact be able to help.

Examples of this were presented in the last chapter, where, in the last situation, characterized by the orientation 'there must be some sense in it', mothers reported that third parties intervened in referring the child to an outside agency. Mrs D's health visitor suggested that she take her retarded child to the local baby clinic regularly, whence after a few months the GP referred the child to the hospital. Mrs D^I was already 'much happier now . . . you hear that many old wives' tales', and was hoping that the nursery would bring him on 'as if I'm working he doesn't get that much attention'. In later interviews she recounted her efforts to help him by playing with him every night 'so that it's not that he is away all day and bedded when he comes home'; they treated Sunday as 'his day', and before the last interview she had bought him a dog which 'had settled him a bit knowing it's his dog, you usually see boys playing outside with their dogs so I thought I'd get him a little one'. However, she continued to 'blame myself in a way, knowing he's the youngest and the girls more or less off my hands'. 'I've taken it for granted he'll be more aggressive so he's got away with it', and did not discount 'stories of children waiting till they are five and still not talking properly and they've had to go to a backward school and I just wouldna' like him to start off on that footing'. She preferred not to discuss the child with most neighbours: 'I just say "Hello" but not get into conversation with them.' One asked her how he was progressing at nursery: 'Further than that I won't talk about him with anyone'. McHugh (1968) found that his subjects preferred any order to none. Parents then may prefer to blame themselves rather than to have no account. Thus 'avoidance' may be a permanent strategy, despite others' attempts to redefine the situation. Korkes (1956) argues that parents who accept personal responsibility for their child's mental illness more often undergo profound changes in personal values, their marital relationship and child-rearing behaviour.

Often, however, parents' strategies change over time. Birenbaum (*op. cit.*) notes that parents may be unable to continue a 'normal-appearing round of life' when the retardate reaches adolescence or adulthood. It follows from the above analysis that if parents define and can present themselves as less 'responsible' for, or more able to influence, the child's condition, then their inter-personal style may change accordingly. Mrs L avoided discussing her child's lack of growth with anyone but her husband. He finally persuaded her to see a specialist, who diagnosed the cause as 'something in the brain'. 'She's got a growth deficiency' then became her account to anyone who commented on the child's size. At the third interview Mrs B reported having been told that her mongol child was a 'one-in-a-million chance'. At the next she described how a girl at the baby clinic had upset her, saying that mongols are 'awfu' wild . . . I said "my one's nae" ' and asking what caused it 'as though it was my fault'. This contrasted with earlier interviews, where she had 'scarcely been out of the home'. Mrs D was asked by the child's nursery school teacher to co-operate with them, using specific techniques to train him. She then seemed much more willing to discuss with me the child's present and future development.

However, adopting one line may constrain future alternatives; especially where the audiences involved are the same, or in contact with one another. Thus, if parents are 'known' to be 'coping' they may not be seen as powerless and thus not offered help. They may project different definitions to different audiences and for different aspects of their activities.

To conclude: interactional styles are related, not to parents or disabilities, but to particular definitions of the situation which remain to some extent negotiable issues. The fact that in the first three situations parents do have a legitimate way of managing encounters, does not mean that any individual parent will never experience other problems of stigmatization, embarrassment and so on. Parents who define themselves as responsible for, but powerless to change, their child's condition may avoid most encounters with others concerning him, because there is no generally acceptable line available to them. Even if they privately 'accept' the child's condition, they may be unable to manage his public presentation – it is difficult to find an audience for endless self-recrimination. The alternative, carrying on as normal, can be sustained only in encounters where both parties are equally willing to honour its claims.

THE DEVELOPMENT OF COMPETENCE

It should be apparent that the management of interaction with others concerning a disabled child is highly complex. Embarrassment is inherent in many 'normal' situations, and parents may face many 'strange' encounters with doctors, social workers and others. Parents must usually indicate the appropriate definition of the situation. Hence, if they are not to withdraw from all social relationships outside the family, they must acquire a special competence in managing encounters.

How do they develop this? As noted, middle-class parents are from the start more likely to possess relevant inter-personal skills. For all parents, specific sources of information are books and magazines written for and by the disabled or their parents, or other such parents met informally or through parent associations. These provide both general and specific prescriptions from which new lines of action may be constructed. This is related to the development of an ideology which, it will be argued in chapter 8, not only prescribes and legitimates, but provides a new basis for calculating costs entailed by particular actions.

Of course, personal experience is crucial. But certain kinds of events may be particularly instructive and it is on these that I focus here. The first performance of 'routine' activities such as taking the child out in a pram (H), on a bus (B), or to the clinic (N), is often crucial. These may constitute 'turning points' after which it may 'never be so bad again'. Indeed, parents often expect such events to be 'the test' of their 'acceptance'. Areas of incompetence may still be revealed in atypical situations. These may by inherently unpredictable – for example, Mrs K's diabetic child started to go into a coma in the street – or they may simply be unpredicted. One mother, whom I visited in the pilot study, took her spina bifida child to a party; only then did she realize how disabled she was compared with normal children and she said: 'It was the first time it really hurt me.' Events which cannot be managed within the parents' existing repertoire may occasion a drastic revision of tactics. Parents discover that 'you have to be rude to some people' when more subtle cues fail to divert a stranger's inquiries. Mr T said that when some people told him his daughter, who would be severely retarded, would be better institutionalized, he felt like 'turning round and saying "It's got God all to do with you" '. He did not, however, say that he had done so. Some situations may remain 'unmanageable' – one cannot prevent people crossing the road to avoid an encounter. Parents may feel like shouting 'Look at him – he's not a monster' (Mrs N), but never regard it as an appropriate strategy.

The skills that parents acquire enable them to typify embarrassing situations and predict *alter*'s response. They learn to define the actions of some categories of other as insignificant and distinguish 'true' sympathy from mere curiosity. Thus they are able to manage interaction so that they are not simply at the 'mercy' of others' definitions. They may certainly continue to be influenced by and value such opinions but they need not just hope that *alter* will be 'considerate'. This seems to be true only in the last situation discussed where parents lack an appropriate line and their alternative 'normal' interactional style requires *alter*'s tactful acceptance. Parents' special skills may further be relevant to other situations. The frequent questioning of their actions by themselves and others may increase parents' awareness of the dynamics of interaction. Like others in 'marginal' situations (cf Scott and Lyman, 1968b), they may become generally more skilled as interactants.

This special competence may then have important consequences for parents' identity and self-conception. The fact that they must treat *alter*'s responses as problematic makes them appear more able to 'take the role of the other' and recognize that 'I'd be the same in their place'. Mrs N described how one woman had told her she would never have stopped to talk had she realized the child was mongol, and said that this did 'irk' her but 'I realize that they're worried how *they're* going to react as much as anything'. Parents of the disabled learn to treat as routine, occurrences which embarrass, distress, anger, or otherwise disorientate 'normal' members of society. Such others may then interpret parents' actions as evidence of 'special' qualities of character – 'kindness', 'understanding', 'self-sacrifice' and related skills. These are the grounds for the 'deep philosophy' that other persons with a stigma are often supposed to hold (Goffman, 1968, p. 147), and which I shall examine in chapter 8. Moreover, such definitions are likely to make sense of their conduct to parents also since, as otherwise normal members, they share the same categories. Hence, they may internalize them and regard themselves accordingly – as Mrs K said, 'I think I'm more mature now'. The relationship between parents' public statements and their private beliefs will be more fully discussed in chapter 8. Here I consider the possible implications of parents' interactional competence for the disabled child's subsequent development.

The child may be affected by his parents' tactics, both directly in that he may learn and adopt them himself, and indirectly in that they may be self-fulfilling. In both respects major problems may arise – not all of which are unique to the child who is disabled. First, parents' presentation may be inappropriate to the child's 'actual' condition, whether present or future. They may claim more or less for him than he can honour and would himself claim were he responsible for his own performance. Second, parents' altercasting of the child may conflict with the identity they present to others. Mr and Mrs J consistently called their son 'fat boy', yet claimed to others that he was 'just sturdy' and in addition told the child to tell others 'you're not fat'. Third, parents may continue to manage the child's person and performance in more spheres and for longer than 'normal'. Thus, if they have developed successful tactics for coping with certain audiences in certain locations they may prevent the child from entering unpredictable or uncontrollable situations and he may rarely leave the safe circle of family and friends. They may continue to choose the child's clothes and hairstyle, supervise his time, his cleanliness and his diet.

There are several reasons for this. First, because their special competence may become routine but includes no prescriptions for change. There are no culturally available timetables for according independence to a disabled child. Further, parents may want to make amends to the child for his suffering: he 'deserves' special treatment, or he may, of course, really lack the ability to manage his own performance.

The disabled child may then be triply disadvantaged. First, because of the identity imputed to him by others on the grounds of his disability, i.e. stigmatization, as analysed by Goffman (*ibid.*). Second, because his disability may prevent him attaining a normal repertoire of inter-personal skills. Weinstein (1969) states that inter-personal competence correlates with IQ and is highly dependent on cue sensitivity. Children refine their tactics in interaction with their peers. Hence, the child is finally disadvantaged if he never acquires the competence to manage his own incompetence. This requires that he experience a normal range of interaction, but this is largely within the control of his parents. To this extent, the child's incompetence may be the product of his parents' competence.

To conclude: parents of a disabled child do not simply deny any differences between their situation and that of normal parents. They do not claim that it creates no problems or has no effect on themselves and their family life. Rather, as they account for acknowledged or observed differences, they make evident otherwise unobservable aspects of their private activities which are 'what any parent would do' in the circumstances in question. They display aspects of the biography of a normal parent, as defined in the official morality, which are relevant to a given event. In formulating particular accounts, they invoke their own, and impute to other members motives which induce others to see otherwise abnormal actions as 'understandable'. Hence, taken in the context of their own and others' reported definitions of the particular ways in which their situation is abnormal, parents' statements can be seen as reconstituting an appearance which is congruent with normal parenthood and family life. This applies even in the last situation discussed, where parents avoid encounters in which they might be called to account.

It may be remembered that one of my criticisms, in chapter 1, of those writers who impute underlying pathology to families with a disabled child was that anything that parents say may be taken as evidence of this state. One example of this was that of parents who bought a pet for their cystic fibrosic child being seen as displaying a 'guilt-denial-of-guilt reaction'. In this chapter I cited Mrs D as having bought a dog for her retarded child in an attempt to make amends to him for her earlier relative neglect. There are, however, several differences in the methods by which the two conclusions were reached.

First, Mrs D herself presented her action as a way of helping the child, having earlier said she had not given him enough attention and had had unrealistic expectations of him. She told me she had bought a dog following a long discussion of the child's continuing destructive behaviour at school and at home, and of his teacher's recommendation of ways in which she might help him. Her observation that 'it has settled him down a bit' followed what I intended as a general question (after a pause in which she spoke to the child): 'Do you notice a difference – are you controlling him more?' Second, this still does not necessarily indicate her intentions at the time of buying a dog; rather, that it was a relevant action to cite in the situation in which the efficacy of actions to help the child were being discussed.

Finally, and most importantly, *not* making evident such actions is as likely to be taken as evidence of underlying pathology as doing so since, taken in context, they appear to be demonstrations of proper maternal concern. Similarly, *not* practising 'avoidance' of encounters in which no good account for the effects of a disabled child on family life is appropriate might not only formulate the individual concerned as a bad parent, but also make publicly available evidence that family life is not always as it is supposed to be.

7   The legitimation of suffering

Parents with a disabled child appear to be good and respectable even if they are held responsible for their situation, because their actions are so presented that they honour the normal order of child-rearing. They make evident or reveal their efforts on behalf of the child and other family members, or avoid encounters in which their own and other members' good identities might be at risk, and thus conceal their deviance. Neither in such cases, nor in those of parents who seem to have managed a good acceptance of or to be coping with their difficulties, need an assumption of individual psychological differences be made. Rather, parents' 'adaptations' are appropriately situated responses organized by their own and others' negotiated definitions of their situation in relation to that of normal parenthood.

Again, even those parents for whom having a disabled child is 'meaningless' in that they can see no congruence between the disability and his behaviour, or those who have not managed to construct a stable order for his appearance, claim a working if precarious definition of him, thus offering assurance of his daily care. Differences between these and those parents for whom 'it all makes sense' do not necessarily indicate more or less common sense, that some parents are more rational than others. Rather, such differences express equally methodical methods of interpreting the disabled child's behaviour in the context of presently available meanings of his condition.

Chapters 5 and 6 could be regarded as constituting an adequate account of the kind of statements made by parents about the disabled child and his effects on their family life. However, it might still be asked: how can parents keep on trying to make sense of their child's condition; appear calm or cheerful; and even sustain their efforts to make amends to him and the rest of the family? In everyday terms these are questions about parents' motivation: how can they 'bear' it? They are based on the assumption that since most parents do not expect, hope, or wish to have a disabled child, then, if most parents with such a child do appear to be good parents, some more-than-normal explanation of their behaviour is required. Of course, I do not intend to abandon my previous argument and invoke psychological qualities of one kind or another, nor to cease to take parents' statements seriously. However, I similarly assume that because they have a disabled child parents' experience is not the same as that of parents of normal children, and therefore their appearance as such does require a different explanation.

In chapter 2, I argued that whether or not they have a disabled child parents are held accountable to a conception of normal parenthood, which bears a questionable relationship to the experience of any parent but which, since it is actively implemented by agents officially empowered to control family-related activities, acts as an official morality to constrain parents' public appearances. Most members co-operate with each other to act as if they agree with and thus maintain the public fiction of this morality, rather than risk incurring the sanctions of such agencies. An understanding of conformity lies not in the assumption of substantial consensus amongst members but in an analysis of the situated uses of the official morality, of the verbal and non-verbal tactics and strategies by which members construct and maintain a working consensus and the appearance of normal parenthood and family life. Parents who have a disabled child likewise make use of 'the family' in claiming the normality of their lives.

The question is: how is it possible that they manage to appeal to quite ordinary motives in accounting for their actions in an extraordinary situation? Basically, I argue that an adequate explanation of the ordinary appearance of parents with a disabled child lies in an examination of the extraordinary activities of agents empowered to deal with family-related problems in general and those pertaining to disability in particular. I take up what Ball (1970) characterizes as the 'moral entrepreneurial' activities of such agencies which attempt to manage the appearance of respectability for others through the constructive use of legitimations of conformity. Such legitimations variously express elements of 'theories' which are culturally defined as more or less appropriate to the situation of parents with a disabled child. In chapter 8 I attempt to show that they constitute an ideology which enables parents to redefine discrepancies between their experience and the normal order of child-rearing so that these discrepancies are symbolically transformed into apparent congruence with that order. The ideology maintains the relevance of the official morality to the parents' situation by legitimating their 'suffering'. In this chapter I examine religion or its commonsense equivalents, medical science, psychiatry and sociology, as they are commonly related to the parents' situation, and in terms of these theories discuss some of the activities of doctors, social workers, voluntary associations, women's magazines and newspapers. From a summary of the similarities and differences between these agencies I suggest that they variously express a substantial consensus as to the appropriate definition of the situation of parents of the disabled, and therefore of action within it.

Scott (1970) has a similar intent in his analysis of the activities of rehabilitation agencies for the blind. He presents some comparison of the typical theories informing such activities in several countries, but his main focus is on the organizational and other constraints under which they operate. I mainly omit such considerations and, in contrast, attempt to spell out the major theoretical grounds of the agents' activities and to show how these may act to legitimate the situation of parents of the disabled. First, however, I summarize the bases of parents' suffering, the discrepancies between their situation and that of normal parents, and present some discussion of the general forms and processes of legitimation.

In chapter 2, several grounds which together account for the congruence between the official morality of child-rearing and the observable behaviour of most parents of normal children were suggested. These were: that parents who are regarded as normally competent adult members of society are, first, generally assumed to acquire child dependents voluntarily and therefore can be held responsible for their position, and, second, to know what activities this entails. Further, most parents may find child-rearing rewarding whatever their reasons and see the family and parenthood as fundamental to our society so that either they do 'agree' with its morality or at least regard public expressions of disagreement as wrong. Hence the morality is constantly reaffirmed and maintained in interaction with others outside the home.

In contrast, not only may parents of disabled children find that their experiences do not make sense in terms of the official morality, but the normal processes by which that morality is maintained are disrupted. Decisions upon such matters as whether the disabled child should be institutionalized, or whether now to have more children, question the grounds of parenthood. An inability to understand or misinterpretation of the disabled child's behaviour resulting in inappropriate treatment of him undermines, as chapter 5 showed, the central task of child-rearing, especially if he looks 'odd' or does not respond to normal stimuli, since it may then be difficult even to feel any affection for him. Changes in the allocation of family tasks and resources involve different costs, and these may be greater than expected if parents find that a commitment to caring for the child entails giving up family holidays, refusing promotion if it means moving to an area where medical and educational facilities are inadequate, or financial hardship if the wife can no longer go out to work. Moreover, such sacrifices may appear pointless when unrewarded by any visible improvement in the child's condition.

Encounters with others, far from being supportive, may aggravate the situation. As chapter 6 showed, parents must often take a more than normal share of the responsibility for managing such interaction. They are called to account for their actions more frequently, as even routine methods are questioned and their 'normal' treatment of the disabled child appears callous to soft-hearted outsiders. Moreover, they more frequently seek or otherwise come to the attention of official agents such as doctors, social workers, or educationalists. To the extent that the normal privacy of the family is thus invaded, more areas of their conduct become subject to public scrutiny.

Hence, parents of a disabled child are *more* than normally held accountable to the official morality of child-rearing, while their experience is *less* than normally manageable within its terms.

What actions might one expect of parents in such a situation, or, what sort of situation is it? Manifestations of 'grief' are commonly associated with instances of 'tragedy'. Mrs B[1] said that the birth of her mongol daughter was 'like a death in the family'; many mothers for whom the onset of disability was sudden said that they cried, were under sedation and they spent some time in the close circle of family and friends where such expressions are appropriate. However, as Sudnow (1967) shows, grief is socially defined as a short-term affair; thus having a disabled child is not like being bereaved. Parents' misfortune is continually made apparent when not only do they lack the normal blessings, but cannot even have the normal worries about their child's progress, cannot expect him to leave home, marry and produce grandchildren. Some mothers said that there might be 'days when I'm back to the bottom of despair' (N) and 'I'll have a good greet' (H), but only Mrs R and Mr N long continued such behaviour and in both cases this was reported by *others*, by Mrs A and Mrs N respectively.

A second possible response is that of 'resentment'. Nietzsche (1969) says that this is typically experienced by persons deprived of proper outlets of action who are then forced to find compensation in imaginary revenge. He sees this as a 'dangerous blasting stuff and explosive' which if not suitably 'channelled' causes rebellion against the prevailing social order. However, Weber (1969) argues that although resentment can provide the grounds for 'revolts in morals' it is not usually a decisive factor.

Resentment may be precluded by locating the 'cause' of a disadvantage. Studies of 'disasters' commonly recount attempts in the aftermath to find a 'scapegoat' (Baker and Chapman, 1962). Two sets of parents (P and U) blamed doctors for their child's condition. Others, as chapter 6 showed, questioned their own guilt, blamed the child or other members of the family for particular aspects of their situations. However, 'Weber made clear above all that there is a fundamental distinction between the significance for human action of problems of empirical causation and what, on the other hand, he called the "problem of meaning" ' (Parsons, 1969, p. 59). Parsons gives the example of premature death through accident when, although the problem of *how* it happened may be easily explained, there remains the problem of 'why such things must happen'. The situation of parents of a disabled child can be seen as presenting problems of a similar order which is generally called the 'problem of evil', or the 'meaning of suffering'. That is, even those parents who blame themselves for the child's condition might be expected to ask 'why should it happen to us?' when similarly guilty parents are not thus punished. They might also ask the more general 'why do such things happen at all?'; that is, according to what law, by what right are we thus punished?

The problem of suffering and evil is inherent in any social world, or, to put it simply, people are sick and die every day. Such phenomena are outwith the normal order of well-being and life, although in practice each is identifiable in terms of the other. The integration and plausibility of a given world or order depends on the availability of categories whereby such phenomena can be defined either as 'not to be taken seriously', as lacking any 'real' status: 'not dead but passed on'; or as being in fact consistent with the categories of that world: 'we all have to die sometime'. This process of legitimation basically consists of producing more abstract or 'second-order' categories which integrate more primary categories. The following account draws heavily on Berger and Luckmann (1967). Integration occurs on two levels: the 'horizontal' and the 'vertical', or, as expressed in chapter 2, it has two dimensions: the 'spatial' and the 'temporal'. Thus postulating an after-life may be seen as inconsistent with the existence of ghosts without the notion of 'troubled spirits' with unfinished tasks on earth; or normal mortality with great variations in longevity without such formulations as 'a short but happy life'.

As these examples suggest, legitimations may be elaborated to varying degrees. Berger and Luckmann distinguish analytically between four such levels. These can be seen more clearly if commonly illustrated with the fact that most parents keep their children. The first 'incipient' level constitutes a simple affirmation that such phenomena are 'how things are done'. It is contained *in* or built into the vocabulary: 'parents do not give away their children.' This level, the 'pre-theoretical', is the basis for all other theoretical formulations. The second level is that of proverbs and moral maxims. 'Those who do, live to regret it.' The third contains explicit theories or bodies of knowledge which 'because of their complexity and differentiation . . . are frequently entrusted to specialized personnel who transmit them through formalized initiation procedures' (*ibid.*, p. 112). Thus 'psychology has shown that parents who give away their children suffer from guilt' or 'are psychologically disturbed'. 'Symbolic universes' constitute the fourth and most comprehensive level of legitimation. These integrate all different provinces of meaning by referring to realities other than those of everyday experience. Since they cannot be experienced in everyday life, they constitute a universe *within* which all experience can be seen as taking place. Such legitimations of parental responsibility in the face of cross-cultural differences, as chapter 2 showed, generally appeal to the well-being of children and the self-realization of adults.

Legitimations at any level have implications for conduct. Most importantly, they not only define what 'is' but what 'ought' to be; they ascribe 'cognitive validity' and 'normative dignity' (*ibid.*, p. 111). Thus, to any normally competent member of our society the ascription of 'parent' implies certain activities, entails certain prescriptions. Berger and Luckmann suggest several important ways in which a symbolic universe can order the experience and action of a given individual. First, it can integrate such 'marginal' experiences as dreams by according definitive reality to the 'wide-awake' world. Thus the 'howling nightmares' of the 'night-side' reality are subjugated to the 'bright reality of everyday life' (*ibid.*, p. 116). Second, it provides the highest level of integration for discrepancies experienced *within* everyday life, so that 'even the most trivial transactions of everyday life come to be imbued with profound significance' (*ibid.*, p. 117). Thus, inappropriate conduct in any social role may be seen as not only 'bad morals' but as an offence against the order of the universe: 'it can readily be seen how this . . . provides powerful legitimation for the institutional order as a whole as well as for particular sectors of it' (*ibid.*). Third, it makes possible the ordering of different phases of an individual's life so that 'the individual . . . can view himself as repeating a sequence that is given in the "nature" of things, or in his own "nature". That is, he can reassure himself that he is living "correctly" ' (*ibid.*). This has its concomitant in the individual's subjective identity, for it enables him to maintain a sense of the 'real me', to 'know who he is' by anchoring his identity in a cosmic reality protected from both the contingencies of socialization and the malevolent self-transformation of marginal experience (*ibid.*, p. 118). Finally, and most importantly, symbolic universes legitimate death. They 'enable the individual to go on living in society after the death of significant others and to anticipate his own death with, at the very least, terror sufficiently mitigated so as not to paralyse the continued performance of the routine of everyday life' (*ibid.*, p. 119). They may take the form of a world view of progressive evolution or of revolutionary history, but without them 'it may readily be seen that such legitimation is difficult to achieve' (*ibid.*).

Any symbolic universe may be challenged by deviant definitions of reality, whether originating from within or outside a given society. Berger and Luckmann discuss several major types of 'conceptual machinery of universe-maintenance': mythology, theology, philosophy and science. Features common to these are that they are grounded in legitimations already present in the society in a more naïve form; their elaboration and maintenance tends to be the responsibility of specialists; and their application in some form of 'therapy' or 'nihilation' acts to keep deviance within a given universe or conceptually liquidate it, respectively. In the latter case this may be by assigning it an inferior status as noted above, or by translating its concepts into those of the prevailing symbolic universe.

In our society religion has been the dominant mode of legitimation. As might be expected from the above presentation, the crucial question for any symbolic universe is the problem of suffering and death. Indeed, Bowker (1970) argues that the different religions might be seen *as* solutions to this central problem. That is, they are differentiated primarily by their symbolic methods of legitimating suffering. For Christianity the problem is at least a logical one since it posits one omnipotent, omniscient and benevolent God. The question is 'How can God permit such evil?' since He must know about it and could be expected to prevent it if He does have the well-being and happiness of mankind at heart. One conclusion is that He does not exist, but other theories or 'theodicies' serve to deny this possibility. Literally translated, a theodicy acts to justify the existence of God in the face of evil. Some of those developed within the Judaeo-Christian tradition will appear in the next section.

In an earlier work Berger and Luckmann (1963) argue that religion has lost its virtual monopoly and much of its effectiveness as various groups have produced alternative definitions of reality. Legitimation has thereby assumed a 'market character' with a concurrent 'privatization of belief' and different legitimating systems competing for the patronage of potential customers. This does not necessarily mean that 'anything goes', for at any one point in time and in particular instances certain legitimations are more subjectively plausible than others. This analogy, however, has largely disappeared in their later work, for there they argue that any given legitimating attempt depends on the 'power' of the legitimator: 'He who has the bigger stick has the better chance of imposing his definition of reality' (1967, p. 127). Moreover, as compared with mythology, the other forms of universe-maintenance are increasingly removed from the naïve level and therefore relatively inaccessible to those uninitiated in their 'secrets'. This does not necessarily mean that they become less convincing since power can include control over 'socialization' processes.

Berger and Luckmann's discussion of legitimation is part of a wider argument which is based on that paradigm of human behaviour which recognizes the social world as humanly created. As such, as they say, it does not require the assumption of a psychological need for integration (*ibid.*, p. 82), although they observe that one may well be built in the psychophysiological constitution of man. However, as the above presentation suggests, they make constant appeal to subjective processes and psychological states which imply precisely that assumption.

The social order is often presented as a 'shield' against the 'terror' of anomie. This is partly a product of the fact that, despite the title of their book, they include no empirical studies of the 'social construction of reality'. More important, as Light (1969) argues, the book cannot itself be accounted for in its own terms. If the construction of reality is transparent to the authors, it could be equally so to those engaged in the work whether as theoreticians or as naïve actors. The 'privatization of belief' remains a possibility.

What parents say about discrepancies between the experience of having a disabled child and normal child-rearing and the relationship between such statements and their private beliefs will be presented and discussed in chapter 8. In the rest of this chapter, I examine the possible sources of what they say in the meanings of their situation that may be made available to them through the various activities of the several agents. I now present what appear to be the principal characteristics of the theories which constitute the grounds of such legitimations of parents' suffering.

THE THEORIES

Four theoretical sources of legitimations will be examined: religion and its apparent commonsense equivalents, medical science, psychiatry and sociology. Evidently, the kinds of questions to which such bodies of knowledge are principally addressed and therefore the answers that they can provide differ. Religion is not centrally concerned with the causation of disability, nor medicine with intra-familial relationships and processes. Of course, there may be disagreements about which phenomena rightfully 'belong' to which discipline, and different theories offer competing explanations of the 'same' phenomena. As chapter 1 showed, the symptoms of subnormal functioning may be seen as evidence of physiological defect, psychiatric abnormality, or social deprivation. 'Pseudo feeblemindedness' or, more topically, 'autism' are cases in point (Soddy, 1972).

The concern here is not with differences in 'empirical' explanations of disability, nor at all with the potential ability of the theories to legitimate the situation of parents of the disabled. Rather, it is only with those aspects of the theories which at present seem to be commonly expressed by or do inform the practices of those agencies discussed in the next section when dealing with parents of a disabled child.[1] Thus, I present the expressions of social workers mainly as appeals to psychiatry but in explanation of the behaviour of parents rather than of the child himself, and the discussion of psychiatry is accordingly limited to issues relevant to normal adults. In any case, Tizard (1966) argues that although services for the mentally deficient were part of mental health services in general, progress in mental deficiency owes little to child psychiatry. Again, I do not discuss how sociology *could* but only how certain of its aspects *do* seem currently to influence agents' activities.

I focus, then, on the theories in so far as they are used to give meaning to any aspect of parents' suffering. This does not, however, exclude empirical explanations of the occurrence of the child's disability. I said earlier that even parents who know the cause of, and blame themselves for, their child's condition may still question the justice or moral requiredness of their disadvantaged situation. Equally, however, they may not. Explanations which refer, or claim to refer, only to realities which, at least to those with the appropriate training and technology, are observable in everyday life, may be seen by parents as constituting an adequate account and no reference to another transcending order be required. Whether or not there is such an order is by definition a metaphysical question. These issues will be further discussed in chapter 8.

1   RELIGION AND COMMON SENSE

From the Middle Ages to the Enlightenment in Europe, abnormal children were commonly regarded as 'changelings'; that is, as the children of demons, pixies, or fairies, who envied men's beauty and his immortal soul and therefore stole a human child to ennoble their race (Haffter, 1968). Having such a child, then, was no fault of his parents provided they had taken the necessary precautions and guarded the child in his early days of life. In the Christianized version, it was the Devil who stole the children and by the seventeenth century he was seen as God's instrument in punishing parents for not fearing him, unchastity, or bearing children outside matrimony. The blame for having a deformed or otherwise abnormal child became increasingly internalized; such a child was a cause of great fear and guilt as parents thought 'Have we offended against God?', and a reason for ostracism by others.

The general decline of religion as an effective means of legitimation seems to be substantiated in the field of disability. Scott (1970) contrasts the theories of blindness held by Italian and, to some extent, French rehabilitation agencies in which the disability is an indicator of being either out of favour with or elect by God, with those of Britain, America and Sweden. In Britain only organizations which are affiliated to religious institutions such as the Church of England Children's Society now appear to legitimate their actions in such terms as 'maintaining the harmony of the normal Christian home'. Similarly, it is only in books like *Taught by Pain*, a collection of personal accounts of suffering which is published by the Church Pastoral Aid Society (1970) that explicit use is made of such theodicies as 'Job's solution',[2] the 'suffering servant' who resigns himself to the will of God and 'gladly accepted God's assurance that I would eventually ["walk and not faint"]' (*ibid.*, p. 82), or the Christian solution – that since Jesus as both man and God suffered for the sins of man this 'helps me to realise just how fortunate I am' (*ibid.*, p. 28).

Only one of the voluntary journals examined[3] – the *Newsletter* of the British Ileostomy Association – appears to include a regular 'Quiet Corner' which presents other theodicies in such quotations as: 'I reckon that the sufferings of this present time are not worthy to be compared with the glory that shall be revealed in us' (Romans 8: 18). Even here, the official aims of the association as expressed in the editorial make no use of such rhetoric, and the writer is in fact also one of the authors of the personal accounts cited above. Neither voluntary association publications nor other periodicals appear to have contributions from the clergy on the subject of disability. Finally, of the parents I interviewed, only Mrs Q found comfort in the explanations offered by a priest and Mrs M in the prayers of her congregation and both their situations were perhaps peculiar. For Mrs Q it was 'like living with a time-bomb' – in that the child was 'officially' dying and yet showed no obvious deterioration over a long period of time, and family M had lost another child in a road accident two years previously. A third mother, Mrs B, whose health visitor suggested that a mongol child was a 'Gift of God', made no use of this explanation in subsequent interviews and her reaction appeared to be less of hostility than of puzzlement.[4]

However, some of the major elements of the Judaeo-Christian tradition do seem to persist in present-day thought so that, though interpretations of the phenomena of disability may be within the context of an empirically observable rather than divinely-ordained world, the type of commitments they entail are similar. Religious and other theories in a society commonly influence each other – commonsense maxims may derive from religious traditions whilst religious theodicies must 'make sense' or be compatible with current conceptualizations. No attempt will be made here to specify any causal relationships but some apparent similarities can be indicated.

First, the question 'Why should this [terrible thing] happen to me?' is felt by many sufferers to be not merely irrelevant or futile but in some sense 'wrong' – as will be seen, parents who did continue to feel resentful at least expressed guilt about this. In other words, the individual is expected to reaffirm through his 'acceptance' of his fate the reality of the social world in which he lives, challenges to that world being illegitimate. Thus, the surrender of self to the order of society, or what Berger (1969) describes as the 'masochistic attitude', remains prevalent.[5]

Second, whether or not parents are held or hold themselves responsible for their child's disability, specific theodicies appear to inform both commonsense and expert legitimations of their suffering. For example, its endurance may not be the road to ultimate redemption in another world but parents can expect compensation in this world. This may take a variety of forms: parents may be rewarded by enjoying a 'closer' marriage, or by their child's progress in response to their efforts on his behalf. Other examples will be seen later. Specific expectations are, of course, open to disconfirmation, and compensation may therefore also be formulated in empirically unverifiable terms – for example, a deeper understanding of the world as expressed by Mrs K, 'I think I'm more mature now'.

Through such constructions 'everything which prevents [men] from attaining their destiny is easily and cheaply transformed into an eternal richness of the soul' (Goldman, 1969, p. 292). Commonsense proverbs and maxims similarly attempt to redefine good and evil. 'Every cloud has a silver lining', or the universally applicable 'Things are never as bad as they seem', are variants on what Ball notes as a common social process whereby 'a potential vice is given the moral meaning of virtue' (*op. cit.*, p. 359). Given the relationship between religion and common sense, such formulae are likely themselves to change with the decline of religion.

A third element of the Biblical tradition that appears to persist is the belief in miracles. This was, of course, central in the New Testament, often constituting proof of divinity, and the concept is still part of our everyday vocabulary. In commonsense usage, it refers to events that are highly desirable and highly unexpected within any explanatory framework known to the actor (Swinburne, 1970).[6] So defined, 'miracle' acts as a residual explanatory category for phenomena that science 'can't explain' and their possibility gives hope in the context of an otherwise uncertain future. Parents of the disabled may thus believe, as chapter 5 showed, that any examples of unexpected progress made by children with disabilities similar to their own child's 'prove' that the doctors 'don't always know best' and that their own child may therefore show similar improvement however unlikely this may appear in the present.

2   MEDICAL SCIENCE

Taber and his associates (1969) present the belief system in which Western medical science is typically grounded as consisting of four major elements: (1) that qualitatively different underlying conditions of the functioning of the human body exist and that therefore these can be diagnosed; (2) that certain conditions, i.e. illnesses, are inherently pathological and upset normal functioning; (3) that they are caused by one or more pernicious agents; (4) that intervention or treatment of some kind can arrest or modify this process. Explanations based on the 'disease model' may recognize other causal factors, e.g. social or psychological, and these may be explicitly related to treatment, but their distinctive nature derives from, and their unique contribution may be defended on the grounds of, their being conceptualized in terms of the structure and functioning of the body (Begelman, 1971).

The current practice of medicine is concerned with phenomena classified as 'illness' or 'disability'. These categories are invoked on different grounds and may have different consequences. Excluding some cases of long-term or chronic illness, the 'ill' person exists in a 'medical' world, the parameters of which are largely defined by the 'nature' of the illness and the doctors in charge. The 'disabled' person, in contrast, remains within social time and space and must therefore make appropriate adjustments to its demands and 'live with' his condition. Medical science cannot therefore provide a total explanation of disabilities since they involve phenomena which cannot be reduced to its terms. Of course, in such cases as coeliac disease or diabetes (where there is a locateable pathological process and this can be shown to be a necessary and/or sufficient condition of disability) medical meanings may be the most important. Medical theory can here provide answers to the major problems raised by disability such as 'Why did this happen to me?'. It can legitimate the occurrence of disability in terms of known pathological processes such as the distribution of chromosomal abnormalities or the genetic basis of certain congenital defects; it may offer some control within its own terms of treatment or by referring the case to another agency on the basis of its expert knowledge; and it can structure the future with a more or less definite prognosis. Disabilities are thereby located in most important ways in the world of medical knowledge so that other possible meanings, whether divine providence or personal liability, can be discounted.

Medical scientists or doctors have extended the applicability of the model to include previously 'incurable' disabling conditions such as phenylketonuria and, earlier, diabetes. However, as chapter 1 showed, some theorists continue to claim as their legitimate field of inquiry phenomena which do not meet the model's requirements. Zigler (1966) says that the majority of theorists regard the mentally subnormal as 'essentially' different from persons of normal intellectual ability and their condition as fixed and largely irreversible. Jacobs (1969) shows how instances of reversibility are interpreted by doctors as evidence of faulty diagnosis. That is, the failure of the medical model to explain such phenomena is taken as evidence of the present intractability of the underlying pathological process and not of the model's inadequacy.

Some doctors themselves express similar criticisms of their discipline. Towers points out that historically medicine acquired the 'aura of objectivity' associated with the 'exact' sciences by adopting their paradigm which is inappropriate to biology as 'the science of the infinitely complex' (1971, p. 159). McKeown argues that there is no question that the seventeenth-century view of the human body is still dominant; that the consequent 'engineering' approach to health has been less important than changes in reproductive behaviour, the provision of food and removal of adverse influences from the environment in reducing the incidence of disease and death, and that there is little prospect of reducing that of congenital disability except by a 'miracle of genetic engineering' (1971, p. 12). In the absence of such advance, medical theory has no adequate explanation of such phenomena.

3 PSYCHIATRY

The psychoanalytic tradition is most relevant to my concerns since it has had the most influence on social work. I do not consider the theoretical differences between various writers, but use Berger's broad definition of 'that assortment of ideas and activities derived in one way or another from the Freudian revolution in psychology' as practised not only by the insti-tutionalized core of psychoanalysis but 'by the ring of satellite organizations and activities ... the counselling and testing complex' (1965, p. 29).

Psychiatry attempts to present scientific propositions about the nature of man. This is not the place to examine their status, nor the various vocabularies in terms of which they have been constructed.[7] Psychiatry offers a theory of the meanings of human actions and experiences which are rooted in psychic rather than cosmic or social processes, but are no more directly available to individual consciousness. Most men act irrationally because they do not understand the mechanisms of repression and projection, learnt mainly in childhood, which defend the conscious self from recognizing its real motives and needs. The 'true' meaning of behaviour lies in the depths of the unconscious mind and can only be discovered by the expert application of scientific methods of interpretation. Through expert guidance the individual can be helped to attain the ideal state of 'self-realization' or 'psychological maturity' in which he achieves a 'healthy adjustment' to the 'realities' of his particular situation.

Psychiatry, then, is 'capable of doing just what institutionalized religion would like to do' (*ibid.*, p. 39). It provides a symbolic universe in terms of which all human experiences can be integrated, legitimating problems in terms of inter- and intra-personal adjustment. 'Conversion' brings the reward of knowledge of oneself. It is no less masochistic in the sense discussed earlier and it too counsels the endurance of suffering, but it may be *experienced* as more liberating since it engages the individual on an active discovery, rather than attending an uncertain future, and it furnishes him with tools to master present and future exigencies of his life.

Moreover, such gains can be contagious. For example, psychiatric students come to believe that not only are they 'better human beings' rather than simply professionals with certain skills, but that even if their patients show no obvious improvement at least they have benefited from contact with such a being (Blum and Rosenberg, 1968). In the field of disability Adams claims that 'the care given by an ordinary family to a backward child may be of very great intrinsic value to the community in providing a focus of compassionate thinking and tolerance' (1960, p. 65).

Berger argues that psychiatry has become part of the taken-for-granted assumptions about the nature of men held by many social groups in America. This seems far less true in Britain – though certain isolated concepts such as 'unconscious' or 'inferiority complex' may figure in the vocabularies of at least some middle-class groups. One reason for this may be that similar counselling services are freely available from other agents, in particular the general practitioner who is not only likely to be less psychiatrically orientated, but whose time to expend on therapy is limited. Commonsense legitimations of the problems caused by disability are more likely, therefore, to be couched in such terms as those analysed earlier.

4 SOCIOLOGY

Formal sociological analyses do not appear to have greatly influenced the activities of agents concerned with parents of the disabled. Rather, as argued in chapters 1 and 2, the reverse has more often been the case. Sociology has taken as its problems those defined by official agencies and based its analyses on an uncritical adoption of commonsense categories. However, certain semi-sociological considerations are sometimes invoked.

First, the concept of 'stigma' has gained some popularity; for example, in discussions of 'community attitudes' to the disabled and their relatives. Second, as noted earlier, there is increasing knowledge of the effects of childhood socialization and the 'importance' of education in general. 'Education' is, in some liberal circles, something of a panacea for all social problems. Third, there is some recognition of structural factors – particularly social class – as important influences on life-style and chances.

In so far as sociology has had any impact on theories held by practitioners in the field of disability, recognition of such factors has led to a shift in the focus of explanation away from the unique individual case towards seeing phenomena rather as typical products of particular socio-economic situations. The origin of suffering is thereby re-externalized: not the Devil or an angry God, but impersonal factors locate an individual's disadvantaged position, and these are largely beyond the present control of any individual. Soddy suggests that 'parents who realise that the chance of the birth of a subnormal child in their own family is at least one in a hundred at every birth ... have gone some way towards acceptance' (1972, p. 46).

Theories of socialization and education have had a more direct influence on treatment of the disabled. The methods of such workers as O'Connor and Tizard (1956) institutionalize such principles in training the mentally handicapped in skills whereby their performance on most routine tasks may reach normal levels. Evidently, the availability of such special training legitimates parents' hopes that their children may attain similar levels of competence and they can therefore invest their faith in the future and the agents who may effect such improvement.

However, given the precedent of others like Itard (*The Wild Boy of Aveyron*, 1799), such programmes may owe less to modern sociology than to eighteenth-century educational philosophy. I argued in chapter 1 that the successes of rehabilitation have provided the most effective arguments against solely medical explanations of disability but that they do not constitute an alternative explanation. Rather, rehabilitation programmes take the identification of an individual's disability as given, thereby perpetrating the belief in his essential difference from persons of normal ability and treat social considerations as conditions which encourage more or less of this underlying difference to be apparent.

THE AGENTS

The central aim in this section is to show how the several theories outlined above may be made available to parents with a disabled child through the various expressions of medical agencies, social workers, voluntary associations, women's magazines and newspapers. That is, to show how in practice the theories may serve to redefine discrepancies between the parents' experience and that of normal parents, thus legitimating their suffering. I regard the agents as moral entrepreneurs who act to reconstruct parents' deviant appearances and contain them within the normal order by asserting alternative moral meanings of the parents' experience. Several points should first be noted.

I attempt no analysis of the relations between an agent's actions and his beliefs, nor impute any intentions whether 'good' or otherwise. Scott observes that 'it is probably impossible for the expert to map out in advance all the implications of a proposed policy . . . expert meanings are not constructed in advance . . . rather they evolve, often unconsciously as the expert "muddles through" [his] day-to-day problems' (*op. cit.*, p. 287). Over time, particular combinations of elements of different theories tend to become institutionalized in the practices of particular agencies but 'only periodically do experts stand back to take a hard look at such things as the consequences of their actions or to attempt to codify the rationale for their activities and to construct explanations for them' (*ibid.*, p. 286). One of Scott's aims is to relate agency practices to socio-economic conditions such as considerations of professional reputation, economic resources, or the sanctions of other powerful agents, e.g. social workers are employed by local authorities. As noted earlier, beyond some discussion of the different 'spheres of competence' I omit such considerations.

Second, I have no direct evidence of contacts between parents and agencies. Discussion of the activities of medical agents is mainly based on parents' statements in the interviews. The main focus is on hospital doctors, since contact with these was a precondition for selection of families; all were the official responsibility of the hospital for all or part of the period of study and during this time the actions of the GP and health visitor were more or less constrained by the hospital's decisions concerning the disabled child. The activities of the latter two agents are considered briefly at the end of the section. Evidently, some of the discussion of the hospital doctor will apply also to the GP.

The discussion of social workers depends more on bibliographic material and as such more properly represents their public statements than their actual practices. I consider this question in the appropriate section, and in addition sought the opinion of several workers as to the adequacy of the analysis. Only three families had any contact with a social work agency, but I include social workers for two main reasons. First, they often influence the national policy of many voluntary associations in either a paid or voluntary capacity and, further, may be active in their local branches. Second, where they do come into contact with parents of the disabled they can provide the most coherent ideology.

Analysis of voluntary associations similarly focused on written reports; magazines and other literature. Few of the parents interviewed had joined or thought of joining an appropriate association and therefore did not attend local meetings. I include voluntary associations, however, since certain of their activities are equally available to non-members. Some associations, e.g. those for epilepsy and diabetes, supply clinics with pamphlets for distribution to parents, and current copies of their various publications which may be displayed in waiting rooms. Many associations mount local and national campaigns (e.g. Spina Bifida Year, 1968; Mental Handicap Week, June 1970) and sponsor television and radio broadcasts. Most parents had had some such contact where an appropriate association existed. Similarly, most parents had read one or more magazine articles relevant to their child's condition and commented on these in interviews. For some these were the only written source of information. Newspapers appeared to be less important, perhaps because the majority of the families took a local paper with little coverage of the topic. The analysis of magazines and newspapers is based on comprehensive files of relevant cuttings and interviews with senior staff of several leading women's magazines.[8]

Finally, it is evident that magazines and newspapers are not
agents of control specifically concerned with parents of disabled
children. Again, like voluntary associations, their mode of
'interaction' with parents is different from that of medical and
social work agencies as are the terms on which such interaction
is initiated and maintained. Parents can choose whether or not
to read relevant publications and disagree with their content
without prejudicing subsequent encounters. I ignore such
differences in treating all the agents as potential sources of
legitimations of the various aspects of parents' suffering.

1   MEDICAL AGENTS

A doctor's major competence lies in the practice of medical
science. No other agent can officially claim this competence and
it is on this that his distinctive status depends and on which he
is ultimately judged (Freidson, 1962; 1970). This is confirmed
in this study by parents who tend to define the hospital as an
irrelevant source of help when they perceive that no medical
skills can help their child. There are, however, two major reasons
why a doctor's everyday practice must also be informed by some
theory of human behaviour.

First, he routinely engages in interaction with the patient,
or, as in the case of a child, his representatives. This involvement
may be necessary, not merely to honour the claims of the client
to respect as a 'person' and to his 'right to know', but to the
proper performance of his medical tasks. It may provide the
documents out of which a diagnosis is constructed and the
co-operation essential to the success of treatment. Second, as
argued earlier, certain disabilities, notably the majority of mental
subnormality, though typically claimed and generally regarded
as a doctor's legitimate concern, do not meet the requirements
of the medical model. Furthermore, no disability can be fully
legitimated within the categories of medical science since the
disabled person, as distinct from the 'sick', remains within social
time and space and must therefore make appropriate adjustments
to its demands and 'live with' his condition.

Given the small part that sociology and psychiatry usually
play in medical training, the theory of behaviour employed by a
doctor is likely to be largely 'commonsense'. It may embody
certain psychiatric concepts that are especially relevant to his
concerns, e.g. the 'over-protective mother' or the 'typical blocking
and distortion' of information by parents dissatisfied with their
child's treatment (Jacobs, *op. cit.*), and sociology may inform the

doctor's actions in several ways. Some may recognize the value of educational programmes, refer patients to them and even help organize them; others may further acknowledge the etiological significance of social factors in producing handicap; but few doctors are likely to have any theoretical knowledge of inter-personal relations. Some doctors confirmed this, telling me of their frequent helplessness and felt incompetence in dealing with parents of the disabled. However, even where neither the doctor nor the parents define his intervention as helpful, it may have significant effects in legitimating the parents' situation.

This can be demonstrated by examining the typical strategies adopted by a doctor in three situations differentiated according to the extent to which they can be defined in terms of medical science: (1) where diagnosis is possible but no treatment is available; (2) where both are possible; (3) where neither is possible. The fourth logically possible type – where treatment is possible but no diagnosis – is excluded since doctors can usually represent it as type (2) through the use of medically 'meaningless' categories, such as 'idiopathic' epilepsy.

(1) Presentation with the 'unavoidable fact' of disability in their child constitutes for parents the loss of normal status and many aspects of Goffman's (1952) analysis of managing another's adaptation to failure are substantiated in this situation. The task is usually performed by a specialist of high status who both carries more conviction and is less likely to incur the parents' hostility. He typically 'stalls' through such tactics as dropping hints that all is not well, allusion to 'strange' tests and procedures or evading questions whilst attempting to take his cue from parents as to how much they want to know. This allows parents to become familiar with their new status whilst not being sure that they will have to accept it, and is apparently often 'successful'. Parents say: 'I knew really before they told me' (Mrs H), or challenge the doctor: 'Are you trying to tell me my child is a mongol?' (Mr N). Moreover, as seen in chapter 5, after the period of uncertainty the news may come as a relief. Doctors then typically allow a short period of 'flooding out' in which they adopt a lay status as 'sympathetic' but this is often terminated by sedation. Such tactics may reflect a concern for hospital routine, but they may constitute an important lesson in the ideology that parents must acquire: 'It's a tragedy but there's no use crying about it.' As Sudnow (1967) indicates, the doctor's 'scientific detachment' may be similar to the attitudes that parents can expect to meet in others.

If parents regard the loss of normal parenthood as reflecting on their competence, or moral character, doctors are well-qualified to reconstruct their definition in clinical terms; that is, though they may feel their expert skills to be irrelevant these may still inform their management of interaction. The meaning of the child's disability is generally presented in medical terms with 'good' reasons for its occurrence, so that other theories of causation, e.g. psychological, which hold the parents liable, can be discounted: 'It can happen to anyone.' Prognosis is presented as more or less uncertain which, as Davis (1960) argues, protects the doctor against future error and avoids provoking 'unmanageable' emotional reactions. More explicitly, it legitimates parents' hopes that their child will be one of the lucky ones and encourages the belief that 'you can never tell' (Jacobs, *op. cit.*).

The doctor then usually engages parents in a programme of 'follow-up' consultations where standardized procedures are used to 'check the child's progress', sometimes regardless of their relevance or efficacy. These provide some control of parents' definitions over time – many become optimistic with their child's initial progress and are reminded that 'he definitely is a mongol though I can't see it' (Mrs H). But they may also be 'supportive', providing expert legitimation for the parents' care of the child, e.g. the important assurance that there is nothing else they should be doing for the child.

(2) In this situation, though 'breaking the news' may still be problematic for the doctor and require similar tactics, medical theory can provide answers to the major problems raised by disability. Not only are both parties likely to define the doctor's intervention as helpful but he can effectively legitimate the occurrence in terms of known pathological processes and offer some control within his own terms of treatment.

Parents are thereby absolved of much responsibility for the child's condition: 'It's all up to them. If they're pleased I am' (Mrs M). Of course, they may retain the everyday management of the child which can include special treatment for his condition and the doctor must attempt to present the disability so that they neither under- nor over-play its severity and regard themselves as able to cope alone. Given this, however, parents regain some control over their situation; major aspects of the child's management become more or less routine, simple 'acceptance' is inappropriate and they may even discover some reward in their special competence.

The effectiveness of legitimations derived from medical science depends on parents' continued belief in their appropriateness. Doubt appears most common where lack of strict management does not lead to a rapid visible deterioration in the child's condition (e.g. obesity, case J; coeliac disease, case S). If they further do not maintain contact with the hospital, then evidently the doctor is powerless and may call in other agents such as social workers or health visitors, the implications of whose activities I examine shortly.

(3) This situation, common in cases of undifferentiated subnormality, is not only the most problematic for the doctor (he is unable to fulfil his professional tasks, yet equally unable simply to admit ignorance) but also the least 'helpful' in any sense for parents. The doctor is often dependent on parents for evidence since they are in a better position to observe the child's everyday behaviour yet, in his terms, this is 'unreliable' and should be elicited without arousing suspicions that he cannot legitimately quell. In this country dissatisfied clients are less able to 'shop around' and the doctor is more likely himself to suffer the repercussions of faulty diagnosis or prognosis.

He is thus highly dependent on inter-personal skills and often is reduced to verbal reassurance – 'Don't worry', or 'Wait and see'. These may have scientific justification in that it is known that some children will later attain normal levels of competence, but to the parent concerned with his individual child they may carry little conviction and rather appear to indicate medical ignorance. Other tactics, however, reflect the attempt to maintain the relevance of the medical perspective and thus the parents' trust in the doctor's competence. Stalling is achieved through presenting 'good' medical reasons for the child's lack of progress (e.g. prematurity; early illness) or, where possible, by concentrating on a specific manageable aspect of the child's condition, such as frequent vomiting, whether or not this is relevant to his presenting complaint. Such methods may be successful in so far as they maintain uncertainty and therefore the parents' hope, as noted above. Parents may themselves seek out further accounts – 'I'm expecting too much of him' (Mrs D) – though these may not absolve them of all blame. Over time, however, they may become less convincing and the doctor may finally use his status to refer his clients to other agencies, e.g. special day-care or nursery school. Such intervention may have more implications for parents' ideology since it may establish the child's disability as a 'fact' to be accepted, but parents may also regain some control over the situation, if, for example like Mrs D, they are requested to co-operate in the special training of the child.

In her study of 180 cerebral palsied children, Hewett (1970) found that only 14 per cent of mothers had received 'specific

help' from their general practioner and this mostly consisted
of regular visiting or obtaining the services of other agencies,
e.g. the Local Education Authority. This finding was generally
substantiated in this study. Though the GP may have less expert
knowledge than the hospital doctor of the child's disability (and
parents are usually aware of this), he can have greater knowledge
of the parents' everyday problems of management. He may
prescribe sedatives for the mother and, where the child is receiving
medical treatment, be important in legitimating changes in the
regime, e.g. in dosage of insulin or phenobarbitone. However,
any explicit attempt to manage parents' adaptations to the
situation – 'You'll just have to accept it' – appear to be defined
as inappropriate by parents. Those mothers who approach their
GP for advice and information found their fears dismissed without
apparent medical justification – 'You mothers worry about
anything' (Mrs B), 'He passed everything off as nothing wrong'
(Mrs G). Such actions may, however, like those of the hospital
doctor, demonstrate to parents that 'really you're on your own'
and 'It's up to you to get what you want' (Mrs K).

The health visitor, with her nursing experience, specialist
training for work with families and knowledge of health and
welfare services, 'seems on the face of it to be the ideal bridge
between the medical world and parents bringing up handicapped
children in their own homes' (Hewett, *op. cit.*, p. 161). However,
her field of competence is indeterminately defined (Jeffreys, 1965)
and, as in Hewett's study, mothers did not expect health visitors
to have special knowledge of their child's handicap nor indeed
to have any special competence relevant to their needs.

In several cases the health visitor did give specific help of
a non-medical kind, e.g. trying to get disposable syringes on
presciption for child E, or, more importantly, talking to Mr N
about his rejection of his mongol child – as Mrs N said: 'We
would have had more trouble without her.' Such cases are sometimes offered as the major justification for the activities of the
health visitor – she may be the only professional in sufficient
contact with families to give help at the appropriate time. In most
cases, however, mothers simply found their health visitor 'nice'
and quite enjoyed their visits. Only one offered explicit ideological
prescriptions, saying that a mongol child was 'God's gift' and that
parents of such children were privileged. However, as noted
earlier, Mrs B was little impressed: 'Everyone has their own way
of looking at it. You know as well as she does' and when she was
told 'You're taking this very well' simply felt depressed: 'I think
I'm too cheery for her.' In general, the health visitors do not

appear to give either direct or indirect help to parents of disabled
children.

2 SOCIAL WORKERS

Social workers do not define themselves as possessing any special
medical competence although they may acquire more than their
lay contemporaries. As Adams says, counselling proceeds 'on the
assumption that all the information possible has been given [to
parents]' (op. cit., p. 47). Social workers' theories about the nature
of disability appear to be those that I argued dominated the
activities of doctors. The 'special problem' with the mentally
handicapped is the permanence of the disability – that 'fundamentally it cannot be altered or even improve beyond certain
rather narrow limits' (ibid., p. 66).

The recognition of social work as a profession was partly
achieved through its adoption of psychiatric theory.[9] Its practice,
at least in this field, can still be regarded as so dominated despite
the evidence of change which I attempt to assess in chapter 8.
One indication of this is that, until recently, casework with the
mentally handicapped was widely regarded as unrewarding. Its
redefinition was based on a rejection of the 'limited view' which
held the 'needs' of the mentally handicapped and their families
to be wholly 'material' and on a recognition of the importance of
emotional factors (ibid.). Second, present-day social work has been
defined as 'the process of helping people with the aid of appropriate
social services to resolve or mitigate a wide range of personal and
social problems which they are unable to meet successfully without
help' (Paisley, 1964, p. 36). The training of social workers is
accordingly aimed at providing a knowledge of the structure of
the social services as well as a competence in 'counselling' skills.
Halmos (1970) argues that there has been an increasing emphasis
on the latter, the general objective being to change the personality
of the client, this being defined as 'therapeutic'. This emphasis
is explicit in the following summary of 'Principles of Casework'
with parents of disabled children, so that far from attempting a
radical critique, or any change of the services available, their
provision may be seen as of secondary importance.

The focus of such work is the 'faulty attitudes and patterns
of behaviour which . . . [prevent] . . . clients from coping satisfactorily with their problems'. Families need careful and skilled
social help through a close personal relationship with the worker
if they are to achieve 'personal acceptance at a deep emotional
level [which] is of course fundamental to arriving at an adjustment

to any serious problem' (Adams, *op. cit.*, p. 64). Not all forms of acceptance are 'healthy'; workers must watch out for denial of the reality of the problem which may be the result of 'instinctive defence mechanism', 'over-compensation', or the attitude that accepts a disabled child as not more than would be expected of life.

Feeling of rejection and blame are 'often rooted in reality experiences' but 'it may be taken that expressions of strong resentment . . . [are] a cover-up for more deep-seated anxieties which are being denied expression' (*ibid.*, p. 69). Families do experience great practical difficulties which may tempt the social worker to offer help but 'though this may often serve a useful ancillary purpose in relieving temporarily some minor pressure, she must remember that the emotional burden is not affected and in some cases material help may even be . . . an irritant because it does not touch the real issue' (*ibid.*, p. 79). It may be hard to watch parents suffering physical strain but often it is through tolerating such stress that the family is able to bear their other problems.

In a later, revised edition of these principles, although the primary focus is presented in the same terms, Adams gives greater emphasis to a social worker's role as 'advocate' for the disabled child and his family, pointing to the responsibility to 'initiate' lines of communication and effective machinery for ensuring co-ordination of services [10] (1972, p. 65). However, the importance of providing such services is justified on the grounds that it 'may fob off immediate breakdown and also lay the foundations for a much more satisfactory long-term adjustment to the situation' (*ibid.*, p. 66). Again, she says that it is vital to investigate the responses of the wider community, e.g. the attitudes of neighbours and employers, but here the social worker's role is to 'take an objective view and . . . give the community angle' so that parents 'may find it easier to tolerate with understanding the less tolerant attitudes they may meet' which may also 'release the parents' own ability to help other people to understand their own special problem' (*ibid.*, p. 83).

The significance of the higher prevalence of mild subnormality in lower social classes is here (cf. chapter 1) given as that 'socially disadvantaged groups are generally susceptible to a range of special pathologies which undermine the general stability of the community' and 'from the opposite angle these socio-cultural factors may have a benign aspect . . . because the subnormal individual is not markedly different from his peers . . . and acceptance as a normal or near-normal member of society is high' (*ibid.*,

p. 72). Resentment is still seen as a cover-up for deeper anxieties since, it is argued, 'relatives who have come to terms with a mentally subnormal member are rarely hostile' (*ibid.*, p. 79).

One can see from such statements how psychiatry can be as powerful a method of legitimation as religion. Any explicitly religious legitimations are likely to be a product of the caseworker's personal beliefs, although Halmos (1960) notes that the quasi-theological language of counselling theorists suggests that they would like to advocate dependence on God. The significance of 'external' factors or the evidence from other perspectives such as sociology is interpreted in psychological terms, and apparent problems as the manifestations of internal psychic disorder of some kind. Some clients have more 'inner strength' than others, but all can be helped to achieve the main end of 'acceptance' with the possible compensatory by-product of contributing to community cohesion.

In practice, few social workers might appear as detached and consistent as the theory advocates. One mother, Mrs B, who did contact a medical social worker found her friendly and easy to chat to; another, Mrs N, definitely helpful in discussing her husband's rejection of their mongol child and telling them both that the child could be taken into care if necessary. In the long run, some parents might indeed come to define social workers as the trustworthy counsellors they set out to be. Social workers are skilled in managing interaction and supposed not to 'interfere gratuitously' but to 'first establish themselves as a recognised source of help' (Adams, 1960, p. 70). Moreover, their common-sense beliefs and assumptions may produce expressions of sympathy as much as of stigmatization. Further, the concepts of psychiatry may not of course be wholly irrelevant. Parents do experience feelings of guilt, resentment, etc., and may find them difficult to discuss with friends and relatives; psychological factors are important in explanations of disability (though in terms of etiology as much as of needs or adjustment. Zigler, 1966).

However, as Hewett says: 'How many of the "anxious", "aggressive" . . . parents . . . would simply "disappear" if both day and residential care were . . . freely available?' (1970, p. 169). Moreover, as argued earlier, the fact that psychiatric legitimations may be experienced as liberating is not incompatible with the fact that they 'scientifically' transform experiences which may be seen as a challenge to the official moral and social order into a means of achieving 'deeper knowledge' of oneself and of that order. Where social workers do come into contact with parents of disabled children they can provide the most coherent ideology: like

Nietzsche's priest, we may see one of their major activities as 'channelling' the course of resentment.

3 VOLUNTARY ASSOCIATIONS

Most voluntary associations were initiated by parents of the disabled with the assistance of other groups such as special foods manufacturers, but their central organization has become increasingly the paid or voluntary responsibility of professional agents, social workers, doctors, public relations officers and so on (Hancock and Willmott, 1965; Katz, 1961). Their publications are therefore informed by a variety of theories, with the general and noted exception of religion.

The special competence of voluntary associations, given official recognition in the 1948 National Health Act, derives from their detailed knowledge of the phenomena pertaining to a particular type of disability. Major components of their publications are accordingly: medical information and reports of research progress, indications of the typical problems that parents[11] face and suggested tactics for managing them. Special equipment is publicized, often by the manufacturers, details of special provisions and facilities, such as special schools and free holidays, are given and members encouraged to explore their rights in such matters. Members contribute news of their own inventions, recipes for those on a special diet and examples of how they coped with problematic situations such as staying in a hotel or going on a long journey.

Such content is not of course without ideological implications. Disabilities are commonly presented as varying enormously in severity, prognosis as uncertain and possible complications or death rarely mentioned. Optimism is thus encouraged. Research work is reported on a world-wide scale; major fund-raising campaigns are often associated with show business or other celebrities, and local ones are shown to be taking place all over the country. All this helps to create the impression that much is being done and many people care. Advice on everyday problems is typically organized by such general principles as 'Routine is the Keyword for the Mentally Handicapped' and stresses the crucial role played by parents, as expressed in such maxims as 'Love is Life' or 'Balance is Life', although with the plentiful help of specialists, thus engaging parents in a team effort to help their child. Special educational provisions are so presented that even training centres for the severely disabled are 'always very happy places . . . staffed by those with a real love for retarded children' (Pamphlet: *The Spina Bifida Child*). Parents are assured that advice is given after full consideration of the individual case; that is, in the final analysis, parents should trust professional agents.

The other distinctive component of the activities of voluntary associations is the publicization of various forms of discrimination against the disabled (e.g. in employment; insurance; the social services) and attempts to rectify injustices. Several associations campaigned in support of the Chronically Sick and Disabled Persons Act (1970) and joyfully claimed much of the credit for its passing. However, though a few associations even assert 'influencing the quality of state provisions for the disabled' as one of their official aims (e.g. the National Society for Mentally Handicapped Children), none appears able to ignore the constraints imposed by 'public opinion'. The ways in which such considerations may influence an agency's practice have been extensively analysed by Scott (*op. cit.*). I shall only note that the three stated aims common to most voluntary associations – (1) helping the disabled and their relatives; (2) furthering research into the disability; (3) informing and influencing public opinion – depend on the presentation of a conception of the disability and its sufferers which will raise money, encourage research and increase state provisions. To the extent that success requires the co-operation of the sufferers, the activities of voluntary associations are centrally and often explicitly directed at managing their ideology.

The strategies used in general illustrate the commonsense theodicies outlined earlier. Thus, parents' efforts on behalf of the mentally handicapped child will be rewarded with 'boundless affection', multiple sclerosis creates devoted marriages as compared to 'those licence-loving intellectuals who . . . tear down the bastions of . . . matrimony' (*Multiple Sclerosis News*, Autumn, 1970). Further, like the converts of psychiatry, the disabled may constitute a benefit to society as a whole. Thus, in the journal last cited: 'Is it only in adversity that the human race shines?' or in *Diabetes in Children* (a pamphlet): 'It is not too much to say that the self-discipline demanded by the diabetic life can help to build in the individual the strength of character and sense of values which render the greatest service to the community, be it local or world-wide'. Thereby parents are encouraged to minimize and redefine their misfortunes and this can act both to provide compensation and to support the public demonstration of their 'strength of character' in adversity, and therefore worthiness of support.

However, simply 'being deserving' is not enough – parents should not take the support given them by normals for granted, and should show that they are willing to help themselves. 'Grate-fulness' and 'self-help' are common themes in the journals, e.g. 'It is up to the NSMHC to educate the public'; 'if the recent Act makes the public complacent who can blame them?' (*M.S. News*, Summer, 1970). Reports of special schools and fund-raising events stress 'the outstanding efforts' of professional agents 'to whom we owe so much' (Scottish ASBAH *Annual Report*, 1969) and the kindness of normals which 'gives one hope for the future' (*M.S. News*, Autumn, 1970). Branch society reports stress the 'hard work, warm hearts and willing hands' of their members, under-playing any difficulties encountered: 'There [has been sorrow] but intermingled with the laughter and fun of building up together' (*Newsletter*, SCMHC, March, 1970). A typical statement of the ideal model for members is 'The generosity of local people gave C his chance and he made the most of it' (Croydon Spastics Society, *Annual Report*, 1965/66).

Members' contributions generally support such prescriptions: 'It was up to me to prove to employers that I was capable' (*The Candle*, British Epilepsy Association, Autumn, 1970). Letters and articles give examples of successes achieved: famous sportsmen who are diabetics; a diabetic member who cycled across Europe; an epileptic who became a nurse after many difficulties. Photo-graphs of children may be accompanied by such statements as: 'I cannot regard my happy, smiling four-year-old boy as a tragedy.' Some members go even further: 'Be grateful you're an epileptic' (*ibid.*);'How fortunate we are only to have an ileostomy'(*Newsletter*, British Ileostomy Association, Winter, 1962).

Such contributions provide models of successful adaptations to disability and thus implicitly help manage the actions of new members. Few instances of deviance from the official ideology appear to be published and those which are may be explicitly sanctioned by other members. One wife of a multiple sclerosis sufferer wrote complaining of the inadequate and unsympathetic treatment she had received from various agencies (*M.S. News*, Autumn, 1969), and in the next issue three letters were printed either expressing outright disapproval of her remarks or sympathy: 'We cannot help feeling bitter about the general indifference of the public', but reiterating that: 'It is up to us to force ourselves on the public. Many people want to help us if only we tell them how.'

4   MAGAZINES AND NEWSPAPERS

Two major characteristics of magazine articles are apparent. First, they are 'personalized' accounts. They focus on individual

cases and usually take the perspective of a mother, though sometimes that of, for example, a benefactress of a rehabilitation clinic
or a 'mother' in a residential home. Titles reflect this emphasis:
'My Child is Different' (*Woman's Own*, 18 April 1970); 'My
Mongol Babies' (*Family Doctor*, February 1965); or often simply
the child's name. Second, they are invariably 'success stories'.
Thus: 'All in Their Stride', 'Of Faith and Love', 'The Purpose
Behind it All' (*Woman's Own*, 11 November 1965; 18 July 1964;
27 April 1963). The introduction to 'Andrew My Son' typifies the
presentation of such accounts. 'The devotion of a mother for her
spastic child is one of the most remarkable human documents
we have ever published. It shows how hope can be plucked from
the seemingly hopeless situation . . . how love and determination
can give the handicapped a very real stake in life' (*Woman*, 25
November 1967).

Some publications prefer to use professional writers, but those
which do accept 'first-person' accounts, reconstruct them as
necessary to produce a beginning, middle and happy end. As one
journalist commented, 'even cats are rarely allowed to die'. The
difficulties parents face are fully documented and they may be
allowed to admit that 'I let myself become sour' or 'at first I
thought – why my family?' (*Woman's Own*, 30 July 1966; 29
March 1969), but they always overcome such problems and
eventually see their efforts as worthwhile. If earlier hopes are
unjustified they are redefined: 'Forget your dreams of building a
cathedral and build a parish church' (*Woman*, 25 November 1967);
if little progress has been achieved at the end there is still hope
though 'the road is longer' (*Woman's Own*, 19 August 1967).
Compensation may come with the realization that 'some things
are worth more than you as an individual'; happiness may lie in
'knowledge of the truth . . . facing up to it and dedicating the rest of
my life to the training of my son' (*Woman's Own*, 26 August 1967).

As in voluntary association publications, few examples of
deviance can be found. In one instance, a celebrity (Brian Rix)
put the case for institutionalization of a mongol child on the
grounds that 'she loves anyone who is kind to her'. This, however,
is juxtaposed with an example of parents who kept their child,
made a direct appeal: 'Help a mother keep her mongol baby – save
her from the anguish of parting from her darling baby', and received
explicit approval: 'Mrs H knows she has done the right thing'
(*Woman's Own*, 9 June 1962). The only unqualified case of deviance
found was in a magazine which the author of a historical analysis
of the development of women's magazines distinguishes as being
edited by a man, having 'blazed a long trial of outspokenness'

and on this account been expected to be short-lived (White, 1970, p. 166). Titled 'Life Sentence? Harriet is For Ever', the mother denies all validity to the above prescriptions: 'special gift? – this is complete nonsense'; parents are not made better, marriages are torn apart and 'in some degree I really do hate her. At the same time I am filled with hate against something unknown that could allow this to happen. If there is some meaning . . . I have not seen it' (*She*, April 1966).

In magazines, therefore, there is further evidence of the commonsense transformation of suffering so that it is contained within and reaffirms the prevailing symbolic order. It does, however, appear to be expressed as a more general principle than has been so far encountered. Articles on disability are included less for their particular content than as 'human documents' of 'triumph over adversity'. No straight medical information is published ('Doctors Corners' are for common and seasonal complaints) nor are there contributions on 'How to Look After Your Spina Bifida Baby'. Moreover, it does seem that editorial staff assume not so much a lack of interest amongst their predominantly 'normal' readership as a positive desire not to know too much. As one said: 'It's a terrible thought to implant [that it might happen to you].' This speaker also said he aimed to produce the 'right kind of emotional attitude' in his readers – one of sympathy and genuine admiration. However, it seems unlikely that the intended corollary, 'Could I do it?', would be answered in the affirmative. As in the explanations of the behaviour of the disabled criticized in chapter 1, heroics, according to an Aristotelian logic, are performed by 'heroes'.

For parents of the disabled such articles, like those in voluntary associations publications, may provide examples of successful adaptations to the problems of disability, indicate what their efforts could achieve and the different rewards that they can look for and that others have been happy to accept. They may, however, have additional implications. First, not only do magazines mostly report successes but they have little control over parents' interpretations of these. They may, therefore, encourage parents not only to hope for the best but to believe in miracles. It is normally atypical achievements that are most remembered: e.g. the diabetic who crossed the Atlantic on a raft; the mongol who learned to type; the spastic who became a novelist. Second, parents, like other readers, may learn to locate their experience within the context of many other forms of suffering, and their identity within the company of all those who have similarly faced adversity.

Newspapers, of course, operate under very different conditions. Unlike magazines, which have to prepare issues several months in advance, they can cover topical events. Most of their coverage of disability consists of reports of, for example, conferences, parliamentary debates, or research findings. The 'tabloids' tend to have less medical and sociological content but certain 'discoveries', e.g. that 4 per cent of all children need some kind of special education, are widely reported. The handicapped appear to be a generally newsworthy group at present. Headlines stressing 'spastic' or 'subnormal' imply that, like 'student', 'drug addict', or age, they are socially significant attributes. Some categories of disability are especially topical – 'newly-discovered' autism was reported almost as frequently as all other disabilities together in 1963–4.

Second, newspapers do appear to adopt a more militant approach, though of course the subject can receive proportionately insignificant coverage. There seem to be more reports and features which criticize existing state provisions. All the papers appeared to support the recent campaign preceding the Chronically Sick and Disabled Persons Act (1970), stressing the 'rights' of the handicapped, to 'fight'. The *Guardian* used an explicit political analogy: 'The Third World of the Handicapped' (9 July 1970). The readers may be more directly implicated: 'What is Britain Doing?' (*Daily Mirror*, 22 December 1969); 'How can people be so heartless?' (*Sunday Mirror*, 24 May 1970). Employers and local authorities are specific targets: 'Spastic Tells of Torture of Life' (because he cannot get a job) (*News Chronicle*, 2 May 1960); 'Bognor Refuses School for the Handicapped' (*Daily Express*, 26 October 1961). Some papers may even sponsor a protest – for example, on the occasion of 'Beach Hut for Spastics Banned' (*Daily Mirror*, 15 January 1964).

Many features on individual cases are interchangeable with those in magazines, though they are rarely first-person accounts. Thus: 'Spastic Marjorie Inspires the Disabled' (*News Chronicle*, 27 August 1966), and 'Private Courage Signing on, Sir' (*Daily Express*, 9 July 1970) (the first spastic soldier) similarly describe the 'tremendous struggles', and 'remarkable achievements' encountered in 'climbing the Everest of normality' (*Manchester Guardian*, 18 October 1961). In these accounts sorrow similarly 'leads from darkness into light'; creates 'good that would never otherwise have been done' and 'we learn so much about ourselves in the process'. But there are examples in all papers of cases without a happy ending, where parents are left in 'drudgery and despair' (*Sun*, 2 October 1969), and which may even argue that the real problems for parents are ordinary and everyday and lead to physical exhaustion as much as spiritual enrichment.

Finally, though cases of deviance are still 'good' news, e.g. 'Nurses Adopt Baby that Mother Turned her Back on' (*Daily Express*, 1 August 1969) they often receive some support: 'It's easy to condemn – how would the rest of us cope?' (*Daily Mail*, 2 August 1969); 'A Plea for Deprived Parents' denies that normals are kind and generous (*Daily Telegraph*, 8 August 1969); 'Must a Mother be a Martyr?' quotes a mother: 'If the most wonderful thing a woman could get was an endless child my position would be ideal. I could always be Mummy' (*Sunday Telegraph*, 6 July 1969).

Together the expressions of the several agents constitute a more or less concerted definition of the situation of parents of the disabled and the appropriate action within it. Doctors are usually the first to introduce parents to their new situation and, with specifically medical or other tactics, manage both their initial and subsequent responses. These include such matters as the behaviour which parents should adopt towards the child and the extent to which they should make special allowance for his disability; parents' attitudes towards themselves, their responsibility for and power to influence the child's condition and hence, indirectly and directly, parents' presentations of themselves to, and identification by, others. Throughout, the doctor acts to sustain parents' hope and trust in his competence, or, where his own skills are inadequate, in that of other agents to which he makes referral.

Both social workers and voluntary associations accept medical definitions of the child's disability as given, either excluding consideration of the issues involved from their own activities, or presenting them in the same, if less esoteric, terms. Both are more explicitly concerned with parents' individual adjustment to the problems of having a disabled child and the repercussions that this may have on other aspects of family life. They discuss the difficulties that parents may encounter in interaction with others in the community, but similarly counsel optimism and tolerance rather than despair. Parents are encouraged to see how they can help others and not to expect help as their automatic right.

Towards those agencies from whom assistance can be expected the appropriate attitude is again one of trust in their goodwill and judgment. Voluntary associations, magazines and newspapers acknowledge that parents do not always receive services to which they are entitled, but similarly approve those who respond with understanding rather than resentment. In general, parents' misfortunes are minimized and their suffering transformed into an unfortunate necessity from which great compensation may yet be gained. This may be on an individual inter-personal or cosmic level where it is presented as a manifestation of a phenomenon experienced by all those who similarly embrace their fate.

Of course, to point to the effective accord with which the several agents legitimate parents' suffering is not to say that in practice inter-agency relations are always harmonious. Paisley (*op. cit.*) presents the ideal model of co-operation and communication when she says that the GP has a central role to play especially if long-term supervision of the disabled child is necessary; the health visitor is well-placed to get early information about the child and his family, and the voluntary associations are important in helping to cope with parents' problems. The individual agencies may take a different view and even make evident such conflicts to parents.

Thus, according to some parents' reports, GPs claim that hospital consultants provide inadequate information for proper management of their patients at home; health visitors make similar complaints about GPs, and I was warned by a social worker not to 'poach' on the territory of a certain health visitor. In both the publications of several voluntary associations and conversations with social workers, complaints were made that doctors often do not refer clients to them. One doctor said of voluntary associations that they provide 'just picnics for the kiddies' and told one mother (Mrs K) that he did not usually recommend them to parents. One senior social worker reckoned that half of their work with the disabled consisted of protecting them from the voluntary associations.

Further, certain differences between the expressions of the agents are evident. The activities of voluntary associations differ from those of doctors in that they discuss everyday problems in detail and provide lay versions of medical explanations. They differ too from social workers, since they do not deny the existence of 'external' problems and may annihilate them through social action rather than psychiatric interpretation. Thus they are more 'radical' than those other agents and do not encourage simple 'acceptance'. Newspapers also adopt a more militant line confronting 'the public' with general and specific instances of parents' suffering, and thus provide some legitimation for such 'deviant' actions as institutionalizing a disabled child, expressing resentment, and refusing to redefine misfortunes. Parents may act on such precedents and challenge the prescriptions of social workers and doctors if, for example, they seek scarce social services to which they are entitled or expect the 'miracle cures' about which they have read.

However, as the recent case of the thalidomide children demonstrated, not publicity alone but organized group action is necessary to any success in legal confrontation. Voluntary associations have, as noted, achieved recognition for similar claims, but they do not provide an alternative to the official morality. They do not constitute an 'own' group for parents of the disabled which, like the 'wise', provides a 'circle of lament to which [the individual] can withdraw for moral support and for the comfort of feeling at home (Goffman, 1968, p. 32). Their most general prescription can be summarized as 'making the best of things with good grace'.

Elements of a radical ideology are then available to parents but the great majority do not, as will be seen shortly, make use of such accounts in face-to-face situations. Some of the reasons why this might be the case are discussed in chapter 8. Here it will be observed simply that the general agreement as to the correct meaning of the experience of having a disabled child can be seen as an expression of fundamental similarities in the theories in which such meanings are grounded and despite any inter-disciplinary demarcation disputes. Evidently, I cannot hope to give here an adequate account of these but shall note several points.

Between the various sciences various patterns of mutual influence have been suggested. Berger (1965) points out that all schools of sociology have been affected in some way by psycho-analytic ideas, and Taber et al. (op. cit.) present the 'medical model' as the model of explanation dominating contemporary psychiatry. In chapters 1 and 2, I argued that much sociology of disability and the family takes for granted commonsense and/or medical categories. Medical science, as noted earlier, is predominantly based on a mechanistic model in which man is treated with the objective attitude once thought appropriate to the inanimate world.

Berger and Luckmann (1967) make the general point that the second and subsequent levels of legitimation are grounded in the 'incipient' or 'pretheoretical' level which constitutes simple affirmations built into the vocabulary of a given language. Bowker argues that all explanations of suffering are grounded in what are taken to be the 'realities of life'. Particular religious accounts

reveal different conceptions of the whole nature and purpose of
existence: they 'conceive differently the nature of the joy
attainable by man. For this reason, they give different accounts
of human nature – that is, of what men are in themselves' (*op.
cit.*, p. 290). Legitimations of suffering appeal to facts which lie
beyond justification. They assert 'such is human life', there is no
other explanation outside or above it.

All the theories assert an essentially similar account of human
life. Whether the concern is with his body or his mind, mankind
is conceived as a collectivity of more or less isolated individuals.
The condition of a disabled child, the problems he presents and
his parents' responses to them are more the product of internal
dysfunctioning or imbalance of some kind than of bad nutrition,
housing, or lack of financial and other resources as themselves
socially-constructed and maintained inequalities.

Kelman (1964) observes that, in practice, such an individual
focus is fostered and sustained by the one-to-one relationship of
the clinical situation. Theoretically, it may be derived from the
Judaeo-Christian tradition. Suttles notes that it is a peculiarity
of this tradition to impute what it regards as small and mean to
man's natural condition, with Original Sin as its 'sacred charter'
for doing so. Hence 'morality is high and lofty, whereas avarice
and greed are low instincts, and generosity and charity are noble
gestures' (1972, p. 130). Suttles argues that Judaeo-Christian
societies have mostly 'relied on these natural vices to distinguish
among the statuses of people and to induce them into the routine
activities which those societies have required' (*ibid.*, p. 131).

In so far as shared cultural or environmental considerations
are now recognized they are treated as uncontrollable facts of
life which, like the incidence of disability, parents must accept,
or as matters which, like the disabled child's diagnosis and
treatment, can only be understood through the appropriate use
of expert categories and techniques. The individual should not
expect to be able to take effective action on his own initiative.

Hence, an individual's knowledge, not only of his particular
problems and of the appropriate ways of dealing with them, but
of his very self is not directly accessible to him; ordinary human
nature as identified with its psychophysiological constitution is
by definition incapable of transcending itself and its situation.
The implications of this will be further discussed in chapter 8,
where it may be seen that the 'theories' as implemented by the
various agencies, whether unintentionally or otherwise, constitute
what Berger (1965, p. 40) characterizes as 'the adjustment
technology without which our society could hardly get along'.

Acceptance and adjustment

As potential sources of legitimation of the suffering of parents who have a disabled child, doctors, social workers, voluntary associations, magazines and newspapers, express substantial agreement. In practice and over particular cases they may come into conflict. According to their theoretical grounds their statements may be of varying degrees of sophistication. However, they similarly define the parents' situation so that it appears consistent with the normal order of child-rearing, and parents have no legitimate claims to be unfairly disadvantaged, nor therefore cause for resentment or challenge to the official morality. I suggested that this is because religion, medical science, psychiatry and sociology as they are generally practised, are founded in a common definition of the facts of life and the possibility of individual action in face of them.

In this chapter, I examine the actual uses which parents make of such legitimations in their statements about differences between their experiences and that of normal parents, and attempt to show that the legitimations expressed by the agencies together constitute an ideology.

Berger and Luckmann define ideology as 'a particular definition of reality [which] comes to be attached to a concrete power interest' (1967, p. 141). They point out that the term only has sense in a pluralist situation: thus one cannot speak of Christianity as an ideology in the Middle Ages when serfs and lords alike 'inhabited' a Christian universe. 'The distinctiveness of ideology is rather that the *same* overall universe is interpreted in different ways depending upon concrete vested interests within the society in question' (*ibid.*). At any one point in time a given ideology may encompass more or less of everyday experience; be held by more or less groups with more or less power. It may be more or less tolerated by groups holding power in the society and be more or less of a challenge and threat to the existing symbolic universe. Through time an ideology may become attached to other and different interest groups, integrated into and even replace the definitions held by those with most power – in which case it may no longer be regarded as an 'ideology' at all.

Geertz (1964) points out that sociology generally lacks a non-evaluative conception of ideology, since it is commonly regarded as a 'distortion' of 'reality'. He argues that this is because, although the sources of ideology have been adequately diagnosed as various kinds of 'strains' in the existing institutional order and it is now taken for granted that they serve the interests of particular groups, the processes by which they operate to alleviate strains and serve interests have been crudely conceptualized in the terms of an 'anaemic psychology'. Ideologies 'reflect' or 'correspond' to psychological strains on the one hand, they produce 'catharsis', 'solidarity' and 'morale' on the other. Geertz observes that the relation between an ideology and social reality is 'much too complicated to be comprehended in terms of a vague and unexamined notion of emotive resonance' (*ibid.*, p. 57). 'Whatever else ideologies might be – projections of unacknowledged fears, disguises for ulterior motives . . . they are most distinctively maps of problematic social reality . . . which attempt to render otherwise incomprehensible social situations meaningful, to so construe them as to make it possible to act purposefully within them' (*ibid.*, p. 64).

As systems of interrelated legitimations, ideologies give cognitive and normative order to particular aspects of social reality; they 'name' situations in such a way as to entail an attitude towards them. Such naming makes disconnected, unrealized private feelings or emotions publicly available. As Geertz argues, the construction and use of an ideology is 'an occurrence not "in the head" but in that public world where "people talk together, name things, make assertions, and, to a degree, understand each other" ' (*ibid.*, p. 60). Hence an ideology is not subject to the standards of scientific rationality which is practised under the assumption of moral neutrality, but, like all common sense (see chapter 5) is 'accurate' if it serves to make sense of action in a particular situation.

Further, as Bittner (1963) points out, it would be 'unrealistic' to expect particular expressions of an ideology to relate uniquely to its organizing elements. Particular actions may be legitimated on a number of grounds, thus 'over-determining' the outcome; the same basic meaning or meanings may be used in many particular instances; hence the illustrations which I give below might have been differently categorized. Indeed, this is a requirement of a 'successful' ideology: the more general the applicability of a legitimation, the less likely it is to be invalidated by actual experience. Thus, the most general 'it's all good experience' can be invoked in any situation.

Goffman presents an analysis of the 'philosophy' or 'code' that the individual stigmatized are 'asked to accept'. He says that this provides not only a 'platform and a politics' – or instructions on how to treat others – but recipes for appropriate attitudes to regarding oneself. None the less, this presentation remains principally at the level of specifically situated recipes for action, dealing with such matters as: the extent to which the stigmatized should present himself as normal or different; how much they should 'face up' to their problems, neither under- nor over-playing them. It prescribes ways of dealing with embarrassment and the reactions of others, the kind of behaviour that should be accepted, attacked, or ignored. Goffman also points out the predominantly psychiatric rhetoric of the stigmatized's philosophy as it is informed by the responses of normals, as opposed to the more 'political' orientation of the 'own' (1968, pp. 129–50). It will be apparent that, in substance, my analysis is very similar to that of Goffman. However, I have attempted not only to examine the apparent theoretical forces of parents' ideology, but to spell out its principal organizing elements or structure.

I present what parents say in relation to six elements of their ideology, and regard these as what Douglas (1970) calls 'deep moral meanings' which can be variously deployed to construct the meaning of a particular instance of suffering in such a way that otherwise 'non-parental' experiences and activities are symbolically transformed into apparent congruence with conventional parenthood as defined in the official morality.

What one 'sees' in parents' uses of the ideology are what were presented in chapters 5 and 6 as accounts which involve appeals to situationally appropriate motives or grounds for their actions which induce *alter* to regard that action as right and moral. What they 'are doing' is 'linking' actions to motives or intentions which are culturally defined as 'possible' for parents to hold, as part of the biography of a normal parent, thus displaying the relevance of that category to interpretations of their actions and enabling others to recognize that parenthood is still 'going on'. This is accomplished despite the discrepancies between the parents' situation and that of normal parents since these discrepancies are reconciled as they are presented in terms of the ideology.

I first present the ideology as a system of the six elements which together are of sufficiently general relevance to be applicable to the situation of any parent who has a disabled child. Evidently the practical usages of the ideology by individual parents, or to which elements they actually do appeal, depends, as chapter 2 showed, upon the contingencies of their immediate situation. Hence, second, I discuss some of these differences and suggest typical relationships between them, summarizing and integrating the analyses offered in previous chapters. Finally, I take up the relationship between parents' statements and their beliefs and attempt to assess what it might 'really mean' to have a disabled child.

THE IDEOLOGY: ITS GENERAL FORM

1 'ACCEPTANCE OF THE INEVITABLE'

This seems to be the secular version of the 'masochistic attitude' which, as noted in chapter 7, persists as a prevalent commonsense theodicy. It entails the submission by an individual to the inscrutability of 'fate', an admission that there are some things one cannot understand since they 'just happen'. Berger (1969) points out that this attitude is in fact prior to any specific theodicy and, theoretically, its expression is sufficient to preclude that of any resentment at the unfairness of one's suffering. Mrs B[I] said 'We've all had a broken heart' and 'some days I am awfu' depressed', but also 'you only say "why should this happen to us?" at first', disclaiming intentionality, 'I couldn't help it . . . you just don't think'. At a paediatric assessment they did not ask about the child's mongolism: 'We knew what it was so what else was there?' Mrs K[I] said 'it's silly really'; that is, there is no sense in resentment if the occurrence is no one's fault and 'it could happen to anyone'. Such expressions are most common where the onset of disability is sudden and parents' responses those of 'meaninglessness' ('I can't see it'), or 'powerlessness' ('I can't believe it'). That is, the meaning of the occurrence is not discoverable in the child's behaviour; the event constitutes, in Schutz's (1964) term, an imposed system of relevancies which, so long as it is not transformed into intrinsic relevancies, remains partly incomprehensible (see chapter 5). 'He doesna' look to me, but there it is' is, in Mrs H[I]'s words, an apparent example of treating the occurrence of disability as data, as conditions for subsequent actions, or of 'accepting' it.

Mrs B[I] put it differently: 'She was the next in line and we got her.' This might be regarded as an expression of the statistical fact that since a given proportion of children are born disabled, it has to happen to somebody. I quoted Soddy as saying that parents who realize that the chance of having a subnormal child is at least one in a hundred 'have gone some way towards accepting it' (1972, p. 46). Simple resignation sometimes appeared mitigated by parents' expressed belief that scientific advance might eliminate the problem for future generations. Several parents accounted for their agreeing to be interviewed in such terms: 'If it can't help us it may help someone.' However, parents appealed to additional grounds in accounting for their continued ability to care for the disabled child. Mrs N reported her GP as telling her 'you'll just have to accept it', and said 'it's not a question of accepting it, I just wondered if there was something I should be doing to help him'.

2 'PARTIAL LOSS OF THE TAKEN-FOR-GRANTED'

This element indicates the suspension of those normal beliefs about the world as analysed by Schutz (*op. cit.*, especially pp. 91–104) by which we assume that life tomorrow will be essentially the same as today, that it will follow a typically predictable course. Thus, the young and healthy plan their activities on the assumption that they will remain alive in the foreseeable future, without which assumption everyday action would be impossible. Of course, people recognize and may say that 'you never know', but for many parents of the disabled this awareness seems to be heightened.

In general, as chapter 5 showed, all parents are more than normally aware of their active part in constructing the meaning of their child's condition. In no case were their methods of doing so the same as those entailed by normal child-rearing. Explicit accounts in such terms as 'taking it from day to day' (Mrs H), or 'we treat her as normal now and wait and see if she needs special training' (Mrs B), were mostly invoked, as chapter 6 showed, where parents neither regarded their child as 'sick', nor were sure that their normal methods of handling him, if appropriate at present, would continue to be so, and did not therefore know how much time and energy they should invest in his care at the possible expense of other members. The ability to claim a working definition of their child's behaviour is essential to parents' appearance as able to care for him. Especially where parents know that the child is not going to be normal whatever his present behaviour, saying 'now he's just a normal baby . . . but we're looking for it that there'll be nothing wrong' (Mrs H) sustains this present appearance. It indicates that parents are prepared for changes in their treatment of the child as they become appropriate and, since they are not being 'over-optimistic', will not suffer great disappointment if the child's development fails to meet their expectations.

However, this is not inconsistent with the expression of positive satisfaction since 'you notice what progress he does make' (Mrs H), and even 'you're glad for each day he's still alive' (Mrs Q). 'Anything can happen' also legitimates a belief in miracles, though in practice this appears to require 'scientific' grounds, if only 'doctors can do wonderful things today' (Mrs F).

Although continuous uncertainty brings some compensations, this claim to 'world-openness' may be difficult to sustain. Weber (1969) argues that most of us require compensation or assurance in the here-and-now; hence the Calvinist doctrine of predestination was often 'corrupted', so that 'good works' could constitute evidence of being elect by God. Those parents who know that their child is going to be disabled seem especially likely to invoke other meanings of their situation.

3 'THE REDEFINITION OF GOOD AND EVIL'

This enables the avoidance of an apparent inability to know the meaning of anything: it preserves the basic parameters by which we evaluate the phenomena in any social world. In general, parents demonstrate their recognition of other forms of suffering compared to which their own is said to be less. As Mrs N said, 'At first it seems all black, but you're quick to realize there's shades of black.' Mothers spoke of cases of polio or the thalidomide children, about whom they had read, or the variety of illnesses and disabilities which they encountered in the hospital or at the baby clinic. Mrs B[1] was immediately confronted by the comparison with her sister-in-law, Mrs F's, spina bifida baby. Initially, she thought herself worse off since 'at least they can do something for F'. Subsequently, however, she revised this interpretation, saying of her mongol daughter: 'At least she's got her health.'

How evaluations are constructed in practice can vary infinitely. The 'same' phenomena can be evidence of 'good' and 'evil' depending on the particular aspects of parents' own and others' situations which they emphasize. Thus, Mrs B said, 'At least she's got the use of her limbs', whilst the mother of a spina bifida child in one of the pilot interviews said: 'I should be thankful she's not mentally retarded.' If the child does die it is still 'a blessing' to Mrs T, whose newsagent's spastic daughters were evidence of her child's possible future. Even the discovery that their child is disabled may, as chapter 5 showed, be seen as better than the preceding uncertainty. Mrs K[I] said, 'It was just a miracle we found out she was diabetic'. Mrs H said, 'We were better off knowing to start with', citing the case of a woman who had not found out that her child was a mongol till he was four years old: 'I think that's much worse.'

Further, evaluations are, of course, always relative. Parents point to ways in which their situation could be worse. Many thought themselves lucky to live in a city where medical facilities were so good, especially Mrs A, since she had heard that children born elsewhere with a breach of the oesophagus often died before they could be transported for treatment. Over all, as Mrs H said, 'there's always someone that wee bittie worse off than yourself'.

However, evaluation of phenomena as good or evil cannot appear arbitrary if it is effectively to legitimate action. It is commonly presented within the context of the next element as constituting a more fundamental and lasting 'discovery'.

4   'THE DISCOVERY OF TRUE VALUES'

This provides a basis for ordering particular evaluations such that they appear to reveal what is 'essentially true' or 'ultimately right'. It thus maintains the necessary 'externality' of the moral order whereby phenomena are located in the nature of God or Being, rather than in the contingent accomplishments of individuals engaged in everyday interaction. Individual sufferings thereby attain some degree of impersonality and parents' accounts appear empirically unfalsifiable, not easily challenged by others or events beyond their control. Mrs B regarded themselves as the poor relations of the family, contrasting her husband's job situation, where he worked long hours with no hope of ever managing his own shop, with that of his brother, whose father-in-law had bought him a business. However, she said 'Money isn't everything. I've realized that now', and 'at least we've got our health'. Mrs K said 'Normally you don't realize how lucky you are', and, as seen earlier, parents who appreciate whatever progress the child does make may contrast this with their attitude to the other children where 'it was all coming natural' (Mrs H).

With this 'deeper knowledge' of the world, like the 'elect' who discover the mysteries of God, everyday trials and tribulations may be discounted as insignificant and no grounds for complaint. Mrs N reported thinking 'what has she got to worry about?', when a neighbour said she was worried about her child's imminent operation for hernia, although she also said that she felt 'mean' at the same time. Such events were the major occasions of parents' expressing any resentment, but as chapter 6 showed, parents generally reported displaying tolerance, imputed good intentions or ignorance on the part of others and asserted: 'It doesn't really matter if other people are unkind.'

5   'THE POSITIVE VALUE OF SUFFERING'

This is the general form of the second major commonsense theodicy discussed in chapter 7. According to this, suffering is the means by which individuals atone for their previous sins and/or earn various kinds of reward or compensation. Examples of these have already been seen in parents' claims to a deeper understanding, greater appreciation of their relative advantages, or of the normal processes of child-rearing. This element is thus more basic than the previous three in and through which it may be seen as constituted.

In general, suffering 'always brings out the best in people'. This can apply to the disabled child himself, or to parents. Mr E thought his diabetic child 'seems more intelligent and reflective now'; Mrs K said, 'I think I'm more understanding'. This can also therefore aid the acceptance of stigmatization by others. Suffering together is presented as favourably influencing inter-personal relationships. It 'brings you closer together', either to the child, 'I feel more for her than I did for the others' (Mrs L), or to one's spouse and the rest of the family. As chapter 6 showed, parents reported, if anything, a greater degree of affection between the disabled child and his brothers and sisters, and Mrs H her pleasurable surprise when her normal children devoted much of their time to their mongol brother, asserting: 'He's my brother, isn't he?' Acknowledged discords between husband and wife were often presented as having ultimately beneficial consequences either for the child or for the parent: as Mrs K said, 'We couldn't leave each other now.'

6   'THE POSITIVE VALUE OF DIFFERENTNESS'

Like religion, an ideology can offer an identity which transcends that which the normal social order confers upon an individual. Parents of a disabled child may be seen as occupying a special status, given which they should not expect their experience to be understandable in normal terms. Parents' appeals to this can account for remaining 'gaps' in the ideology and thus constitute a final defence against appearing incompetent.

Parents' differentness is of course potentially evident wherever it is known that they have a disabled child, and they are held accountable for their actions as parents to a greater than normal extent. When others treat the child as more or less disabled than his parents think him to be, or when the child behaves in such a way as to discredit his parents' claims on his behalf, their normal identity is impaired. As chapter 6 showed, this may occur where the parents appear to overplay the child's normality, in which case they may be accused of 'not facing up to reality' or, in seeking help, to over-play his disability, when they may be seen as 'over-protective'. Hence, parents' attempts to honour the official morality may often be misinterpreted and taken rather as evidence of their deviance. Invoking the parents' differentness resolves such 'internal contradictions' and is most important in constituting inter-personal relations.

For parents the immediate 'value' of differentness is that it legitimates what Scott and Lyman (1968a) call 'meta-accounts', that is strategies for avoiding giving accounts. They identify three such strategies: 'mystification', 'referral' and identity-switching. The first of these suggests that *alter* does not possess certain specialized knowledge which would explain parents' actions. Thus parents may say 'it's very complicated' or otherwise invoke the underlying physiological basis of their child's condition – 'It's something in the brain' (Mrs L) – rather than attempt a detailed explanation which anyway might reveal their own relative ignorance. 'What the doctor said' may be a constant source of referral. Mrs M referred to her GP's recommendation when she said how excitable her epileptic son became in company: 'he said "If you can stand it, let him carry on".' Mrs E and Mrs C invoked their identity as the child's medical agent as well as mother when they refused him sweets, 'It's for his own good', or kept him home from school with a cold, 'With him next thing you know it's pneumonia.'

Such accounts may provide some control of others' expressions of sympathy and ignorant advice. Thus Mrs E could appear legitimately angry with her sister-in-law who wanted to give sweets to the child, and Mrs B at an acquaintance's suggestion that her mongol daughter would be aggressive, saying: 'They give advice when really they don't know at all.' As noted in chapter 6, some situations may remain 'unmanageable' because parents cannot force their company upon those who avoid them. In such cases, though appealing to their special status as a public account is impossible, it may, however, be a source of private consolation, and in other situations, like the interview, parents discount the importance of any such stigmatization. This, as will be seen shortly, may be especially important where parents' general appearance is categorized as 'avoidance'.

In general it can be seen that the ideology acts to define the situation of parents with a disabled child in such a way that it appears congruent with the normal order of child-rearing. Evident discrepancies between the parents' situation and that of normal parents are symbolically transformed so that, far from constituting a challenge to, they appear to affirm, the validity of that order. Uncertainty about the future encourages hope; concentrating on the present appears 'realistic'. The inability to take for granted the appropriateness of normal child-rearing practices makes one appreciate the process of child development; even finding out that the child is disabled is better than not knowing or finding out later. Marriages are closer than they would otherwise have been, and normal children discovered to have hitherto unsuspected resources of maturity and unselfishness.

In chapter 7, I said that parents of the disabled were more than normally held accountable to the official morality whilst their experience might be expected to be less than normally accountable within its terms. However, not only are particular discrepancies legitimated, but the fact that parents' normal privacy is invaded by public and private agencies may be a further source of consolation as they share in the mysteries of medical science and make this evident to uninformed others. Hence parents' claims to be adequately fulfilling the tasks of normal parenthood are understandable. Though they may suffer, they are not unfairly disadvantaged since they are amply rewarded with a family life which affords them greater personal satisfaction, acts more than normally as a means of self-realization. They have no grounds for resentment or deviance from the official morality. However, not all parents are equally rewarded, or in the same way. To which legitimations parents make appeal depends upon the particular contingencies of their situation.

SITUATED USES OF THE IDEOLOGY

How parents of the disabled use the ideology in practice evidently depends primarily on what particular 'problems' or discrepancies they face. These might be expected to occur differentially according to such structural considerations as the size, sex- and age-structure of the family concerned; the age of the disabled child and his type of disability, and the social class of the parents. Irish (1966) points out that the number, sex and relative ages of siblings provide different possibilities of role-playing and suggests that each child develops on the basis of and in relation to the roles that have already been taken by others in the family. In a large family, a disabled child may then more readily be identified as, for example, 'the baby', whilst the others fulfil their parents' aspirations and provide adequate emotional satisfactions. As noted in chapter 2, Le Masters (1957) treats having a first child as a 'crisis' for any parent. Hence this may be compounded where this child is disabled and case R, where the mother remained in a state of shock months after the birth of the child, might be evidence of this.

Farber (1964), as seen in chapter 1, found that to middle-class parents the birth of a retarded child was a blow to their expectations, whilst lower-class parents treated it as a problem of day-to-day care. Mercer (1965) argues that lower-class parents with different standards of normal child-development are more likely to reject official definitions of their child as retarded (see chapter 2). In chapter 6, I noted that financial resources can mitigate the problems entailed by a commitment to constant care of the disabled child, and that middle-class parents are more likely to obtain preferential treatment from formal agencies and possess inter-personal skills relevant to managing such encounters. I do not, however, have evidence for making an adequate analysis of such issues and only present some illustrations.

Parents themselves may invoke structural factors over which they have no control as a further means of accounting for discrepancies between their situation and that of normal parenthood, or of identifying compensations. Mrs B made an oblique reference to social class when she said that she thought having a disabled child only happened to 'people who live in bungalows' implying, I think, that living in a tenement is disadvantage enough. Mrs A[I] spoke of the 'boon' that her telephone and father's car had been in ordering groceries and visiting the child in hospital, wondering how she would have managed without them.

Chapter 6 showed the differences in parents' accounts of their relationship with their disabled child according to his age – for example, whether he was 'sensible enough' to be trusted out alone (case M); particular disability – for example, whether he appreciated parents' efforts on his behalf (case F); and individual character. Mrs J ascribed her inability to keep her child to a diet to his long-established food preferences; Mrs E said that she was thankful it was not her older daughter who was diabetic since she was far more difficult to control than her brother. The disabled child's sex may also be invoked. Mrs D said that her retarded child's aggressive behaviour was partly her fault, but that this was because she had been treating him as leniently as she had her two older daughters. Mrs N[I] had very much wanted a daughter and thought it would have been worse had her mongol child not been a boy: 'As if anything could be worse.' The age of the normal children may similarly account for their jealousy or difficult behaviour, 'He's just at that age', and also provide a blessing. Mrs A[I] was glad that she had had a miscarriage prior to the birth of her disabled daughter since her first child was due to start school and would thus be away all day; Mrs H observed that it was as well that her two other children were almost adult, since 'we'd have had mair problems if they'd been small'. She was also thankful that, just at the age when she and her husband would have got 'sorta' into a rut', the disabled child gave them something new to live for. Mr T[I], on the other hand, thought it good that 'we're young and healthy' because they would be able to care for the child for years hence.

Whatever the size of family, parents report it as an advantage. Both Mrs Q and Mrs T said that having other children to care for was the most important defence against breaking down when their disabled children were thought or known to be dying. Mrs F was glad she had only two children as this gave her more time to devote to her spina bifida son; Mrs L said she did not need to send the disabled child to a nursery since with eight children 'we've got our own nursery'. A large extended kin network was identified as making an important difference to parents' responses to the onset of disability. When Mrs B[I] said that 'We've all had a broken heart' and that she had wanted to go home to her mother's for a week after leaving hospital she observed that 'It seems to be like that wi' a large family'. Mrs H reported how her many relatives and neighbours had constantly visited and cheered her: 'Our family, they dinna' let you get down in the dumps.'

Evidently such structural factors have implications for parents' experience of having a disabled child in so far as they enter into the interpretive processes by which interaction is established and maintained. Parents' ideology, like any other, is constructed in and through 'talk' with others. I have already shown in chapter 6 how parents' inter-personal styles are typically different according to their own and others' negotiated definitions of their responsibility for and power to do something about their child's disability. Here I shall attempt to show that as parents' normal appearance is informed by appeals to the ideology in general, so differences in their appearance or identification by others may be related to the invocations of different combinations of some of the elements.

The appearance of 'stoic acceptance' is typically grounded in appeals to most if not all the elements of ideology. As already noted, stoic acceptance is often associated with congenital disability, and 'acceptance of the inevitable' with sudden onset, which is common in cases of congenital disability. The demonstration of acceptance is essential to a normal appearance since there are no immediate problems with which parents can claim to be actively engaged once they can offer assurance of their competence in the child's everyday management. The explicit account of 'taking it from day to day', or the second element, claims the grounds for this. Making comparisons with other cases in terms of the relative good of their situation is important since parents have little means of actively improving their situation and therefore can only show how it might be worse, as is claiming the discovery of true values in the absence of visible reward (e.g. the child's progress in response to his parents' special techniques), or even improvement on the previous situation (of uncertainty). Together these constitute evidence of the positive value of parents' suffering and also of their differentness. However, in this situation, there are typically less specific medical legitimations to which to appeal. As noted in chapter 6, the major interactional problems for 'accepting' parents is the control of others' expressions of unwanted sympathy and advice. That is, parents are less able to make evident their special status; are more dependent on others making this ascription. None the less, the accounts that they can use – 'It can happen to anyone' – create the impression of humility which is grounds for such identification.

In contrast, parents who are not responsible but have power appear to be 'coping splendidly' as they demonstrate their new and special skills in managing the child, familiarity with hospital routine and medical vocabulary, and can even claim to be known to the consultant paediatrician by name (Mrs F). Their specific rewards are more tangible also in that since they can do something to help the child, their situation could evidently be worse and they may have medical legitimation for any long-term uncertainty.

'Asthma takes seven years to work itself out' (Mrs C); 'We know that they can't say for sure' (Mrs A). Acceptance is more a prerequisite to subsequent routinization and adjustment; it is implicit in the evidence of the child's continual care rather than actively displayed. Lastly, parents in this situation make less claim to the discovery of true values. They can appear to be exerting control over and therefore acting effectively under present conditions, hence, as for most people most of the time, the question of moral requiredness, or 'the purpose of it all', is less apparent. Strictly speaking, their conduct does not require an extraordinary account. However, heroic qualities are still commonly imputed, the possible reasons for which will be discussed later.

'Making amends' requires no extraordinary explanation; it is what any normal person who has caused a child's suffering would do. Parents who so appear do not claim acceptance of their situation, rather active attempts to change it. Nor do they claim to 'take it from day to day'; rather, displaying their efforts to make sense of the child's behaviour may be evidence of such attempts. They do not claim that their situation could be worse or make comparisons with persons in similar situations. Parents' own sufferings are not unfair punishment from which compensation should be expected, but retribution for their earlier actions. Any identified rewards, such as the child's improvement in response to his parents' efforts, are acknowledged with gratitude and a resolve to live by, rather than exult in, deeper understanding of the true value of family life. Mrs O avowed her determination to keep her temper in the face of her epileptic son's frequent enuresis and 'psychopathic' tendencies; Mrs K, as noted in chapter 6, acknowledged that accusing her husband of genetic responsibility for their child's diabetes was 'rather than blame myself, I suppose' and affirmed that 'we could never leave her now . . .. You should have a responsibility for your children – we are responsible for it, you see.'

Parents to whom responsibility is attributed but who have no power similarly constitute no public threat to the legitimacy of the normal order of child-rearing. They similarly do not say that their situation could be worse, nor talk of deriving compensation from their suffering. They do not claim acceptance, but nor can they demonstrate attempts to change their situation. As noted in chapter 6, these ascriptions of responsibility and power typically occur in cases of 'undifferentiated' mental subnormality where, as in Case D, no stable definition of the child's condition is available. Such parents do not know whether their situation is that of having a disabled child, and hence even those who do not blame themselves have nothing to accept. In either case, their situation is 'pre-ideological'. Whilst they may experience continual discrepancies as their expectations of the child are constantly revised, there are no grounds on which they can make public appeal to legitimate their situation. Although they may in fact be engaged in active, constructive work, demonstrate this where they cannot avoid accounts, and thus show that they have not abandoned the attempt to care for their child, making this evident also reveals their uncertainty and therefore relative incompetence. Hence, parents 'avoid' all encounters where they are not afforded 'consideration' or moral credit on other grounds.

Parents to whom responsibility is attributed might yet be expected to feel some resentment and question the justice of the permanence of their punishment, especially as they see others who appear to 'get away with it': not all parents who fail to provide adequate care and control have a disabled child; no one can change his genetic heritage. They can, however, derive positive value from their differentness. Those who have power may employ meta-accounts, and they similarly act to turn away unwanted inquiries. Those who have none may rather derive some consolation from their abnormal status. Their knowledge of the true value of family life may constitute a private feeling of 'superiority' and in so far as it is evident to others, the 'silent suffering' of such parents may be seen as the ultimate affirmation of the official morality.

RESPECTABILITY AND REALITY

In fact, there seem to be several grounds for expecting change over time towards an appearance of coping splendidly, both in individual cases and in general. As observed in chapter 6, the majority of parents displayed this style.

In all cases, an ability to make sense of the disabled child's condition is a prerequisite to the management of a respectable appearance; the success of parents' inter-personal strategies depends on a knowledge of the child and his appearance to others. The focus in chapter 5 was on parents' methods of constructing such knowledge rather than its substantive origins. Hence, there is no clear relationship between different methods and uses of the ideology. Thus cases D and L were both categorized as 'there must be some sense in it'. O and E as 'distrusting appearances', but at the same time these parents appeared to be practising 'avoidance', 'coping' (L and E) and 'making amends' respectively. Some relationships between particular legitimations and methods of construction have been indicated in presenting the ideology in its general form. Explicit appeals to 'acceptance' and 'taking it from day to day' were said to be most common in cases of sudden onset or of 'meaningless' and 'powerless' responses. The fact that some parents delayed seeking a medical opinion was related in chapter 5 to fears of being seen as responsible for the child's condition.

The majority of parents did not abandon the attempt to make sense of their child's behaviour and claimed that their constructions were in accordance with medically-given definitions. However, as chapter 7 showed, this cannot be interpreted as a simple product of a normal moral requirement to continue caring for the child, nor necessarily of automatic deference to expert opinion. Increased knowledge of the objective meaning of the disability was crucial to parents' ability to see its relevance to their individual child, but even where a doctor could provide little such information, the ways in which he managed interaction with parents served to maintain parents' interpretive attempts and their trust in his competence. Where parents did express doubt, doctors often employed explicit sanctions: 'You'll just have to accept it'; 'You mothers worry about anything', directly asserting the validity of their perspective.

Parents' constant efforts to make sense of their child's condition despite any uncertainty may, over time, constitute some power as particular hypotheses or themes become more tenable in the light of past and present experience. These, where parents are called to account, provide the basis for some demonstration of proper parental activities. McHugh (1968) found that powerless subjects were preoccupied with cause; parents with some power appear correspondingly less to question the origin of their child's disability and of their suffering. When seen from their own perspective, parents' definitions were seen to be rational and 'realistic' and most thereby appeared to be coping to some degree and in a legitimate way.

Not, of course, that this is necessarily how they appear to others. However, none of the expert theories examined legitimate holding parents responsible for their child's condition and, as practised, encourage parents' assumption of power in co-operation with official agencies. Medical theories are formulated in terms of bodily structures and functions which are largely independent of individual control and for which therefore he is not liable. Psychiatry counsels adjustment to reality as defined by the relevant experts, and an active quest for understanding of self and others. Sociology locates disability as a random occurrence or one which is subject to impersonal external forces to which adjustment via education or rehabilitation is the major course.

Such theories are increasingly made available to the public in general. Magazines and newspapers are of course aimed at 'normals'; as are research projects and education campaigns designed to change community attitudes. Further, as seen, expert definitions give parents some control over others' definitions in face-to-face situations. The examples given in chapter 6 of changes in parents' strategies over time were informed by expert meanings. Mrs B and Mrs L became able to appear 'not responsible' as the accounts 'she's got a growth deficiency' and 'it was a one in a million chance' were made available to them. Mrs D acquired some power when asked by the nursery school teacher to co-operate with them in training her retarded child.

Parents' ideology is mainly expressed in commonsense terms and explicitly includes what were identified as elements of commonsense thought. Some of the agents make explicit appeal to similar grounds especially where their special theories are inadequate, but in any case parents' expression of the ideology seems to produce an appearance which is essentially the same as that common course of action which the agencies legitimate. Parents do not speak of 'unconscious fears' and 'repression', but 'the back of your mind'; not 'self-realization' but 'more understanding'; only Mrs O used the word 'stigma'. They do not express resentment or show despair, but a determination to do whatever is best for the child and the rest of the family, and to seek help when it becomes necessary, recognizing that their own opinion is not always a reliable guide to action. Mrs H discharged herself from hospital as soon as she discovered that her child was mongol, but in the last interview talked of getting help to train him before he reached school age. At the third interview Mrs B still said '[the hospital] can't do much – it would be the welfare', but at the next, on a social worker's recommendation, was considering sending her mongol child to a day centre, saying: 'We must let her get any chance to learn more than I can learn her . . . . I suppose they can, they've had them all before.'

As parents acquire and use the ideology, so their competence in interaction with others is increased. They can demonstrate their ability to care for the disabled child, make evident the ways in which their situation has compensations or is a positive improvement on that prior to having him, counter or forestall others' imputations of incompetence, and thus claim to be fulfilling the responsibilities of parenthood and maintaining a normal family life.

At the beginning of chapter 7 I said that others might ask how parents of the disabled manage to appear predominantly calm and cheerful; in chapter 6 that such an appearance provided the grounds for the imputation of special psychological qualities constituted in a special philosophy of life. Those sociological studies of disability and the family examined in chapter 1 similarly invoked essentially psychological explanations of parents' behaviour in the research situation, either in the form of pathological mechanisms of guilt and denial or as social rules in the form of 'attitudes' to socialization, 'expectations' and 'dispositions' to act. Both of these types of explanation required reinterpretation of what parents actually said in order to sustain the assumption that having a disabled child disrupts normal family life, and both, I argued, rested on an unexamined notion of that life.

I have attempted throughout to 'take parents' statements seriously'. That is, not to discount them in order to assert the pathological nature of the effects of a disabled child on his family, but neither simply to present them in their own context which provides no orderly explanation of similarities and differences amongst them. Rather, I have started from an explicated conception of the 'normal family' and argued that it is a set of basic rules which defines the constitutive activities of parenthood, but which 'constrains' individual action in so far as it enters into the interpretive processes of interaction. In any situation in which the category of parent is ascribed to an individual he must account for his actions or 'use' the category in such a way as to appear to satisfy the basic expectancies which it entails. Hence, I have treated statements made by parents of a disabled child as accounts informed by the normal order of child-rearing and family life, only assuming their correspondence to parents' conscious processes in chapter 5, and attempted to show the different ways in which these make an orderly appearance of normal family life, observable to me or to others.

However, partly because I, like those other writers, do not believe that having a disabled child is an unproblematic experience, and partly because, for reasons given in chapter 2, the normal family appears to bear a questionable relationship to the experience of any parent, I do not treat parents' uses of it as 'matters of course'. Rather, I argue that they do so act because the normal family is a moral category sanctionably implemented by agencies empowered to control family-related activities.

Whatever their particular appearance, the statements made by parents who have a disabled child are organized or informed by the official morality of child-rearing and family life as it is implemented both routinely and by agents specifically concerned with managing the phenomena of having a disabled child. Parents use 'normal parenthood' and the 'normal family' in their variously deviant situation in methodical ways which are negotiated in observable encounters with identifiable others. They manage to appeal to normal motives despite the differences between their situation and that of normal parents because the definitions of their situation, or the meanings of having a disabled child that are available, and the ways in which these are made available to them, constrain them to redefine such differences and present themselves and their situation as understandable within normal terms. They appear respectable because that is how others require them to appear, even if those same others then marvel at their achievement. Indeed, the fact that others express such amazement may, as will be seen shortly, ultimately constitute the strongest sanction upon parents' performance.

At the beginning of chapter 1, I said that most research into the effects of a disabled child on family life raised two questions. Earlier, I have been concerned with providing some answer to the first of these: why parents of a disabled child say what they say when interviewed. I now consider the second: what, if anything, does what they say indicate about the experience of having a disabled child?

Up to this point, I have sought sociological authenticity by 'treating what others take to be an essential identity as a convenient disguise' (O'Neill, 1972, p. 217). Throughout, it has been implied that parents may not believe in what they say, that there was 'something else' behind these polite, public appearances. What, then, might this something else be? What does it 'really' mean to have a disabled child and is family life so reconstituted that it is phenomenologically continuous with life as it was before? In the rest of this chapter, I examine some of the answers that can be given to such questions and interpret these as evidence of certain critiques of the contemporary social, political and moral order. Equally, the fact that I raise these questions can be taken as evidence of my attitude to such critiques.

What people really think, despite what they say, is not of course a problem peculiar to sociology: it routinely confronts members going about their everyday affairs. Moreover, the methods employed are the same. As I said in chapter 3, sociological analyses are based in the documentary method of interpretation through which orderly everyday action is accomplished. To assume that the only way to know what another person is thinking is to *have* his thought is to commit what McHugh calls 'the general error of privatism' (1968, p. 134). We always infer another's intentions from his observable actions. Hence, if I have shown how the observable actions of parents of a disabled child create particular impressions or enable others to make particular interpretations, the question of what other appearances they might display could be said to be 'out of bounds'.

Hellmer (1970) suggests that the 'man without qualities' as presented most consistently by Goffman (1955), might be the proper focus of sociological inquiry. Goffman argues that 'to be' a type of person is not merely to possess the required attributes but to sustain standards of conduct and appearance that are appropriate, and that this is a performance whether or not the actor is aware of it. Persons can stand in a number of relationships to their outward behaviour, under-, over-, or otherwise presenting their 'real feelings' (1969, p. 65). The fact that I am not happy with what parents say could then be regarded as evidence of the inadequacy of my research design. I should have observed parents' encounters with official agencies, sat in clinics, gone to voluntary association meetings and become a temporary 'member' of a family with a disabled child.

O'Neill rejects the man without qualities as an appropriate model for sociological analysis since he argues that 'the sense of possibility and its technique of impression management is false to the naïve inter-subjectivity which is the unarticulated structure of our everyday trust in and competence with social reality' (*op. cit.*, p. 217). Appealing to Garfinkel's experimental production of incongruity, he says that the 'universality of consciousness is prior to the particularities of the personal biography which becomes its expressive vehicle' (*ibid.*). In other words, we can potentially know what another person in our culture thinks because we both think in terms of categories given in the language that forms the symbolic base of our society. In Schutzian terms, the universality of consciousness is the world-taken-for-granted constituted in those assertions about the nature of reality (the basic rules or facts of life) that every competent member of a society believes as a matter of course. According to this position, I do not believe what parents of the disabled say because I have a different conception of the nature of reality and do not share the same categories.

However, as Light (1969) says of Berger and Luckmann, if O'Neill or any sociologist can recognize and question matters of course so can every competent member of society. Light points out that people can be aware that they are deluding themselves, hence recognize that the symbols with which they interpret their experience are not the same as, nor 'true to' that experience. One can add that people can also 'not know what to think' or 'not know what I really believe'. They can regard the symbols available to them as inadequate for expressing their feelings, and construct new ones as in 'slang' or 'argot'. Hence the man without qualities may be not just the best model that sociology can find but a common mode of consciousness.

Berger argues that this 'identity crisis' is the psychological concomitant of advanced industrial society in which 'individuals . . . do not know to which of a number of selves which they experience they should assign priority status' (1965, p. 36). Hence it might be argued that parents experience having a disabled child as I have presented it: not as a simple matter of motivation, but as a product of their interaction with others, informed by the meanings of their experience which are culturally defined and officially sanctioned as appropriate.

No one of these three interpretations is likely to be wholly appropriate. No doubt I should have had other ideas had I adopted other research strategies; parents are unlikely to 'lie' systematically, or, on the other hand, to confide wholly in me. Accounting for their situation in terms of the official morality is, in any case, part of the experience of having a disabled child. Hence, as in the discussion in chapter 2 of the relationship between the official morality of the family and the experience of parents, I shall present what evidence I have of statements made by parents of the disabled which counter official legitimations of their situation, and discuss the general grounds which together account for the near absence of such deviance.

As already reported, several mothers did say that they felt 'depressed', 'nervy', 'panicked' or they cried. This might of course be interpreted as an appropriate display of caring and not appearing 'too cheery' as Mrs B put it. In any case, they reported that this occurred occasionally, on 'some days', or in response to particular events such as a hypoglycaemic reaction, or when they continued such behaviour, that they had been told by their husbands to 'pull yourself together' or 'you'll just have to get used to it' (Mrs K).

This seems to be an expression of cultural definitions of sex-appropriate behaviour. In our society men are typically supposed not to 'show their feelings', do not have to appear upset or concerned, and if they do it is likely to be seen as inappropriate. They can appear callous yet still be assumed to 'care really' and can appeal to their traditionally accredited grounds of 'rationality', 'level-headedness', etc., to justify actions inappropriate for women, such as putting the child in an institution. Women, on the other hand, are supposed to have a 'maternal instinct' and therefore expected to both feel and show greater distress, want to keep the child at any cost to themselves. Doctors demonstrate such expectations in their use of the father as mediator to break the news of a child's disability to his wife – he can normally be expected to 'take it like a man'.

Hence, although I have throughout referred to 'parents', the analysis is more applicable to mothers. However, this is justifiable on several grounds: they were in any case the main respondents; they generally have more contact with official agents and it is more to the mothers that these direct their efforts; the mother is the 'centre' of the family and moreover principally responsible for the day-to-day care of the child. Therefore it is 'in fact' her management of the experience of having a disabled child that is likely to be more important: it is she most of all who has to espouse publicly the official morality concerning child-rearing in our society. This does not, however, mean that fathers are free of its constraints. To the extent that he is called to account for his actions, the 'family man', as seen in chapter 2, does constitute a moral category to which any of his behaviour is potentially relevant. For both sexes, getting married and having children is the main qualification for normal adulthood and hence full membership in our society.

Parents typically discover others in the surrounding community in a similar position to their own. Strangers may identify themselves as having already 'adjusted' to their situation and become regular counsellors: friends (in one case the mother's own mother) reveal that they or a relative have or had a disabled child. Neighbours bring reports of the progress of children in the next street; others may give 'material' assistance such as baby-sitting or simply visiting, which alleviates the parents' situation. However, parents generally reported that even sympathetic others 'don't really understand', or 'only get upset', and it appeared that the more 'support' parents were given by others, the less problems they acknowledged and the more they defined their situation in terms of the official morality.

Every parent may know that family life is not as it is normally presented. Everyone can remember their life as it was before they married, may recall dreams and ambitions the fulfilment of which the assumption of family responsibilities curtailed, or may simply wonder what life would have been like had they married someone else. Normal parents discuss such matters amongst themselves, but having a disabled child sets parents apart in such respects. As shown in chapter 6, the effect of interaction with others, far from legitimating expressions of discontent, is to require parents to act 'as if' they had the special qualities that the ideology provides for them, to produce the 'differentness' which accounts for their heroic behaviour. As others treat more of their activities as relevant to their parenthood, parents of the disabled become more committed to fulfilling their responsibilities. Hence their identities as parents may attain greater salience than normal, which may be one reason why they are often held to be a 'model for us all'. This may be a source of public and private consolation to parents but it may also constitute the most effective, since ubiquitous, form of control.

The one case, Mrs N, who denied the validity of most of the elements of the ideology demonstrates the failure of these normal legitimating processes. Following usual practice, the hospital first informed her husband of the child's condition. For several days he refused to tell his wife that their son was a mongol, whilst she became increasingly aware that something was very much the matter. When she did find out, she found no doctor to give her a satisfactory explanation of the child's condition. Her husband at first threatened suicide, called the baby a vegetable and wanted him put away. Both his own mother, with whom he always spent more time than at home, and even the GP (to the mother's surprise and horror) supported him in this. Many friends and acquaintances avoided her and for some time only her sisters could provide (weekly) support. Hence she had very 'good' reasons for feeling resentment, though she made little direct appeal to such grounds herself. More significantly, she lacked an adequate audience at the start for such feelings of resentment and thus had little opportunity to learn their appropriate expression. The subsequent intervention of a social worker, and a chance encounter with a specialist on mongolism transformed her expressions in so far as she then regarded her marriage as better than it had been previously, but she still did not claim that family life was as it ought to be, nor display a proper acceptance.

Over time, she did become more hopeful – 'you have to be – you've got to face it', but thought that had she known her child would be mongol, she would have had her pregnancy terminated, although 'maybe that's only because I've had the experience of having him'. She also realized that she could not be told for certain how the child would develop, but 'really I think I was hoping they'd tell me what they thought of him'. She could see that things could be worse – a friend's mongol child had heart disease as well – but not many people qualified as 'worse off'. Hearing of a child with diabetes, she said to her husband: 'Don't expect me to break my heart for him – he can live a normal life'; and when a mother confessed her anxiety at her baby's overdue arrival she thought, 'You've nothing to worry about'. She did say, 'I know it's silly'; 'I consciously didn't want to think that'; 'I felt so small'; that is, she acknowledged that it is wrong to feel like this, but still said, 'I do feel a bit resentful of people with normal children – especially with two normal children'. Finally, far from discovering the positive values of suffering and being different, she was desperately worried that she was becoming *less* understanding – most especially towards her other child: 'I'm always on at him and out of all proportion. I know it's all in my imagination but the worry of it might affect [the normal child]. He [the mongol] would be my reason for doing it but none the less it's not him, it's me that's doing it.'

The processes through which parents' ideology is constructed may further give it a 'reality basis'. Discontinuities between life before and after having a disabled child support a perceived change in self-conception and identity. The very fact that taken-for-granted assumptions about parenthood and child-rearing are thrown into doubt and questioned may be said to constitute a 'deeper understanding of them'. Husbands and wives may become 'closer' because they talk through matters arising from having the disabled child more than previously. As Davis (1963) suggests, abnormal actions such as husbands crying may contribute to feelings of solidarity. As judged by the standards of the official morality, parents may be 'better' because they have been advised by official agencies on issues normally left to their own discretion. They may *be* better 'trained' as their public competence implies.

Further, in using the ideology parents may discover and then reconcile inconsistencies and incoherencies, or become committed to certain courses of action such as not going out as others cease to offer to baby-sit. They may privately maintain standards of behaviour that they do not personally believe in for an 'unseen audience'. Any knowledge can become detached from 'actual' social conditions and act back on those conditions, so that legitimations may become more convincing as parents interpret their experiences through them and thus 'discover' their 'real' meaning.

Moreover, in contrast to many deviants (cf. Bryan, 1966), though some problems became routine, others became greater and new ones appear (a mongol adult is less appealing and more difficult to manage) precisely as parents' ability to cope diminishes. Ideology then may become more highly developed and more deeply held. On the other hand, specific aspects of the situation may remain permanently unaccounted for: 'It's the look of it upsets me' though even then 'I know it sounds shallow' (Mrs B).

Any normative order, as observed in chapter 5, may be preferable to none. To the extent that parents believe in the legitimations available to them they can continue to exist in society not 'as if nothing had happened' but 'in the knowledge that even these events or experiences have a place within a universe that makes sense . . . it is not happiness that a theodicy primarily provides, but meaning' (Berger, 1969, p. 58). 'That's what they're for, epitaphs, Joel suddenly realized, so you can feel you've got some control over the death, you *own* it, you choose a name for it. The same with wanting to know all you can about how it happened . . . any poor subterfuge will do . . . .' (Agee, 1958, p. 174).

However, it is not any order which the ideology reconstitutes. Child-related activities are not only central to the contemporary conception of the normal family, and their proper performance one of its major identifying characteristics for both outsiders and members, they are also an important source of its stability. Berger and Kellner regard marriage as a crucial nomic instrumentality, in that it is 'the main social arena for the individual's self-realization, as opposed to the immensely powerful and incomprehensible alien world', yet as being 'the most unstable of all personal social relationships' (1964, p. 57). However, with the entry of children, parents' more-or-less consciously negotiated order attains some degree of 'facticity' for its authors, and parents become committed to treating their tacit agreements as unquestioned 'laws' in the process of initiating new members to the group. Hence, the discovery and imputation of incompetence in such respects is likely to have fundamental implications for parents' self-conception and identity. They may not only see themselves and be seen as potentially inadequate parents but be highly committed to re-presenting themselves as 'good' and hence welcome the reconstituting power of the ideology.

In general, one might predict that ideology 'fails' frequently, but strictly in private and briefly, since accompanied by the feeling that despair and resentment are not only pointless but wrong. What one can certainly say is that any explanations of how parents manage to maintain the unity of a family containing a disabled child which appeals to independent personality attributes, to equilibrating forces, or to the normal strength of the family as an institution, do no justice to the hard work in which parents must continually engage, and refuse to recognize the constraints under which they do so. Further, to the extent that parents do believe in what they say, this tells us more about our moral and social order than it does of any unavoidable facts of life. It can still be asked: why do others not know what to say, or why is the family the most important source of identity for the majority of members of our society?

Berger says that locating the 'real me' in their occupation is 'not very seductive for the great masses of people in the middle and lower echelons of the occupational system' (1965, p. 36). More explicitly, he argues that, with increasing industrialization, economic institutions have become progressively separated from (and repressive of) traditional political institutions on the one hand and from the family on the other. The stability of the economic system depends on legitimating this separation of spheres of activity; that is, upon presenting it as an ahistorical and inevitable fact of life. To put it crudely: the vast majority of people must not mind that whatever they say or do makes little or no difference to the conditions under which they live. For most people, the only conditions which they can influence are those in the sphere of the family. Family-related activities must then be legitimated as 'decisive occasions for self-discovery' (*ibid.*, p. 37). Legitimation of the family is then fundamental to the present social order, though it is of course possible that other institutions might do as well or better, and the situation of parents with disabled children constitutes a test of its legitimating power.

Berger argues that institutionalized psychologism, as derived more or less directly from the psychoanalytic tradition, is ideally suited to the task. The notion of the unconscious is subjectively congruent with the equally opaque social world – 'the individual is unconscious of the fundamental forces which shape his life' (*ibid.*, p. 39). The themes of sexuality (realized in marriage) and the primary formativeness of childhood experiences legitimates the family as 'the most "healthy" locale of identity affirmation . . . . The understanding of the self as an assemblage of psychological mechanisms allows the individual to deal with himself with the same technical, calculating and objective attitude that is the attitude par excellence of industrial production' (*ibid.*, p. 40).

Most important of all, it does provide an ultimate order in terms of which man can locate his essential identity, and this is located within human consciousness itself.

I argued that psychiatry has had less influence on the facts of life in British society and that medical science as practised by doctors was more likely to legitimate suffering. However, I also suggested at the end of chapter 7 that the model of man, excluding the unconscious, is the same in all the sciences which are concerned with him, and that this is essentially 'medical'. Freidson (1961) examines the extension of the concept of 'disease' to diverse forms of social behaviour, arguing that it thereby calls pathological and amenable to scientific treatment what was once regarded as the consequence of a responsible person's choice. It 'creates a rhetoric by which behaviour the actor believes to be serious and responsible, even if deviant, is reduced to a mere symptom of disease for which he is not truly responsible'; 'moral arguments for social reform become displaced by "scientific" arguments' (*ibid.*, p. 125).

In a symbolically medical world, the appropriate action for the individual is that presented by Parsons and Fox (1952) as the 'sick role'. The sick person is relieved of many of his normal responsibilities but this is conditional on his co-operation with those treating him in order that he may get well. The correct way of being sick is determined by the 'nature' of his sickness as it is defined by the doctors in charge. O'Neill says that 'the sick role is society's last chance of seducing the deviant into recommitting himself to social gatherings, objects and loyalties' (*op. cit.*, p. 18). Critics of advanced industrial society have more generally presented this as the abandonment of judgment, humility and acceptance whereby man invests his 'faith' in the ever-increasing mastery of the world through scientific methods by the experts (see e.g. Habermas, 1969; Shroyer, 1970).

Any symbolic universe is itself a theodicy; it entails the submission of an individual to its order. But the prevailing social order rests on a presentation of knowledge as a neutral picturing of fact, as 'information' divorced from its socially constructed base. It rests on what Mueller (1970) analyses as 'repressive communication', since it thereby denies human intentionality, or the fact that man has language and is therefore capable of transcending and changing any 'given' situation. An individual cannot then 'identify and understand himself independently of his position in the existing social structure'; he cannot 'find grounds both for criticizing the status quo and for believing that it is possible to act with others in changing it' (Macintyre, 1969, p. 4).

At the risk of over-extending my own analysis, one might see the ideology of parents of the disabled as an expression of this mode of consciousness.

It is evident that the majority of the elements of parents' ideology are commonly available to, and routinely employed by, members of our society in the face of everyday frustrations and disappointments; they appeal to 'quite ordinary motives'. Hence the ideology may be seen as a general symbolic method of achieving 'triumph over adversity', giving meaning to a variety of forms of suffering, and in this sense, the situation of parents of the disabled is different only in degree. Their normal expectations are so fundamentally thrown into doubt and in that sphere in which the majority of individuals enjoy their greatest freedom from wider social groups that the ideology may not immediately appear appropriate. 'Coping splendidly' then characterizes the ideal form of action. It does not encourage the discovery of 'true values', entails no re-vision of the prevailing social order. Rather, it entails a day-to-day 'pragmatic' approach to piecemeal problems, giving mastery of an individual's own immediate situation. Its reward is the realization of the justice of the prevailing social order. The reward of 'differentness', however, is evidence of the moral bankruptcy of that order.

'Persons', defined in chapter 2 as necessarily moral entities, have no place in the present social order, since the freedom to exercise moral responsibility is denied. The identity which man is offered is de-humanizing: it requires him to conceive of himself in terms of a model which requires him not to exercise his ability to act. To the extent that this is recognized, then, the moral authority of the prevailing order is undermined. O'Neill (*op. cit.*) observes that this authority draws on medieval credit; one might say on Judaeo-Christian credit, for, as Macintyre (*op. cit.*) says, Christianity, like all the great religions, did have a revolutionary potential, did provide a transcendent identity for the individual.

The special status of differentness is not such an identity. Its ascription commits the individual to an ever greater affirmation of the prevailing social order. Family life is the best arena for an individual's self-realization: despite the loss of individual freedom which parenthood presently entails, it is the means of becoming a proper person. The contemporary hero is he who gladly accepts his fate but his only alternative is to be symbolically liquidated by his fellow men. The non-expert cannot change the course of events, control the natural order of things, but he can achieve greatness precisely by acknowledging this fact and suffering in the correct way. The consequence of such repressive communication is not that the questions raised by the problems of suffering and evil are now answered by scientific interpretations of man and nature, as the thinkers of the Enlightenment hoped, but rather that 'the questions are increasingly no longer asked, that men are largely deprived of any overall interpretation of existence' (*ibid.*, p. 2).

Hence, if parents of a disabled child do believe in what they say, it may be because they have no available means of taking action and articulating their interests. They have no other meanings available with which to interpret their experience, to transcend their immediate situation and make it shareable with others. They may be silent because they do not have anything else to say. It is in this sense that only parents themselves know what it means to have a disabled child.

Certainly, there is some evidence of the formulation of an alternative response, whether this be in parent groups as the voluntary associations once were, or in the actions of certain sectors of the official agencies themselves. I can only attempt a brief assessment of these. Thus, within medicine, groups like the Young Socialist Medical Association, and magazines such as *Needle* include in their programme the need for 'Patient Power' to counteract the mystification of medical practice. Also 'community medicine' projects have been instituted aiming at preventive social measures which require that doctors be informed of other disciplines (see e.g. Mitchell, 1971). Against this, the increase of research and the complexity of medical science may be adduced in support of a prediction that the medical tasks of diagnosis and treatment will become more specialized and 'computerized'.

In social work, dissatisfaction with the psychiatric domination of casework, articulated earlier in the USA, receives collective expression both in 'official professional journals' (Cooper, 1971) and in the conference and publications of *Case Con*. Apart from the question of how far such discussion has affected practice, Popplestone (1972) argues that 'radical' social workers represent a wide range of ideological positions, a consequence of which being that they currently lack a consistent programme. Individual social workers do organize groups where parents of disabled children may discuss their common problems, and where these do not retain a psychoanalytic basis they may legitimate the expression of specific grievances and resentment. However, one worker has observed that this phenomenon is strictly confined to the group situation – even 'over coffee' parents reassert their respectability.[1]

Some voluntary associations in particular appear to have adopted more militant strategies recently: the Spastics Society asserts: 'Anybody's child can be a spastic'; the NSMHC: 'Community care means you'. However, this appears to reflect not the increased participation of members but rather the professionalization of charity work with an emphasis on good administration, and effective fund-raising campaigns based on a reconstruction of the public image of the organization informed by the techniques of public relations (Exley and Exley, 1971).

I shall not speculate as to the possible implications of such changes for the legitimation of suffering and our society. It is still commonly said that it is a 'tragedy' to have a disabled child. Macintyre says that 'the tragic is a category which . . . remains a possibility wherever the attempt is made both to live within, and to transcend a society' (1964, p. 74). If parents, like the majority of the members of our society, are deprived of an overall theory of existence, then having a disabled child 'cannot' be a tragedy. The only categories available to them construct their experience as 'a constant burden'.

Notes

CHAPTER 1   UNDERLYING PATHOLOGY AND APPARENT
            NORMALITY

1 The same criterion is often used in decisions as to whether to send a
  juvenile offender to approved school (Cicourel, 1964).
2 For comparisons in the area of mental illness see Sampson *et al.* (1962) and
  Yarrow *et al.* (1955).
3 Zigler (1966) discusses the issues involved and argues, not that tests should
  be abandoned, but that workers should turn their attention away from
  the superficial content of tests, i.e. the right or wrong answers, and towards
  the problem of the cognitive structures and processes that give rise to
  content, e.g. thought, memory, concept formation and reasoning. He
  argues that had intelligence tests been developed by cognitive theorists
  rather than test constructors and psychometricians, the problems
  encountered in trying to define intelligence might never have arisen.
  Despite the statistical rigour involved, no satisfactory theory of intelligence
  has come out of the correlational or factor analytic methods. Zigler
  attributes the fact that intelligence became the province of the testers
  rather than the theorists to the practical demands of society for a test
  which would measure intellectual functioning. He also says, 'for a variety
  of reasons, American thinking was not receptive to the approach taken
  by the cognitive theorists' (*ibid.*, p. 112) but does not expand on this.
4 The statutory definition for the purposes of registration as 'blind' given
  in the National Assistance Act (1948) is: 'so blind as to be unable to perform
  any work for which eyesight is essential.'
5 Zigler (1964) shows that this is typical of developmental studies in general.
  These have produced either naturalistic observations on the one hand,
  or rarefied concepts which place divergent behaviour within them on the
  other; e.g. both 'resistiveness' and 'ultra-conformity' may be attributed
  to 'developmental disequilibrium'.
6 In his analysis of coding behaviour, Garfinkel demonstrates that *ad hoc*
  practices such as reconstructing some features of an instance so that it
  fits a given rule are an irremediable feature of research and everyday
  action. 'To treat [coding] instructions as though *ad hoc* features in their
  use were . . . grounds for complaint about the incompleteness of instructions
  is very much like complaining that if the walls of a building were only
  gotten out of the way one could see better what was keeping the roof
  up' (1967, p. 22). The point is not then that *ad hoc* practices can be avoided,
  but rather that they should become the topic of analysis.

CHAPTER 2   NORMAL APPEARANCES AND OFFICIAL MORALITY

1 For interactionist accounts of deviance see e.g. Becker (1964; 1966); Lemert (1951; 1967). Rubington and Weinberg (1968) provide a selection of readings and introductory summaries of the main issues. Garfinkel (1967) is the source of ethnomethodological studies some of which are presented in Dreitzel (1970). Douglas (1971b) devotes the first chapter to discussing the differences between 'linguistic' and 'phenomenological' ethnomethodology. The influence of phenomenology on British and American sociology has come mainly through the writings of Schutz (e.g. 1962; 1964; 1966).

2 Piliavin and Briar (1964) show how the demeanour of juveniles who have been apprehended influences police action towards them. Those who act respectfully are more likely merely to be cautioned.

3 The protection of privacy is of course currently seen as a social problem with the growth of centralized stores of information about many aspects of individuals' characteristics, interests and activities. Beaney (1966) examines the development of rights to privacy as a series of actual conflicts in the form of lawsuits. The conception of a 'right to be let alone' arises as soon as a civilization has distinguished between 'inner' and 'outer' man, or the life of the 'soul' and of the 'body' (Konvitz, 1966); it is meaningless in the absence of self-consciousness which Bates (1964) says is why it is not accorded very young children. The importance of privacy may be defended on psychological grounds. 'It is perhaps an absolute necessity to withdraw to repair one's energies, to ruminate over the significance of past events, and to plan. It is only in moments in which one is not reacting to other people that communication with self can be at its best' (Lindesmith and Strauss, 1956, p. 213). Negley (1966) points out, however, that there is no non-moral answer to the question of why privacy is necessary, since even if it is argued that privacy ensures for the individual the possibility of moral choice and action, this begs the question of what *ought* the moral status of the individual to be. Konvitz observes that 'to mark off the limits of the public and the private realms . . . is an activity that touches the very nature of man' (*op. cit.*, p. 274). However, although such general delimitations may constitute differences between societies' conceptions of individual rights, within any one society such rules must of course be invoked and honoured in specific situations and the availability and enjoyment of privacy is differentially structured. Handler and Rosenheim (1966) argue that social class is one most important determinant. Lower-class individuals (a) lack resources to interpose screens around their private activities and (b) are more vulnerable to official and quasi-official inquiry and surveillance.

4 However, Goldschmidt (1966) makes a similar criticism of anthropologists who seek a universal definition of marriage. They have either abandoned the attempt in the face of cross-cultural variations, or have identified a simple criterion, e.g. the provision of birth status rights to children which strips the concept of marriage of its commonsense meaning, and in any case is not satisfactorily cross-cultural since it excludes ritual acts which are called marriage but which do not legitimate children, e.g. between two men. Both accounts founder on the assumption that something called 'marriageness' might be discoverable.

5 Some of the extensive literature on such topics is critically reviewed by Wootton and Illsley (1970) who focus on differences in child-rearing

practices, and Safilios-Rothschild (1970) who examines studies of family power structure and decision-making.

6 Harris (1969, pp. 93–121) examines the contributions of three major authors to this debate: Parsons (1952); Litwak (1961) and Goode (1963). He argues that they all pay too little attention to the process of industrialization itself; the continued existence of extended kin relationships may point less to inadequacies of theories of the family than to those of industrialization. He suggests two key characteristics of industrial society, the level of skill required and the degree of job differentiation, as 'ways of referring indirectly to the conditions of action of men in societies with advanced technologies' (*op. cit.*, p. 115). Since these differ at different stages of industrialization and between different sectors and geographical areas one would expect to find variations in family structures. Moreover, the family is important in creating the conditions for industrialization partly because different systems of inheritance affect the availability of capital. However, it is not a necessary prerequisite; industrial enterprises actively used it in taking family units into the factories.

CHAPTER 5   DEFINITIONS OF THE DISABLED CHILD AS RATIONAL CONSTRUCTIONS: SOCIAL CONTEXTS AND COMMON SENSE

1 For how this might be brought to bear on parents see chapter 7, but this might be how some parents 'can' refuse to have their children home; apparently heartlessly, it has no reality to them. For parents who later institutionalize their children it is phenomenologically different. Equally, of course, one would expect parents' accounts to be different in the two situations. In the first, 'we didn't really know what we were doing' might be honoured, whereas in the second, an appeal to the welfare of other family members is more likely to be offered.

CHAPTER 6   THE PRESENTATION OF NORMAL PARENTHOOD: PRIVATE ACTIVITIES AND PUBLIC PERFORMANCES

1 See Goffman (1959) for his analysis of teams and teamwork (pp. 67–91) and of impression-management in general (pp. 181–209).
2 See Goffman (1961a, pp. 13–117) for a discussion of the characteristics and examples of total institutions.
3 Gross and Stone (1964) discuss the various possible sources of embarrassment in interaction and the strategies that participants may adopt to overcome its disruptive effects. A more detailed analysis of the peculiar interactional status of young children is available in Strong (1971).
4 From now on, when I cite individual cases the notation [1] indicates that a response was given in the first interview. No additional notation indicates that it occurred in the second or subsequent interviews.
5 This was suggested by Sudnow's discussion of similar problems facing the bereaved (1967, p. 137).
6 Edgerton (1965) developed this model in the context of the mutual suspicion that informs interaction between white colonialists and natives. It refers to the strategies adopted by natives in attempting to evaluate the sincerity of apparent offers of friendship on the part of the white man.

CHAPTER 7 THE LEGITIMATION OF SUFFERING

1 The outline of the theories is, however, as will be indicated by the references, partly based on bibliographic material which is written sometimes from a sociological perspective and therefore is not necessarily how the agencies themselves might present them.

2 See Berger (1969) and Obeyesekere (1968) for this and other theodicies elaborated within the Judaeo-Christian tradition.

3 I examined recent copies of official reports, magazines and other literature produced by twelve associations which operate on a national and local basis, out of a total of about forty listed in the *Handbook and Directory of Voluntary Social Services*, National Council of Social Services, 1964. Those included were: The Multiple Sclerosis Society of Great Britain and Northern Ireland; Cystic Fibrosis Research Trust; British Polio Fellowship; Ileostomy Association of Great Britain; British Migraine Association; National and Scottish Associations for Spina Bifida and Hydrocephalus Ltd (ASBAH); National and Scottish Societies for Mentally Handicapped Children; British Diabetic Association; the Spastics Society and the British Epilepsy Association.

4 However, Farber says 'there are numerous contradictions in the findings on the role of religion in families with handicapped children . . .. Little is known about the specific relationships between the belief system, religious practices, sense of guilt over the responsibility for the child's illness, or guilt over rejecting the child and kind of parental activities concerning the child' (1964, p. 421). I can only say that I have no evidence of its importance in any way.

5 Berger (1969) points out that this 'irrational' attitude is pretheoretical or prior to any specific theodicy, however rational, since every nomos or order entails a transcendence of individuality. The masochistic attitude is, however, an important motif in many theodicies.

6 Swinburne regards this commonsense definition of miracle as highly derivative and limits his discussion to events of religious significance. So defined, he points out that, although miracles are not in accordance with the nature of objects or laws, they are very much in accordance with the divinely ordained natural order as a whole: 'Miracles are events with a point in the overall structure of things and so in a sense very much regular' (1970, p. 9). Bernard Shaw, however, suggests something of the more worldly processes by which the category is ascribed in practice:

> LA TREMOUILLE: Well come. What is a miracle?
>
> THE ARCHBISHOP: A miracle, my friend, is an event which creates faith. That is the purpose and nature of miracles. They may seem very wonderful to the people who witness them. That does not matter: if they confirm or create faith they are true miracles.
>
> LA TREMOUILLE: Even when they are frauds, do you mean?
>
> THE ARCHBISHOP: Frauds deceive. An event which creates faith does not deceive: therefore it is not a fraud, but a miracle.
>
> *(Saint Joan, 1967, p. 70).*

7 Macintyre makes a number of criticisms of psychoanalytic claims to scientific status. He says that whilst Freud made a lasting contribution in pointing to hitherto unnoticed facts, unrevealed motives and facts of life, many of his followers in the very process of attempting to systematize his concepts have transformed them into a religion, treating them as a closed system rather than examining the evidence on a particular topic and then generating the concepts from this. Most importantly, he argues

that what is *normal* in man's behaviour – his work, art and social life –
cannot be seen as 'the outcrops of infantile patterns' (1971, p. 35) and
therefore evades psychoanalytic explanation.

8 They wish to remain anonymous but I should like to record my gratitude
to them and the staff in the library at IPC Magazines Ltd. The method of
analysis of all the printed material was what Riley and Stoll (1968) call
'exploration' in content analysis, which attempts to isolate what appear
to be the most important themes without subjecting the material to
systematic itemization and enumeration.

9 For the general point that social work is one of the recent professions
that owes its recognition partly to the adoption of an established body of
theory, see Goode (1960a). For an historical discussion of some of the
reasons for social work's adoption of psychoanalytic theory, see
Borenzweig (1971).

10 The concept and strategies of 'social advocacy' were developed in the
USA as a 'radical' alternative to those of casework and counselling (see
e.g. Terrell, 1969). Earlier, Kelman (1957) wrote of the 'illusory' aim of
achieving parental 'acceptance' and argued that parents should be
encouraged not to accept the *status quo* and that any personal therapeutic
benefits should be regarded as a (desirable) by-product of social work
intervention. Similarly, Morris points out that parents assume that 'they
are being asked to be as contented with a retarded child as they are with
one who has a normal learning potential' (1955, p. 513). This contrast
between British and American theories is different from that found by
Scott (1970) with reference to blind rehabilitation agencies. He says
that British agencies tend to think in terms of 'mood states', counselling
cheerfulness and good nature, whilst the American emphasis is on an
adjustment which involves the production of a 'new self' that accepts
disability, having learned to live with it. My analysis is no more comprehensive than Scott claims for his own, but it does seem that the British
approach includes both these elements, whilst the American is far closer
to that practised in Sweden – focusing on practical difficulties and
regarding disability as but a defect in one modality.

11 For convenience, where statements may be applicable to both the disabled
themselves and to their relatives, I shall refer to 'parents'.

CHAPTER 8   ACCEPTANCE AND ADJUSTMENT

1 I thank Jan Carter for this point.

Bibliography

ADAMS, M. (ed.) (1960), *The Mentally Subnormal: The Social Casework Approach*, Heinemann, London.

ADAMS, M. and LOVEJOY, H. (eds) (1972), *The Mentally Subnormal: Social Work Approaches*, Heinemann, London.

AGEE, J. (1958), *A Death in the Family*, Gollancz, London.

APTER, D. E. (ed.) (1964), *Ideology and Discontent*, Free Press, New York.

BAKER, G. W. and CHAPMAN, D. W. (eds) (1962), *Man and Society in Disaster*, Basic Books, New York.

BALL, D. W. (1967), 'An abortion clinic ethnography', *Social Problems*, 14, pp. 293–301.

BALL, D. W. (1970), 'The Problematics of Respectability', in Douglas, J. D. (ed.), *Deviance and Respectability*, Basic Books, New York, pp. 326–71.

BALL, D. W. (1972), 'The "family" as a *sociological* problem: conceptualization of the taken-for-granted as a prologue to social problems analysis', *Social Problems*, 19, pp. 295–307.

BARKER, R. (1948), 'Social psychology of physical disability', *Journal of Social Issues*, 4, pp. 28–38.

BARKER, R., WRIGHT, B., MEYERSON, L. and GONICK, II. (1951), 'Adjustment to Physical Handicap and Illness: A Survey of the Social Psychology of Physique and Disability', *SSRC Bulletin*, 55, Washington, DC.

BATES, A. P. (1964), 'Privacy: a useful concept', *Social Forces*, 42, pp. 429–34.

BEANEY, W. M. (1966), 'The right to privacy and American Law', *Law and Contemporary Problems*, 31, pp. 253–71.

BECKER, H. (ed.) (1964), *The Other Side: Perspectives on Deviance*, Free Press, New York.

BECKER, H. (1966), *Outsiders: Studies in the Sociology of Deviance*, Free Press, New York.

BECKER, H. (1967), 'Whose side are we on?', *Social Problems*, 14, pp. 239–47.

BECKER, H. and GEER, B. (1970), 'Participant Observation and Interviewing: a Comparison', in Filstead, W. J. (ed.), *Qualitative Methodology*, Markham, Chicago, pp. 133–42.

BEGELMAN, D. A. (1971), 'Misnaming, metaphors, the medical model and some muddles', *Psychiatry*, 34, pp. 38–58.

BERGER, P. L. (1965), 'Towards a sociological understanding of psycho-analysis', *Social Research*, 32, pp. 29–41.

BERGER, P. L. (1969), *The Social Reality of Religion*, Faber & Faber, London.

BERGER, P. L. and KELLNER, H. (1964), 'Marriage and the construction of reality', *Diogenes*, 46, pp. 1–24.

BERGER, P. L. and LUCKMANN, T. (1963), 'Sociology of religion and sociology of knowledge', *Sociology and Social Research*, 47, pp. 417–27.

BERGER, P. L. and LUCKMANN, T. (1967), *The Social Construction of Reality: A Treatise in the Sociology of Knowledge*, Allen Lane, London.

BIALER, I. (1968), 'The Relationship of Mental Retardation to Emotional Disturbance and Physical Disability', Conference on socio-cultural aspects of mental retardation, June 10-12, George Peabody College for Teachers, Nashville, Tenn.

BIRCH, H. G. (ed.) (1964), *Brain Damage in Children: The Biological and Social Aspects*, Williams & Wilkins, Baltimore, Md.

BIRCH, H. G., RICHARDSON, S. A., BAIRD, SIR D., HOROBIN, G. and ILLSLEY, R. (1970), *Mental Subnormality in the Community: A Clinical and Epidemiologic Study*, Williams & Wilkins, Baltimore.

BIRENBAUM, A. (1970), 'On managing a courtesy stigma', *Journal of Health and Social Behaviour*, 11, pp. 196–206.

BIRNBAUM, N. and LENZER, G. (eds) (1969), *Sociology and Religion*, Prentice-Hall, Englewood Cliffs, New Jersey.

BITTNER, E. (1963), 'Radicalism and the organization of radical movements', *American Sociological Review*, 28, pp. 928–40.

BITTNER, E. (1965), 'The concept of organization', *Social Research*, 32, pp. 239–55.

BLOOM, S. (1963), *The Doctor and His Patient*, Free Press, New York.

BLUM, A. F. (1970), 'Theorizing', in Douglas, J. D. (ed.), *Deviance and Respectability*, Basic Books, New York, pp. 320–36.

BLUM, A. F. and MCHUGH, P. (1971), 'The social ascription of motives', *American Sociological Review*, 36, pp. 98–109.

BLUM, A. F. and ROSENBERG, L. (1968), 'Some problems involved in professionalizing social interaction: the case of psychotherapeutic training', *Journal of Health and Social Behaviour*, 9, pp. 72–65.

BLUMER, H. (1956), 'Sociological analysis and the "variable"', *American Sociological Review*, 21, pp. 683–90.

BLUMER, H. (1965), 'Sociological implications of the thought of G. H. Mead', *American Journal of Sociology*, 71, pp. 535–48.

BORENZWEIG, H. (1971), 'Social work and psychoanalytic theory', *Social Work*, 14, pp. 7–16.

BOWKER, J. (1970), *Problems of Suffering in the Religions of the World*, Cambridge University Press.

BRUYN, S. T. (1968), 'The new empiricists: the participant observer and phenomenologist', *Sociology and Social Research*, 51, pp. 317–22.

BRYAN, J. H. (1966), 'Occupational ideologies and individual attitudes of call-girls', *Social Problems*, 13, pp. 441–50.

BUTTERFIELD, E. C. and ZIGLER, E. (1965), 'The effects of success and failure on the discrimination learning of normal and retarded children', *Journal of Abnormal Psychology*, 70, pp. 25–31.

CICOUREL, A. V. (1964), *Method and Measurement in Sociology*, Free Press, New York.

CICOUREL, A. V. (1968), *The Social Organization of Juvenile Justice*, Wiley, New York.

CICOUREL, A. V. (1970), 'Basic and Normative Rules in the Negotiation of Status and Role', in Dreitzel, H. P. (ed.), *Recent Sociology No. 2*, Macmillan, London, pp. 4–48.

COOPER, D. (1971), 'Politics and the helping professions', *Social Work Today*, 2, pp. 2.

COVENEY, P. (1967), *The Image of Childhood*, Penguin, Harmondsworth.

CRESSEY, D. R. and WARD, D. A. (eds) (1969), *Delinquency, Crime and Social*

Process, Harper & Row, New York.

DAVIS F. (1960) 'Uncertainty in medical prognosis: clinical and functional', *American Journal of Sociology*, 66, pp. 41–7.

DAVIS, F. (1961), 'Deviance disavowal: the management of strained interaction by the visibly handicapped', *Social Problems*, 9, pp. 120–32.

DAVIS, F. (1963), *Passage Through Crisis*, Bobbs-Merrill, Indianapolis, Ind.

DEXTER L. (1964), 'On the Politics and Sociology of Stupidity in Our Society', in Becker, H. (ed.), *The Other Side*, Free Press, New York, pp. 37–49.

DHSS (1970), *Industry: Disablement Benefit for Accidents at Work*, NIG, HMSO, London.

DOUGLAS, J. D. (1967), *The Social Meanings of Suicide*, Princeton University Press.

DOUGLAS, J. D. (ed.) (1970), *Deviance and Respectability*, Basic Books, New York.

DOUGLAS, J. D. (1971a), *American Social Order: Social Rules in a Pluralistic Society*, Free Press, New York.

DOUGLAS, J. D. (ed.) (1971b), *Understanding Everyday Life: Towards the Reconstruction of Sociological Knowledge*, Routledge & Kegan Paul, London.

DRABEK, W. and BOGGS, J. (1968), 'Families in disaster: reactions and relatives', *Journal of Marriage and the Family*, 30, pp. 249–63.

DREITZEL, H. P. (ed.) (1970), *Recent Sociology No. 2: Patterns of Communicative Behaviour*, Macmillan, London.

EDGERTON, R. B. (1965), 'Some dimensions of disillusionment in culture contact', *Southwestern Journal of Anthropology*, 21, pp. 231–43.

EDGERTON, R. B. (1967), *The Cloak of Competence: Stigma in the Lives of the Mentally Retarded*, University of California Press, Berkeley.

EDWARDS, J. N. (ed.) (1969), *The Family and Change*, Knopf, New York.

ELLIS, N. R. (ed.) (1963), *Handbook of Mental Deficiency*, McGraw-Hill, New York.

EXLEY, H. and EXLEY, R. E. (1971), 'What price charity?', *Nova*, December, IPC, London.

FARBER, B. (1959), 'Perceptions of crisis and related variables in the impact of a retarded child on the mother', *American Journal of Sociology*, 64, pp. 337–51.

FARBER, B. (1964), *The Family: Organization and Interaction*, Chandler, San Francisco, California.

FARBER, B. (ed.) (1966), *Kinship and Family Organization*, Wiley, New York.

FARMER, M. (1972), *The Family*, Longman, London.

FILMER, P., PHILLIPSON, M., SILVERMAN, D. and WALSH, D. (1972), *New Directions in Sociological Theory*, Macmillan, London.

FILSTEAD, W. J. (ed.) (1970), *Qualitative Methodology: Firsthand Involvement in the Social World*, Markham, Chicago.

FLETCHER, R. (1966), *The Family and Marriage in Britain*, Penguin, Harmondsworth.

FOWLE, C. M. (1968), 'The effects of the severely mentally retarded child on his family', *American Journal of Mental Deficiency*, 73, pp. 468–73.

FREIDSON, E. (1961), 'The sociology of medicine', *Current Sociology*, 20, pp. 123–39.

FREIDSON, E. (1962), 'Dilemmas in the Doctor–Patient Relationship', in Rose, A. (ed.), *Human Behaviour and Social Processes*, Routledge & Kegan Paul, London, pp. 207–24.

FREIDSON, E. (1965), 'Disability as Social Deviance', in Sussman, M. (ed.), *Sociology and Rehabilitation*, American Sociological Association and Vocational Rehabilitation Administration, Washington, DC, pp. 71–99.

FREIDSON, E. (1970), *The Profession of Medicine: A Study in the Sociology of Applied Knowledge*, Dodd Mead, New York.

GARFINKEL, H. (1956), 'Conditions of successful degradation ceremonies', *American Journal of Sociology*, 61, pp. 420–4.

GARFINKEL, H. (1963), 'A Conception of and Experiments with "Trust" as a Condition of Concerted Action', in Harvey, O. J. (ed.), *Motivation and Social Interaction*, Ronald Press, New York, pp. 187–238.

GARFINKEL, H. (1967), *Studies in Ethnomethodology*, Prentice-Hall, Englewood Cliffs, New Jersey.

GEERTZ, C. (1964), 'Ideology as a Cultural System', in Apter, D. E. (ed.), *Ideology and Discontent*, Free Press, New York, pp. 47–75.

GERGEN, K. and GORDON, J. (eds) (1968), *The Self in Social Interaction*, Wiley, New York.

GLASER, B. and STRAUSS, A. (1967), *The Discovery of Grounded Theory*, Aldine, Chicago.

GOFFMAN, E. (1952), 'On cooling the mark out: some aspects of adaptation to failure', *Psychiatry*, 15, pp. 451–63.

GOFFMAN, E. (1955), 'On facework: an analysis of ritual elements in social interaction', *Psychiatry*, 18, pp. 214–31.

GOFFMAN, E. (1956), 'Deference and demeanor', *American Anthropologist*, 58, pp. 473–501.

GOFFMAN, E. (1959), *The Presentation of Self in Everyday Life*, Doubleday, New York.

GOFFMAN, E. (1961a), *Asylums: Essays on the Social Situation of Mental Patients and Other Inmates*, Anchor Books, New York.

GOFFMAN, E. (1961b), *Encounters: Two Studies in the Sociology of Interaction*, Bobbs-Merrill, Indianapolis, Indiana.

GOFFMAN, E. (1968), *Stigma: Notes on the Management of Spoiled Identity*, Penguin, Harmondsworth.

GOFFMAN, E. (1969), 'The insanity of place', *Psychiatry*, 32, pp. 357–85.

GOLDMAN, L. (1969), 'The Hidden God', in Birnbaum, N. and Lenzer, G. (eds), *Sociology and Religion*, Prentice-Hall, Englewood Cliffs, New Jersey, pp. 292–303.

GOLDSCHMIDT, W. (1966), *Comparative Functionalism: An Essay in Anthropological Theory*, University of California Press, Berkeley.

GOODE, W. J. (1960a), 'Encroachment, charlatanism and the emerging professions: psychology, sociology and medicine', *American Sociological Review*, 25, pp. 902–14.

GOODE, W. J. (1960b), 'A theory of role strain', *American Sociological Review*, 25 (August), pp. 483–96.

GOODE, W. J. (1963), *World Revolution and Family Patterns*, Macmillan, London.

GOODE, W. J. (1967), 'The protection of the inept', *American Sociological Review*, 32, pp. 5–19.

GOSLIN, D. A. (ed.) (1969), *Handbook of Socialization Theory and Research*, Rand McNally, Chicago.

GOULDNER, A. (1971), *The Coming Crisis in Western Sociology*, Heinemann, London.

GROSS, E. and STONE, G. (1964), 'Embarrassment and the analysis of role requirements', *American Journal of Sociology*, 70, pp. 1–15.

HABER, L. D. and SMITH, R. T. (1971), 'Disability and deviance: normal adaptations of role behaviour', *American Sociological Review*, 36, pp. 87–97.

HABERMAS, J. (1969), 'Technology and Science as Ideology', mimeographed, New School for Social Research, New York.

HAFFTER, C. (1968), 'The changeling: history and psychodynamics of attitudes to handicapped children in European folklore', *Journal of History of the Behavioural Sciences*, 4, pp. 55–61.

HALMOS, P. (1960), *The Faith of the Counsellors*, Constable, London.

HALMOS, P. (1970), *The Personal Service Society*, Constable, London.

HANCOCK, A. and WILLMOTT, P. (1965), *The Social Workers*, BBC, London.

HANDLER, J. F. and ROSENHEIM, M. K. (1966), 'Privacy in welfare: public assistance and juvenile justice', *Law and Contemporary Problems*, 31, pp. 377–412.

HARRIS, C. C. (1969), *The Family*, Allen & Unwin, London.

HARVEY, O. J. (ed.) (1963), *Motivation and Social Interaction*, Ronald Press, New York.

HEEREN, J. (1971), 'Alfred Schutz and the Sociology of Commonsense Knowledge', in Douglas, J. D., *Understanding Everyday Life*, Routledge & Kegan Paul, London, pp. 45–56.

HELLMER, J. (1970), 'The face of the man without qualities', *Social Research*, 37, pp. 547–79.

HEWETT, S. (1970), *The Family and the Handicapped Child*, Allen & Unwin, London.

HOFFMAN, L. W. and HOFFMAN, M. L. (1966), *Review of Child Development Research*, Russell Sage Foundation, New York.

HOROBIN, G. and VOYSEY, M. (forthcoming), 'Sociological perspectives on brain damage', *Impact Journal on Mental Handicap*, Impact International, Dublin.

IRISH, D. P. (1966), 'Sibling Interaction: A Neglected Aspect in Family Research', in Farber, B. (ed.), *Kinship and Family Organization*, Wiley, New York, pp. 149–58.

JACKSON, J. (1954), 'The adjustment of the family to the crisis of alcoholism', *Quarterly Journal of Studies on Alcoholism*, 15, pp. 564–86.

JACOBS, J. (1969), *The Search for Help*, Free Press, New York.

JEFFREYS, M. (1965), *An Anatomy of Social Welfare Services*, Michael Joseph, London.

KATZ, A. H. (1961), *Parents of the Handicapped*, Charles C. Thomas, Springfield, Illinois.

KELMAN, H. (1957), 'Some problems in casework with parents of mentally retarded children', *American Journal of Mental Deficiency*, 61, pp. 595–8.

KELMAN, H. (1964), 'The Impact on Families of Children with Cerebral Damage', in Birch, H. G. (ed.), *Brain Damage in Children*, Williams & Wilkins, Baltimore, pp. 77–99.

KONVITZ, M. R. (1966), 'Privacy and the law: a philosophical prelude', *Law and Contemporary Problems*, 31, pp. 272–88.

KORKES, L. (1956), *A Study of the Impact of Mentally Ill Children upon their Families*, Department of Institutions and Agencies, Trenton, New Jersey.

LADIEU, G., ADLER, D. and DEMBO, T. (1948), 'Studies in adjustment to visible injuries: social acceptance of the injured', *Journal of Social Issues*, 4, pp. 64–8.

LAING, R. D. (1960), *The Divided Self*, Tavistock, London.

LEACH, E. (ed.) (1968), *Dialectic in Practical Religion*, Cambridge University Press.

LE MASTERS, E. E. (1957), 'Parenthood as crisis', *Marriage and Family Living*, 19, pp. 352–5.

LEMERT, E. (1951), *Social Pathology*, McGraw-Hill, London.

LEMERT, E. (1967), *Human Deviance, Social Problems and Social Control*, Prentice-Hall, Englewood Cliffs, New Jersey.

LIGHT, I. H. (1969), 'The social construction of uncertainty', *Berkeley Journal of Sociology*, 14, pp. 189–99.

LINDESMITH, A. and STRAUSS, A. (1956), *Social Psychology*, Dryden Press, New York.

LITWAK, E. (1961), 'Geographical mobility and extended family cohesion' and 'Occupational mobility and extended family cohesion', *American Sociological Review*, 26, pp. 9, 258.

LOFLAND, J. (1971), *Analysing Social Settings*, Wadsworth, Belmont, California.

MCHUGH, P. (1968), *Defining The Situation: the Organization of Meaning in Social Interaction*, Bobbs-Merrill, Indianapolis, Indiana.

MACINTYRE, A. (1964), 'Pascal and Marx on Goldman's Hidden God', *Encounter*, 23 (4), pp. 69–76.

MACINTYRE, A. (1969), *Marxism and Christianity*, Duckworth, London.

MACINTYRE, A. (1971), *Against the Self Images of the Age: Essays on Ideology and Philosophy*, Schocken Books, New York.

MCKEOWN, T. (1971), 'A Sociological Approach to the History of Medicine', in McLachlan, G. and McKeown, T. (eds), *Medical History and Medical Care*, Nuffield Provincial Hospitals Trust, London, pp. 3–18.

MCLACHLAN, G. and MCKEOWN, T. (eds) (1971), *Medical History and Medical Care*, Nuffield Provincial Hospitals Trust, London.

MCMICHAEL, J. K. (1971), *Handicap: A Study of Physically Handicapped Children and Their Families*, Staples Press, London.

MADDOX, G. L., BACK, K. W. and LIEDERMAN, V. R. (1968), 'Overweight as social deviance and disability', *Journal of Health and Social Behaviour*, 9 (December), pp. 287–98.

MARX, M. (1963), *Theories in Contemporary Psychology*, Macmillan, New York.

MEAD, G. H. (1956), *The Social Psychology of G. H. Mead* (ed.) with an Introduction by Anselm Strauss, Phoenix Books, University of Chicago Press.

MEADOW, K. P. (1968), 'Parental response to the medical ambiguities of congenital deafness', *Journal of Health and Social Behaviour*, 9, pp. 299–309.

MERCER, J. R. (1965), 'Social system perspective and clinical perspective: frames of reference for understanding career patterns of persons labelled as mentally retarded', *Social Problems*, 13, pp. 18–433

MEYEROWITZ, J. H. and KAPLAN, H. B. (1967), 'Familial responses to stress: the case of cystic fibrosis', *Social Science and Medicine*, 1, pp. 249–66.

MEYERSON, L. (1948), 'Experimental injury: an approach to the dynamics of disability', *Journal of Social Issues*, 4, pp. 68–71.

MITCHELL, R. G. (ed.) (1970), *Child Life and Health*, Churchill, London.

MITCHELL, R. G. (1971), 'The community paediatrician', *British Medical Journal*, 3, 10 July, pp. 95–8.

MOORE, B. JR (1969), 'Thoughts on the Future of the Family', in Edwards, J. N. (ed.), *The Family and Change*, Knopf, New York, pp. 455–67.

MORRIS, E. (1955), 'Casework training needs for counselling parents of the retarded', *American Journal of Mental Deficiency*, 59, pp. 510–16.

MUELLER, C. (1970), 'Notes on the Repression of Communicative Behaviour', in Dreitzel, H. P. (ed.), *Recent Sociology No. 2*, Macmillan, London, pp. 101–15.

MUSGROVE, F. (1966), *The Family, Education and Society*, Routledge & Kegan Paul, London.

NAGI, S. Z. (1965), 'Some Conceptual Issues in Disability and Rehabilitation', in Sussman, M. B. (ed.), *Sociology and Rehabilitation*, American Sociological Association and Vocational Rehabilitation Administration, Washington, DC, pp. 100–31.

NEGLEY, G. (1966), 'Philosophical views on the value of privacy', *Law and Contemporary Problems*, 31, pp. 319–25.

NIETZSCHE, F. (1969), 'The Principle of Resentment', in Birnbaum, N. and Lenzer, G. (eds), *Sociology and Religion*, Prentice-Hall, New York, pp. 101–9.

NIMKOFF, M. F. (1969), 'Biological Discoveries and the Future of the Family: A Reappraisal', in Edwards, J. N. (ed.), *The Family and Change*, Knopf, New York, pp. 445–55.

OBEYESEKERE, G. (1968), 'Theodicy, Sin and Salvation in a Sociology of Buddhism', in Leach, E. (ed.), *Dialectic in Practical Religion*, Cambridge University Press, pp. 7–38.

O'CONNOR, N. and TIZARD, J. (1956), *The Social Problem of Mental Deficiency*, Pergamon, Oxford.

O'NEILL, J. (1972), *Sociology as a Skin Trade: Essays Towards a Reflexive Sociology*, Heinemann, London.

PAISLEY, M. E. (1964), 'The Historical Development from the mid Nineteenth Century of Services for Physically Handicapped Children with Special Reference to the Development of Social Work and its Place in those Services Today', unpublished M.Sc. dissertation, London School of Economics.

PARKES, C. M. (1970), 'The first year of bereavement', *Psychiatry*, 33, pp. 444–65.

PARSONS, T. (1952), *The Social System*, Tavistock, London.

PARSONS, T. (1969), 'Religion and the Problem of Meaning', in Robertson, R. (ed.), *Sociology of Religion*, Penguin, Harmondsworth, pp. 55–60.

PARSONS, T. and FOX, R. C. (1952), 'Illness, therapy and the modern American family', *Journal of Social Issues*, 8, pp. 31–44.

PENROSE, L. S. (1963), *The Biology of Mental Defect*, Sidgwick & Jackson, London.

PERRY, S. (1954), 'Some theoretical problems of mental deficiency and their action implications', *Psychiatry*, 17, pp. 45–73.

PILIAVIN, I. and BRIAR, S. (1964), 'Police encounters with juveniles', *American Journal of Sociology*, 69, pp. 206–14.

POPPLESTONE, G. (1972), 'Who is being radical?', *Case Con*, 7, pp. 14–17.

PUCCETTI, R. (1968), *Persons: A Study of Possible Moral Agents in the Universe*, Macmillan, London.

QUARANTELLI, E. (1960), 'Images of withdrawal behaviour in disasters: some basic misconceptions', *Social Problems*, 8, pp. 68–73.

RICHARDSON, S. A. (1965), *Interviewing: Its forms and Functions*, Basic Books, New York.

RICHARDSON, S. A. (1969), 'The Effects of Physical Disability on the Socialization of a Child', in Goslin, D. A. (ed.), *Handbook of Socialization Theory and Research*, Rand McNally, Chicago, pp. 1047–64.

RICHARDSON, S. A. (1970), 'Age and sex differences in values toward physical handicaps', *Journal of Health and Social Behaviour*, 11, pp. 207–14

RICHARDSON, S. A., GOODMAN, N., HASTORF, A. H. and DORNBUSCH, S. M. (1961), 'Cultural uniformities in reaction to physical disabilities, *American Sociological Review*, 26, pp. 241–6.

RILEY, M. W. and STOLL, G. S. (1968), 'Constant Analysis', in Sills, D. (ed.), *International Encyclopaedia of the Social Sciences*, 3, Free Press, New York, pp. 376–81.

ROBERTSON, R. (ed.) (1969), *Sociology of Religion*, Penguin, Harmondsworth.

ROBINSON, W. S. (1951), 'The logical structure of analytic induction', *American Sociological Review*, 16, pp. 812–18.

ROSE, A. (ed.) (1962), *Human Behaviour and Social Processes*, Routledge & Kegan Paul, London.

RUBINGTON, E. and WEINBERG, S. (eds) (1968), *Deviance: The Interactionist Perspective*, Macmillan, London.

SAFILIOS-ROTHSCHILD, C. (1970), 'The study of family power structure: a review 1960–9', *Journal of Marriage and the Family*, 32, pp. 539–52.

SAMPSON, H., MESSINGER, S. L. and TOWNE, R. D. (1962), 'Family processes and becoming a mental patient', *American Journal of Sociology*, 68, pp. 88–96.

SARASON, S. B. (1953), *Psychological Problems in Mental Deficiency*, Harper & Row, New York.

SARTRE, J.-P. (1964), *Saint-Genet: Actor and Martyr*, W. H. Allen, London.

SCHATZMAN, L. and STRAUSS, A. (1955), 'Social class and modes of communication', *American Journal of Sociology*, 60, pp. 329–58.

SCHEFF, T. J. (1964), *Being Mentally Ill*, Weidenfeld & Nicolson, New York.

SCHEFF, T. J. (1967), 'Towards a sociological model of consensus', *American Sociological Review*, 32, pp. 32–46.

SCHEFF, T. J. (1968), 'Negotiating reality: notes on power in the assessment of responsibility', *Social Problems*, 12, pp. 3–17.

SCHOTTLAND, C. I. (1969), 'The Changing Roles of Government and Family', in Weinberger, P. E. (ed.), *Perspectives on Social Welfare*, Macmillan, London, pp. 132–47.

SCHUTZ, A. (1962; 1964; 1966), *Collected Papers: Volumes I, II, III*, Martinus Nijhoff, The Hague.

SCOTT, M. B. and LYMAN, S. M. (1968a), 'Accounts', *American Sociological Review*, 33, pp. 46–62.

SCOTT, M. B. and LYMAN, S. M. (1968b), 'Paranoia, homosexuality and game theory', *Journal of Health and Social Behaviour*, 9, pp. 179–187.

SCOTT, R. (1970), 'The Construction of Conception of Stigma by Professional Experts', in Douglas, J. D. (ed.), *Deviance and Respectability*, Basic Books, New York, pp. 255–90.

SHALLENBERGER, P. and ZIGLER, E. (1961), 'Rigidity, negative reaction tendencies, and cosatiation effects in normal and feebleminded children', *Journal of Abnormal and Social Psychology*, 63, pp. 20–6.

SHAW, G. B. (1967), *Saint Joan*, Penguin, Harmondsworth.

SHROYER, T. (1970), 'Toward a Critical Theory for Advanced Industrial Society', in Dreitzel, H. P. (ed.), *Recent Sociology No. 2*, Macmillan, London, pp. 210–34.

SILLS, D. (ed.) (1966), *International Encyclopaedia of the Social Sciences* 3, Free Press, New York.

SODDY, K. (1972), 'The Clinical Picture', in Adams, M. and Lovejoy, H. (eds.), *The Mentally Subnormal: Social Work Approaches*, Heinemann, London, pp. 18–61.

STRAUSS, A. (ed.) (1956), *The Social Psychology of G. H. Mead*, Phoenix Books, University of Chicago Press.

STRONG, P. M. (1971), 'Parent–Child Interaction', unpublished paper, Department of Sociology, University of Aberdeen.

STRYKER, S. (1968), 'Identity salience and role performance: the relevance of symbolic interactionism for family research', *Journal of Marriage and the Family*, 30, pp. 558–64.

SUDNOW, D. (1967), *Passing On: The Social Organization of Dying*, Prentice-Hall, Englewood Cliffs, New Jersey.

SUSSMAN, M. B (ed.) (1965), *Sociology and Rehabilitation*, American Sociological Association and Vocational Rehabilitation Administration,

Washington, DC.

SUTTLES, G. D. (1972), *The Social Construction of Communities*, University of Chicago Press.

SWINBURNE, R. (1970), *The Concept of Miracle*, Macmillan, London.

TABER, M., QUAY, H. C., MARK, H. and NEALEY, V. (1969), 'Disease ideology and mental health research', *Social Problems*, 16, pp. 349–57.

TERRELL, P. (1969), 'The Social Worker as Radical: Roles of Advocacy', in Weinberger, P. E. (ed.), *Perspectives on Social Welfare*, Macmillan, London, pp. 355–64.

TIZARD, J. (1966), 'Mental subnormality and child psychiatry', *Journal of Child Psychology and Psychiatry*, 7, pp. 1–15.

TIZARD, J. (1972), 'Implications for Services of Recent Social Research in Mental Retardation', in Adams, M. and Lovejoy, H. (eds), *The Mentally Subnormal: Social Work Approaches*, Heinemann, London, pp. 269–90.

TOWERS, B. (1971), 'The Influence of Medical Technology on Medical Services' in McLachlan, G. and McKeown, T. (eds), *Medical History and Medical Care*, Nuffield Provincial Hospitals Trust, London, pp. 157–75.

TURNER, R. (1953), 'The quest for universals in sociological research', *American Sociological Review*, 18, pp. 604–11.

TURNER, R. (1968), 'The Self-conception in Social Interaction', in Gergen, K. and Gordon, J. (eds), *The Self in Social Interaction*, Wiley, New York, pp. 93–105.

VOYSEY, M. (1972a), 'Impression management by parents with disabled children', *Journal of Health and Social Behaviour*, 13, pp. 80–9.

VOYSEY, M. (1972b), 'Official agents and the legitimation of suffering', *Sociological Review*, 20, pp. 533–51.

WALLACE, A. F. C. (1956), *Human Behaviour in Extreme Situations: A Survey of the Literature and Suggestions for Further Research*, National Academy of Sciences, National Research Council Committee on Disaster Studies, Publication No. 390, Washington, DC.

WALSH, D. (1972), 'Varieties of Positivism', in Filmer, P. *et al.*, *New Directions in Sociological Theory*, Macmillan, London, pp. 37–56.

WEBER, M. (1969), 'Major Features of World Religions', in Robertson, R. (ed.), *Sociology of Religion*, Penguin, Harmondsworth, pp. 19–41.

WEINBERGER, P. E. (ed.) (1969), *Perspectives on Social Welfare: An Introductory Anthology*, Macmillan, London.

WEINSTEIN, E. (1969), 'The Development of Competence', in Goslin, D. A. (ed.), *Handbook of Socialization Theory and Research*, Rand McNally, Chicago, pp. 753–75.

WEINSTEIN, E. and DEUTSCHBERGER, P. (1964), 'Tasks, bargains and identities in social interation', *Social Forces*, 42, pp. 457–65.

WERTHMAN, C. and WERTHMAN, J. (1969), 'Delinquency and Moral Character', in Cressey, D. R. and Ward, D. A. (eds), *Delinquency, Crime and Social Process*, Harper & Row, New York, pp. 613–32.

WHITE, C. L. (1970), *Women's Magazines 1693–1968*, Michael Joseph, London.

WIEDER, D. L. (1971), 'On Meaning by Rule', in Douglas, J. D. (ed.), *Understanding Everyday Life*, Routledge & Kegan Paul, London, pp. 107–35.

WILSON, T. P. (1971), 'Normative and Interpretive Paradigms in Sociology', in Douglas, J. D. (ed.), *Understanding Everyday Life*, Routledge & Kegan Paul, London, pp. 57–79.

WINCH, P. (1963), *The Idea of a Social Science*, Routledge & Kegan Paul, London.

WOOTTON, A. J. and ILLSLEY, R. (1970), 'Social Influences on Parents and Their Children', in Mitchell, R. G. (ed.), *Child Life and Health*, Churchill,

London, pp. 298–318.

WYNN, M. (1972), *Family Policy*, Penguin, Harmondsworth.

YARROW, M. R., SCHWARTZ, C. G., MURPHY, H. S., and DEASY, L. C. (1955), 'The psychological meaning of mental illness in the family', *Journal of Social Issues*, 11, pp. 12–24.

YOUNG, M. (1954), 'The role of the extended family in a disaster', *Human Relations*, 7, pp. 388–93.

YOUNIE, D. (1964), 'The predictive value of a register of pre-school handicapped', *Health Bulletin*, 22, pp. 56–61.

ZBOROWSKI, M. (1952), 'Cultural Components in Responses to Pain', *Journal of Social Issues*, 8, pp. 16–30.

ZEAMAN, D. and HOUSE, B. J. (1963), 'The Role of Attention in Retardate Discrimination Learning', in Ellis, N. R. (ed.), *Handbook of Mental Deficiency*, McGraw-Hill, New York, pp. 159–225.

ZIGLER, E. (1964), 'Metatheoretical Issues in Developmental Psychology', in Marx, M. (ed.), *Theories in Contemporary Psychology*, Macmillan, New York, pp. 341–68.

ZIGLER, E. (1966), 'Mental Retardation: Current Issues and Approaches', in Hoffman, L. W. and Hoffman, M. L. (eds), *Review of Child Development Research*, vol. 2, Russell Sage, New York, pp. 107–66.

ZIGLER, E. and HARTER, S. (1969), 'The Socialization of the Mentally Retarded', in Goslin, D. A. (ed.), *Handbook of Socialization Theory and Research*, Rand McNally, Chicago, pp. 1065–1103.

ZNANIECKI, F. (1965), *Social Relations and Social Roles: The Unfinished Systematic Sociology*, Chandler, San Francisco, California.

Index

181–2, 186–90 *passim*; recognition of disability, 136, 137; resentment,, 162, 184, 191, 192, 203, 208, 216, 222; responses and statements, 1–2, 4, 16, 22–3, 25, 26, 27, 36, 39, 40, 42–3, 56–7, 74, 116; responsibilities, 50, 146, 147–53; rules of, 48–9; sex-appropriate behaviour, 214–15; status, 201–2; *see also* Fathers, Mothers

Parkes, C. M., 105

Parsons, T., 162, 226; and Fox, R. C., 220

Penrose, L. S., 6, 10

Perry, S., 5, 7, 11

Person, concept of, 31, 32, 36, 58, 133, 140, 141, 176, 213, 221; conceptions, 34, 35

Phenomenology, 23, 26, 60

Phenylketonuria, 6, 171

Piliavin, I. and Briar, S., 225

Play-schools, 88

Poliomyelitis, 18, 199

Popplestone, G., 222

Pringle, Mia Kellmer, 54

Private, 42, 218; activities, 128–57 *passim*; agreement, 56; performance, 95; place, family as, 51; privacy, 203, 225; privatism, 213; privatization of belief, 165, 166

Psychiatry and psychiatrists, 32, 171–3, 181, 192, 194, 209, 219–20, 222, 227

Public, 41; labellers, 124; morality, 42; rules and appearances, 41, 43, 50, 95, 128–57 *passim*, 160

Puccetti, R., 31, 56

Q

Quarantelli, E., 47

Questionnaires, 66–7

R

Religion, 21, 160, 164, 167–70 *passim*, 183, 193, 194, 201, 221, 227

Respectability, 55, 56, 57, 158; and reality, 208–23 *passim*

Richardson, S. A., 12, 14, 31, 32, 67, 100, 123

Rickets, 8

Riley, M. W. and Stoll, G. S., 228

Robinson, W. S., 71

Rousseau, Jean-Jacques, 53

Rubington, E. and Weinberg, S., 27, 124, 225

Rules in social order, 24, 37, 40–1

S

Safilios-Rothschild, C., 226

Sampson, H., 105, 224

Sarason, S. B., 10

Sartre, Jean-Paul, 53

Schatzman, L. and Strauss, A., 147

Scheff, T. J., 32, 100, 136, 147

Schottland, C. I., 153

Schultz, A., 70, 99, 105, 125, 197, 198, 213, 225; on common sense, 96–8; on typifications, 101–2

Scott, M. B. and Lyman, S. M., 154; on 'accounts', 55, 56, 202

Scott, R., 160, 167, 174, 185, 228

Self, 28, 35, 124, 154, 217; *see also* Identity

Shallenberger, P. and Zigler, E., 11

Shaw, George Bernard, 227

She, 188

Shroyer, T., 220

Sick, definition as, 143; role, 220; treatment as, 148

Smallpox, 9

Social services, 53–4

Social workers, 3, 160, 166, 179, 181–4, 191, 222

Sociology, 52, 173–4, 192, 194, 210, 212; sociological versus social problem, 1, 44, 45, 47

Soddy, K., 6, 14, 166, 173, 198

Spastics, 187, 188, 199–200; Society, 223

Spina bifida, 85, 118, 141, 142, 153, 199, 205

Spock, B., 98

Stigmas and stigmatization, 28, 29, 30, 123, 124, 125, 129, 130, 152, 155, 173, 201; curability of, 30; individual, 196; management of, 133

Strong, P. M., 226

Stryker, S., 49

Subnormality, *see* Disability, mental